Covenant Economics

Also by Richard A. Horsley from Westminster John Knox Press

Hearing the Whole Story: The Politics of Plot in Mark's Gospel

Scribes, Visionaries, and the Politics of Second Temple Judea

*In the Shadow of Empire: Reclaiming the Bible
as a History of Faithful Resistance* (editor)

Covenant Economics

A Biblical Vision of Justice for All

Richard A. Horsley

WESTMINSTER
JOHN KNOX PRESS
LOUISVILLE · KENTUCKY

First edition
Published by Westminster John Knox Press
Louisville, Kentucky

09 10 11 12 13 14 15 16 17 18—10 9 8 7 6 5 4 3 2 1

Unless otherwise indicated, Scripture quotations are from the New Revised Standard Version of the Bible, copyright © 1989 by the Division of Christian Education of the National Council of the Churches of Christ in the U.S.A., and are used by permission.

Book design by Sharon Adams
Cover design by designpointinc.com

Library of Congress Cataloging-in-Publication Data

Horsley, Richard A.
  Covenant economics : a biblical vision of justice for all / Richard A. Horsley.
     p. cm.
  Includes bibliographical references and index.
  ISBN 978-0-664-23395-2 (alk. paper)
  1. Economics in the Bible.   2. Covenants—Biblical teaching.   3. Economics—Religious aspects—Christianity.   4. Covenants—Religious aspects—Christianity.
5. United States—Economic conditions.   6. Christianity and justice—United States.
I. Title.

  BS670.H67   2009
  261.8′5—dc22

                                                          2009001896

PRINTED IN THE UNITED STATES OF AMERICA

Contents

Acknowledgments

I am deeply indebted to a number of colleagues and friends in biblical studies for their mentoring over the years on literary, historical, and economic issues in books of the Hebrew Bible. Principal among these are Marvin Chaney, Norman Gottwald, Roland Boer, and Gale Yee. I have also learned much from recent conversations with Steve Friesen on people's economic situation in the Roman Empire and Pauline communities, and with Warren Carter on the Gospel of Matthew. Robert Bellah first opened up for me the importance of the Mosaic/Sinaitic Covenant in American history. Tom Conry has become my principal mentor on economic history in the United States. Noelle Damico and Ran Huntsberry read the early drafts of the chapters and made many very helpful suggestions. Particularly helpful, probably in ways I will never recognize, were the intense discussions of the initial draft of the book with twenty or so ministers and community organizers connected with the Industrial Areas Foundation in the Southwest, led by Ernesto Cortés, Paul Buckwalter, and Frank Pierson. Jon Berquist made important suggestions for the shaping of the presentation. And I greatly appreciate Dan Braden's close attention to details in the production of books at Westminster John Knox.

Introduction

"All People Are Endowed by Their Creator…"

Many Americans understand themselves as a biblical people. Historically politicians as well as preachers have boldly claimed that the United States is God's New Israel, a chosen people with a destiny to embody "justice and liberty for all." This sense of a special calling as the New Israel is deeply rooted in the origins of the country. The groups of English Protestants who settled in New England crossed the stormy Atlantic to escape tyranny, just as the ancient Israelites had crossed the Red Sea to escape hard bondage under the pharaoh of Egypt. They then created new covenant communities patterned after Israel's Covenant at Mount Sinai. The Mayflower Compact made by those who settled in Plymouth is the most famous covenantal charter. John Winthrop's sermon "A Modell of Christian Charity" provides a fulsome statement of the Covenant for those who settled Boston. Many such new covenantal communities in New England adopted the Covenant delivered through Moses in Exodus 20 and the restatement of the Covenant by Jesus in the Sermon on the Mount (Matt. 5–7) as their charter documents.

A century and a half later the Revolutionary War for independence was understood as a new exodus. Just as the Hebrews of old had asserted their liberty from Pharaoh's oppression, so now the colonists were asserting their liberty against the British monarchy. Moreover, the Declaration of Independence was strongly covenantal in substance. The adamant assertion that all people are "endowed by their Creator with certain unalienable Rights, that among these are Life, Liberty, and the pursuit of Happiness," is a restatement of the most fundamental assumption of Israel's Covenant with God. The language is that of eighteenth-century natural rights, but the substance is what God declares to the people in the biblical Covenant (as we shall see in chapter 2 below). In their Declaration the American revolutionaries stated boldly that "with a firm reliance on the protection of Divine Providence, we mutually pledge to each other our Lives, our Fortunes and our sacred Honor." In that declaration Jefferson and his compatriots sound very much like Joshua and the Israelites renewing the Covenant at Shechem in Joshua 24.

Most significantly of all, the Constitution of the United States, the foundation of the people's self-government, was understood as a new Covenant. Advocates of its ratification declared that, just as the twelve tribes of Israel had received the Covenant on Mount Sinai as a model of civil government, so now the thirteen states were creating a new model of civil government. The Constitution, like the Covenant, is focused on the protection of people's rights, as articulated explicitly in the first ten amendments, usually called the Bill of Rights. It follows the Covenant in having no human sovereign. It assumes what the Covenant affirms, that the transcendent Deity is the guarantor of people's rights. Like the Covenant, the Constitution asks the inner commitment (ratification) of the body politic. And like the Covenant, the Constitution, while providing for the active participation of the people in the creation of positive law, understands law as derived ultimately from a higher source, God or Nature. In Jefferson's terms, law is ultimately the "law of nature and of nature's God."

In carrying out their new exodus, however, arrogantly presuming that they were "the chosen people," the "founding fathers" were violating fundamental principles of the Covenant designed to protect people from tyranny and oppression. They not only took the land away from the peoples already living on it, but they slaughtered those peoples. While declaring that all people are "endowed by their Creator with certain unalienable Rights," they systematically denied the rights and the very humanity of the Africans whom they enslaved.

Attended by the inconsistency and hypocrisy involved in its adaptation to North American democracy, the Covenant continued to play a prominent role in political life. In their inaugural addresses, presidents referred to the Covenant that the people had made with God, the land, and one another, often with explicit reference to covenantal images and statements in the Bible. It might not be too much to argue that, following the election by the people, the inauguration of the President before the people's representatives and Supreme Court justices every four years has been a covenant renewal ceremony. As symbolized in the newly elected President's solemn oath to uphold the Constitution, the rule of law rather than tyranny has prevailed. And, however fitfully and inconsistently, the political rights of the people guaranteed by the covenantal Constitution have been protected. Albeit belatedly, the Constitution was finally amended to extend civil rights to the descendants of former slaves and to extend the franchise to women.

Political Rights—But What about Economic Rights?

In retrospect it is clear that the founders' principal motive in drawing on the covenantal tradition in the Bible in the foundational documents of the United States was to establish political liberty and to guarantee political rights. In the 1770s and 1780s the driving concern was to assert independence from the English monarchy and to establish self-government. Political rights were again the principal concern when the covenantal tradition figured prominently in the emancipation of slaves in the 1860s and the civil rights legislation in the 1960s.

The biblical Covenant, however, like the exodus with which it is linked, is focused as much on economic rights as on political rights. The hard bondage under Pharaoh in Egypt that the Hebrews escaped in the exodus was not only political subjugation but economic oppression. The covenant that they received on Mount Sinai focused on principles meant to keep them from falling back into economic as well as political subservience (as we shall see in the chapters below).

Earlier generations of Americans, from Plymouth Plantation to Abraham Lincoln, were aware that the covenant was concerned with economic rights as well as political rights. In his sermon founding the covenantal community in Boston, John Winthrop declared that as "wee entertaine each other in brotherly Affeccion, wee must be willing to abridge our selves of our superfluities for the supply of others' necessities." The framers of the Pennsylvania Declaration of Rights even seriously considered including the explicit economic statement that "an enormous proportion of property vested in a few individuals is dangerous to the rights, and destructive of the common happiness of mankind." In 1865, in his second inaugural address, President Abraham Lincoln interpreted the mutually destructive Civil War as the delivery of the divine curses for having broken the covenant:

> Yet, if God wills that it continue until all the wealth piled up by the bondsman's two hundred and fifty years of unrequited toil shall be sunk, and every drop of blood drawn with the lash shall be paid by another drawn with the sword, as was said three thousand years ago, so still it must be said "the judgments of the Lord are true and righteous altogether."

Clearly the founders and the subsequent generations of citizens of the United States knew that the Covenant was concerned with economics as well as political liberty. The founding documents of the United States and the development of institutional guarantees focused on political rights while somewhat neglecting economic rights.

This was surely at least partly because in the formative and early history of the United States a rival ideology rapidly displaced the biblical covenantal tradition in economic affairs. For the founders at the time of the Revolution and the framing of the Constitution, liberty may have meant mainly liberation from British tyranny. But it was understood in a broader framework of social moral values of freedom to do the good for the common welfare. For Jefferson and others familiar with Roman history, freedom was closely identified with "republican virtue," which meant doing what was good for the body politic. Freedom, however, quickly came to mean the freedom to pursue self-interest. A new faith was emerging that social concord could still be maintained when individuals sought their own private interests without worrying about the social-economic consequences for others. This ideology of freedom as pursuit of self-interest reinforced and shaped the strong sense of individualism in U.S. society. The ideology of individual self-interests gave license to entrepreneurs in nascent capitalist enterprises.

The recognition by the courts of corporations as persons with the same rights as individual citizens gave a considerable boost to the multiplication and expansion of corporations. The marriage of capitalist corporations with industrialization and international trade brought about a complete transformation of the economy in the United States—from agricultural to industrial, from family businesses to huge corporations, from rural to urban, from self-sufficient farming to dependence on wage labor. In all of this the "captains of industry" came to control the economy. Workers became dependent on the owners and management. Fewer and fewer people came to own and control more and more of the wealth and resources. Through most of this development, government in the United States, local, state, and federal, supported the corporations against the efforts of workers to assert their economic rights.

Capitalism, which requires an economic return on capital invested, thus became *the* economic system, with no effective challenge and little serious criticism. One of the principles on the basis of which the American colonists had made their exodus out from under the English monarchy was "no taxation without representation." They refused to render up a portion of their family income, usually from the sale of their produce, unless they had a voice in its determination. Once the political revolution was successful and entrepreneurial capitalist enterprises were expanding, however, the equivalent principle was not applied to economic relations. Perhaps because in principle all supposedly enjoyed equality of opportunity, those who worked for others did not rebel against the owners of factories who made a profit by keeping a portion of the value of their labor. Most citizens who bought into "the American dream" accepted as natural and inevitable an economic system in which a vast majority yielded up a portion of the value of their work as profits for the company for which they worked. Until recently little objection was made that executives make a hundred or a thousand times as much as workers, and that the big investors have billions while millions of workers have barely enough to live on. It is even accepted that, since capitalism is a dynamic system, it must grow. Each corporation must grow, and every national GNP must grow, whatever the effects on people or the environment.

The biblical Covenant and its concern for economic rights, however, had not disappeared. Although economic rights had not been institutionally protected in the same way as political rights, the Covenant was still integral to public life in the United States. While the Constitution prohibited the establishment of a religion—"separation of church and state"—churches and synagogues continued to cultivate biblical tradition, including the Mosaic Covenant. Meanwhile the Covenant had become central to what has been called the American "civil religion," the sacred documents (Declaration of Independence, Constitution), celebrations (Fourth of July, Thanksgiving), and ideology ("liberty and justice for all") that lend cohesion to the different peoples, regions, and parties that make up the body politic of the United States. Presidents referred prominently to the covenant in their inaugural addresses. In political discourse and debate of a century ago, moreover, the ten commandments were referred to alongside the Declaration of Independence and Constitution as one of the founding documents of the country, including its economic relations.

In Progressive Era presidential campaigns (around the beginning of the twentieth century), for example, both the Republicans and the Democrats appealed to the ten commandments as the authority for their respective positions and accused the other of abandoning the principles of both Covenant and Constitution. Both sides saw the implications of the eighth commandment in particular for the huge corporations and the trusts they were establishing. Theodore Roosevelt, the great Republican champion of the ten commandments, insisted that "thou shalt not steal" meant that individual corporate heads and politicians should be honest. Each corporation should receive "its exact rights and nothing more," but honest politicians would not propose laws that would restrain those corporations. William Jennings Bryan, populist advocate of workers and farmers, on the other hand, accused the Republicans of revising the eighth commandment to read "thou shalt not steal on a small scale." He appealed to the original commandment as a basis on which to restrain and regulate the large corporations that many feared had become so powerful as to threaten democracy and individual liberty. Gradually sensing the implications of the commandment, Roosevelt moved increasingly toward Progressive policies. When his friends on Wall Street and the Republican Party accused him of attacking their corporations, his defense was that "most of what I preach you can find in the Ten Commandments."

Influenced by the principles of the biblical Covenant the U.S. government did enact reforms and regulations, first in the Progressive Era and later in the New Deal. The reforms attempted in various ways to restrain the worst abuses of corporate power, with labor laws, environmental regulations, taxation of excessive profits, and a progressive income tax. Labor unions were able to bargain for better wages and a modicum of job security, which provided a minimum of economic security to families. Such reforms, of course, were only attempts to check abuses by those who wielded power in the system, not a fundamental change in the system itself.

With deregulation in the last few decades, however, corporations were cut loose to make profits and "grow" capital regardless of the impact on the environment and on individual and community life, in the United States or elsewhere in the world. The reforms protecting workers and gains in wages and job security had made labor too expensive in the United States. Accordingly, in a relentless process that escalated in the 1980s, giant corporations in major industries steadily closed their plants and laid off millions of workers. Whole industries, such as steel, and many cities along with them were decimated, as the corporations moved their manufacturing to "undeveloped" countries with very cheap labor and no protective labor laws. To avoid layoffs labor unions had to give back wages, while CEOs' compensation escalated. Weakened unions could no longer defend workers' rights to decent wages and job security, and transnational corporations could effectively ignore the rights of workers in developing countries. The U.S. government promised that plenty of new jobs in high-tech and service industries would replace those lost. But the service jobs were low paying, and in the last decade those who eagerly trained for high-tech jobs received their own pink slips, as large corporations outsourced the technical support increasingly important to their operations. The U.S. government promised job-retraining programs, but did not fund them.

In recent years we have experienced the further erosion of economic rights. The profits of the huge corporations and the enormous expansion of wealth among the very rich come at the expense of their workers, whether the ones who lost well-paying jobs in the United States or those working in sweatshops elsewhere. The now globalized capitalist economy does not recognize the economic rights of its workers. Far from protecting such rights, moreover, the U.S. government yielded to the power of the huge corporations. Workers have shrinking wages and little or no job security. As the cost of increasingly high-tech health care escalates, corporations eager to maintain their profit margins have either eliminated or reduced their contribution, forcing employees to pay more and more of the inordinate costs. To avoid or emerge from bankruptcy, corporations expropriate pension funds to pay their institutional creditors, such as huge banks, leaving their employees without pensions. Bankruptcy laws designed to protect families and small businesses from unforeseen contingencies that might mean financial ruin are revised to provide less protection. Simultaneously the bankruptcy laws are manipulated to protect the credit card companies (which charge 18 to 25 percent interest and escalating fees) against cardholders, driving the latter deeply into debt. There are huge government bailouts for corporations, but not for families. In the increasingly globalized capitalist economy dominated by transnational corporations, it is difficult to find laws, programs, or mechanisms that provide economic security for individuals and families.

In the capitalist system, however, it has been deemed necessary for capital to grow, for corporations to make profits, to provide a return on investments, regardless of the effect on individual people, families, and communities. Increasingly the U.S. government has been serving the interests of huge conglomerate corporations at the expense of the interests of the people. Having started out with an assertion of their liberty over against the political tyranny of the English monarchy, the people of the United States are now seeing their lives heavily determined by enormously powerful transnational corporations and their super-wealthy CEOs who claim that their only responsibility is to their investors.

This situation bears a striking resemblance to that of the ancient Hebrews caught in hard bondage under Pharaoh, the enormously powerful head of the imperial economy in Egypt. Those ancient Hebrews, however, once they asserted their liberty from Pharaoh, formed the Covenant, which was concerned with economic as well as political rights. Thus a new look at the prominent and extensive covenantal texts in the Bible may help us discern the economic concerns that have been missing in the American appropriation of the biblical Covenant. A broader survey of economics in the Bible will reveal that biblical economics more generally centers on the Covenant. We will discover in the biblical Covenant that the "unalienable rights" with which all people are "endowed by their Creator" include economic rights, rights necessary for "Life, Liberty, and the pursuit of Happiness." In the covenantal economics of the Bible, moreover, God-given economic rights are inseparably connected with public communal values. The erosion of these rights and values by the power of huge corporations is a fundamental violation of the Covenant that so informed the foundational events and documents of the United States.

The Bible and Economics

The Bible might seem like the last place one would look for information and guidance on economics. Despite the prominent role that the exodus and Covenant played in the formative history of the United States, the assumption has grown during the last century that the Bible is religious literature about religious matters. This is reinforced by the modern separation, particularly in "secular" societies, of religion and politics and the belief that economics are and ought to remain independent of religious concerns.

As our American ancestors from John Winthrop to Abraham Lincoln recognized in the biblical Covenant, however, economic concerns run throughout the Bible. The foundational event for Israel, the exodus, was an escape from economic as well as political oppression. Books of the Pentateuch include many laws and teachings on economic matters, from prohibition of interest on loans and cancellation of debts to damages for injury to draft animals and damage to crops. Tithes and offerings are the transfers of economic goods to the control and consumption of the priests. The people who are clamoring for a king to reign over them are warned that a king will take their goods and their property. King Solomon imposes forced labor, the very oppression from which God had liberated Israel in the exodus. Ahab and Jezebel frame Naboth so that Ahab can seize his vineyard, against God's guarantee that ancestral land was inalienable. The prophets rail against royal officers' economic exploitation of the people.

Economic concerns are central also in the teachings of Jesus. The petitions of the Lord's Prayer focus on enough food to eat each day and the cancellation of debts. Jesus declares that it is harder for a wealthy person to enter the kingdom of God than for a camel to pass through the eye of a needle. He advises the wealthy young man who insists that he has kept the covenantal commandments to sell all his goods and give to the poor. In the Gospel of Luke, the decree by Augustus Caesar, the Savior of the Empire, that people must pay tribute forces Joseph and Mary to journey to Bethlehem, where Jesus is born as the alternative "Savior." In his confrontation with the client rulers of Rome in Jerusalem, Jesus is forced to address this same question of the tribute to Caesar—and does so in a way that does not assume the separation of religion from politics and economics. The apostle Paul is not just preaching his gospel, but gathering a collection from the assemblies of Christ for the poor in the Jerusalem community. The revelatory prophetic visions of John on Patmos include an uncompromising condemnation of the merchants and kings of the earth who supply the Roman imperial elite with expensive luxury goods.

Despite the prominence of economic issues throughout the Bible, the field of biblical studies has generally neglected economics. In recent years, however, a few scholars have given special attention to the economic system assumed in biblical books and/or to economic concerns evident in particular texts. Studies of laws about cancellation of debts and inalienability of land in biblical and Mesopotamian law codes have significant implications for economic concerns in the Mosaic Covenant in particular. Sophisticated studies of key prophetic oracles have opened up a far more precise sense of the situation that the prophets were addressing and what they were protesting. Similarly, investigation of the political-economic context in which Jesus and his movement emerged has enabled us to hear previously undetected economic implications in his teachings.

Drawing on these recent studies we can formulate a provisional picture of the economic structures and dynamics in which the ancient Israelites lived and we can gain a sense of the economic concerns of the prophets and of Jesus and the Gospels. In the explorations of key texts in the following chapters it will become clear that a distinctively covenantal concern for economic rights and mutually supportive and cooperative community runs strongly throughout the Pentateuch, the Prophets, the Gospels, and the Letters of Paul.

Procedure

I have attempted to sketch a broad overview both of how economics worked in the society reflected in biblical texts and of how those biblical texts thought it ought to work—and their relationship. The critical historical analysis in the chapters on Hebrew biblical books depends heavily on the investigations by several key scholars and my own teaching of these materials for many years. For the analysis of the Gospels and Paul I depend heavily on my own research and reflection laid out in many articles and books.

No attempt will be made to apply the academic field of economics to biblical texts. Analysis in the field of economics has been developed to try to understand the working of a modern industrial economic system. Many of its basic assumptions and concepts would therefore be anachronistic with regard to the economic system presupposed or advocated in biblical texts that originated in the ancient world. Indeed, at many key points we will have to make a conscious effort not to impose concepts and generalizations about economics that we simply assume.

This book will be mainly an exercise in historical investigation of biblical texts, examining the relations between the physical environment (land and water), social structure, and culture (religious beliefs, laws, etc.). Often this will mean looking at what biblical texts say that social-economic relations ought to be (or ought not to be) and how that affected or did not affect economic behavior and development.

To take a modern example, a century ago now the German sociologist and economic historian Max Weber argued that "the Protestant ethic" was conducive to the development of capitalism. Calvinism taught that self-indulgent consumption of surplus resources was sinful. Faithful Calvinists saved some of their money rather than consume or spend it on immediate gratification. This led to the accumulation of capital, which in turn could be invested at interest, leading to a further accumulation of capital. Or, for a biblical example, covenantal law forbade the taking of interest on loans as a way of helping the family unit remain economically viable in hard times. But some disobeyed and did charge interest, which led to the concentration of their control of land and labor and the increase in their power and wealth.

Outline of the Book

A quick overview of the sequence of chapters and their argument may help orient the reader to the treatment of economic relations in biblical texts, which has been generally neglected in critical study of the Bible.

Israel, in the multilayered texts that it produced, sets itself off from the dominant ancient Near Eastern civilizations of Mesopotamia and Egypt.

The foundational narrative of Israel's formation as a people is the story of their exodus from hard bondage under the Egyptian Pharaoh. The obvious starting point in chapter 1, therefore, is to sketch the economic structure of those great imperial civilizations. Particularly important for their relevance to biblical economics will be to identify the features that are so oppressive as to lead the Hebrews to withdraw and the other features that carry over into Israel.

The books of the Pentateuch, or the Torah, combine the historical narrative of Israel's origins and its foundational laws. At the center of the Pentateuch/Torah, both substantively and as the organizing structure, is the Mosaic Covenant. From Exodus 19 through the rest of Exodus, all of Leviticus, and up to Numbers 10, Israel is encamped at Mount Sinai receiving the Covenant and covenantal law. The whole book of Deuteronomy is then a "second (covenantal) law" taught by Moses as the Israelites prepare to enter the land. As became quite clear a half-century ago, the Covenant has a constitutive structure of integral components that lay out basic principles for social-economic life. Chapter 2 explores the implication of the basic components of the covenantal structure and the economic principles that they articulate. The rest of the covenantal law-giving in the books of the Pentateuch elaborate on and apply those fundamental principles. Included are a number of mechanisms designed to make the basic guiding principles work. These are the focus of chapter 3.

The second division of the Hebrew Bible, the Prophets, includes both the historical narratives of the rise and actions of monarchs in Israel and collections of oracles delivered by prophets under the kings. The historical books include key passages that summarize and elaborate the political-economic structure of the monarchs, including how they replicate the structure of ancient Near Eastern empires. The earliest oracles of the classical prophets pronounce God's indictment and punishment of kings and their officers for violating the principles of the Covenant and the economic rights of the people. Chapters 4 and 5 examine these developments.

As background and context for examination of the economic concerns of Jesus and the movement that responded to his ministry, chapter 6 examines how Roman domination of Judea and Galilee complicated the economic structure. I focus particularly on how Roman rule brought additional pressure on the already difficult economic circumstances of the Galileans and Judeans.

That Jesus was every bit as concerned with economic issues as the Hebrew prophets has often gone unnoticed. The biblical tradition of covenantal principles and mechanisms continued into the time of Jesus. This can be seen particularly in the covenant renewal and extensive covenantal teachings evident in some of the Dead Sea Scrolls. The renewal of the Mosaic Covenant was also central to Jesus' proclamation of the kingdom of God. This is most evident in the covenantal speech of Jesus that stands behind both the Sermon on the Mount in Matthew and the Sermon on the Plain in Luke. In this speech, to which I will devote most of chapter 7, Jesus pronounces a new declaration of deliverance ("blessed are you poor . . .") and then lays out renewed demands for covenantal mutual sharing and cooperation. The renewal of the Mosaic covenant also runs throughout the Gospel of Mark, particularly in a series of dialogues in Mark 10 focused mainly on covenantal economics, which will be explored in chapter 8.

In chapter 9 we look briefly at the economic concerns of Paul in the assemblies of Christ he was catalyzing among non-Judean people in Greek cities. Historically unprecedented was the collection that he was gathering for "the poor among the saints in Jerusalem," a unique experiment of "international" economic sharing among peoples subject to imperial rule.

Chapter 10 is devoted to how the Gospel of Matthew continues and further schematizes the economic teaching of Jesus, both the economic sharing and justice within the communities, and the condemnation of rulers for their economic exploitation of subject peoples, in new communities of Diaspora Judeans in Syria. This happens most clearly in the Sermon on the Mount, but also throughout the book.

The conclusion focuses on ways that covenantal principles and mechanisms that protect people's economic rights may be relevant to the very different economic situation today.

The first five chapters could be used independently from the chapters on the Gospels and Paul. Any one of these chapters could even be used separately, although it is difficult to understand the significance of the Covenant and its declaration of economic rights without a sense of the imperial economy of the ancient Near East. The chapters on Jesus' renewal of the covenant community, including covenantal economics, would be difficult to understand without previous acquaintance with both the Roman imperial economy and the original structure, principles, and protective mechanisms of the Mosaic Covenant laid out in chapters 2 and 3 and the prophetic protests of violation of people's economic rights in chapter 5.

A Note to Readers

I strongly encourage you to read the key passages in the Bible that are discussed in the chapters below—indeed to read them repeatedly as you reflect on the texts and their implications. (Often comparing different translations generates additional insights into the texts.) Only in some cases has it been economically feasible to reprint the key passages in these chapters. So have a Bible handy as you use this volume.

Chapter One

Serving the Sacred Forces of Imperial Civilization

The ancient Near East has often been called "the cradle of civilization." High civilization emerged independently in a number of places, including China, India, and the Americas (among the Incas and Aztecs). Schooling in Western societies, however, has focused on the origin of civilization in the fertile river valleys of the Nile in Egypt and the Tigris and Euphrates in Mesopotamia. The abiding symbols of those civilizations are the great pyramids in Egypt and the massive stepped towers, called ziggurats, in Mesopotamia. We stand in awe of these grand structures, especially at how, long before the explosion of technology in the modern world, it would have been possible to erect monuments on such a huge scale.

What we do not necessarily learn in our "secular" education is that the high civilizations were sacred. They were all focused on the service of the sacred superhuman natural and civilizational forces that determined the people's lives, forces that we usually refer to as "the gods." The pyramids and ziggurats were sacred monuments, the tombs of the Pharaohs, who were the sacred CEOs of imperial Egypt, and the palaces of the divine cosmic-civilizational Forces of imperial Mesopotamia, respectively.

But precisely as religious monuments they are clues to the sacred *economic* structure of Egyptian and Mesopotamian civilizations. Lacking heavy construction equipment, the ancients had only their own muscle power and that of their donkeys and oxen. The construction of those huge pyramids and ziggurats would have required thousands and thousands of workers all toiling closely together in careful coordination. That work required captains and commanders whose authority the thousands of workers would have heeded and whose orders they would have obeyed. In addition to the pyramids and ziggurats, these ancient civilizations also

1

featured the palaces of kings, the mansions of the high-ranking officers, the pleasure gardens for these ruling elite (such as the hanging gardens in Babylon), and irrigation dikes and canals.

What is more, the tens of thousands of workers had to be fed. There were two possibilities. If the same gangs of thousands of laborers worked throughout the year on construction, then the "surplus" produce (in addition to the produce necessary to support the producers) of ten thousand farmers would have been needed to feed every thousand laborers. Or, if the constructional laborers worked in shifts while also still working the land during the crucial farming months, then ten months' farming was required to support each month's labor on the sacred monuments of civilization. In addition, of course, the sacred kings/CEOs and their officers, not to mention their military forces, had to be supported in the style to which they had become accustomed.

Given the limited productive capacity of ancient agriculture, the massive monuments of ancient civilizations thus required the labor of hundreds of thousands of farmers and laborers, mainly in the production of food. The high civilizations of the ancient Near East depended on an extensive agrarian economy. At the base of the economy of the great civilizations of antiquity was the agricultural and construction labor of the masses. At the top were the rulers and their supporting officials and military forces who organized and coordinated the people's labor. Moreover, those at the top required the authority and power to persuade or coerce those at the base to obey their commands. Most of our sources pertain to the rulers and the religion that authorized their power. But the sources also allow us to deduce a few conclusions about the role of the producers who obeyed the commands of the rulers.

Study of economics in ancient Near Eastern societies tends to focus on the plethora of documents (such as records of tax collection) that have been unearthed in the last century or so. Little attention has been given to broad patterns of economic structure and relationships. Interpreters tend to apply concepts and categories derived from modern capitalist economics, such as "the market" and "private property." But a market economy did not become dominant in any society until modern times. Trade was limited to the wealthy and powerful in the ancient Near East. To think in terms of "private property" and of a "public sector" and a "private sector" may simply prevent us from discerning the different overlapping and often competing claims on economic resources.

Most important is to keep constantly in mind that, in contrast to modern society, there was no separation between economics, politics, and religion. In most cases there were no words and concepts for what we think of as particular functions or roles. Our textbooks may label Hammurabi as the Babylonian king or emperor. In Akkadian, however, he was called simply "Great One," which we would have to translate with multiple overlapping terms: emperor of Babylon = high priest of Marduk, the chief sacred Power of Babylon = CEO of the Babylonian imperial economy. What scholars usually refer to as "temples" were literally the "houses" of particular gods where their chief servants offered sacrifices. But these "temples" were also the storehouses in which the tithes and offerings brought to the gods were kept. They were also the political center of the area that they controlled. The economy and politics were thus always sacred, done in service to the cosmic-civilizational Forces or Powers that determined the people's lives.

The particular structure of economics in ancient Near Eastern societies varied according to topography, climate, and historical development. Thus any broad picture of the ancient Near Eastern economy will involve oversimplification. Nevertheless we can discern certain basic common structures that were shared in the ancient Egyptian and Mesopotamian empires and Canaanite city-states.

The "Great Ones"

The empires of the ancient Near East were built up like elaborate pyramids. The basic unit of production and consumption was the family. Smaller or larger numbers of families lived in villages, and numbers of villages supported temple towns and cities with taxes, tithes, and offerings. After the emergence of large cities, centered around the great temples of several Forces, in both Mesopotamia and Egypt, one city conquered the others and headed an imperial structure. In both Egypt and Mesopotamia these empires also included the great temples, their towns and lands. When another great city became dominant, the center of power changed, but not the fundamental structure of the empire and its economy. The conquered cities were subordinated to and paid tribute to the imperial city or court. But the imperial regime generally did not interfere much with the structure and operations of the subordinate cities and temples. They may have designated their high officers to be governors with oversight over certain cities or areas. But they left the basic local structure intact as the instrument by which they could both control the area and extract their revenues.

The most fundamental structure in the ancient Near East was a relatively simple one. Rulers in command of instruments of persuasion or coercion demanded that producers who farmed the land (called "black-headed ones," the term for ordinary humans) produce more than enough to feed themselves, which the rulers expropriated as taxes, tithes, and/or tribute. The rulers also demanded that producers spend a certain number of days or weeks working on their construction or other projects, some of which might be ostensibly also for their benefit. The "great one" of the temple should not be thought of as owning the land. The concept of (private) property does not appropriately describe the economic relationship of ruler and land. Nor can the producers/laborers be thought of as the rulers' slaves. Everyone in a given society was understood as a "servant of the god(s)" and the farmers/laborers and officials alike were called the "servants" of the rulers as well. But the rulers did not own them. The rulers rather had a claim to a portion of the people's produce and labor.

There were usually at least two layers of rulers, the local and the imperial. Both (or all) layers had claims on the produce and often the labor of the producers. Local kings levied taxes, temples expected tithes and offerings, and emperors demanded tribute. The imperial rulers usually had the local rulers collect their tribute. Also, since most revenues were extracted in produce—money had not yet been "invented"—and transportation over long distances was prohibitively expensive, imperial rulers did not have all tribute sent to the imperial capital. They rather used tribute to support their military forces in the local area and for local or regional projects.

Rulers provided support for their military forces and officials who carried out functions such as revenue collection in one or both of two ways. One was to give them rations from general tax revenues. This was the principal way of supporting the military forces, which consumed much or most of the revenues in subjected areas. To support high-ranking officers and collateral branches of the royal family, rulers often turned over to them the operation and revenues from estates of various sizes. Many of the latter involved one or more village communities of producers. These holdings were attached to the office, not property owned by the officials. If son succeeded father in the office, the estate could appear as hereditary, although a change of rulers often resulted in reassignment.

While the structure and relationship between rulers and their subjects sketched above continued as the base of the ancient Near Eastern economy, complications and variations had developed over a period of generations and centuries. As rulers and their officers also became creditors, they could extract produce as interest on loans in addition to taxes and tribute. When they came into greater control of the land of heavily indebted producers, they became in effect absentee landlords who took much of the produce of the people who had become their tenants.

Some such arrangement probably explains the origin of two forms of enhanced control of both land and labor by the rulers and their officials. One was "royal land" and "royal peasants/people." Both local kings and great emperors held estates, often large tracts of land worked by dependent farmers tied to the soil or tied to the monarchy. In some cases these were the result of a long process of making loans, charging steep interest, and eventually "foreclosure," in which the land and even the farming families themselves came under the more complete control of the rulers. Some of the vast tracts of royal land and the workers on the land were royal projects to expand production onto new lands.

In the second form of control of land and labor, officials of local and imperial kings and of temples engaged in the same practices of making loans, charging interest, and foreclosing on debts, albeit on a lesser scale. In this way they brought land and peasant producers increasingly under their control. Royal or imperial officers thus ended up holding many small scattered plots (not continuous large tracts of land). They could thereby handsomely enhance their own wealth, prestige, and power in ways that made them semi-independent of the rulers. In effect these officials and their heirs became absentee landlords who lived in considerable wealth supplied by the rents paid by their tenants who worked the land that had come under their creditors' control. It is worth reminding ourselves that documents mentioning what appears to us as sale of real estate or of persons and rental contracts were written for the elite, mainly high-ranking officials. Hence we should not imagine, on the basis of such documents, that large numbers of "citizens" of ancient Near Eastern cities owned "private property" that was commonly bought and sold or that the persons "sold" had become chattel slaves. The aim of the rulers and their officers alike was to control land and labor to enhance their income.

Since the economy was largely agricultural, the principal way for rulers to "grow" their economy was to conquer more territory, to subject additional cities and smaller kingdoms. Ancient rulers had no sense that wealth could be reinvested in order to enhance productivity. Instead wealth was simply accumulated and used in display, the more grandiose the better. Rulers constructed ever grander temples for the gods, palaces and tombs for themselves, even completely new capital cities for the greater glory of their reign. Palaces and temples were adorned with precious metals. In some cases silver and gold were simply stockpiled. Royal officials also had a passion for display, but on a less elaborate scale.

The elaborate lifestyle to which rulers and their officers became accustomed required support services. Here what might otherwise appear to modern Westerners as markets, merchants, and commerce fits into the economy. Trade was sponsored, although probably not completely controlled, by the rulers. The latter sent or contracted traders to acquire materials or fancy foods not locally available, such as timber or precious metals or gems, and provided them with the products or precious metals to trade for them. Such trade was a very limited part of the overall economy. Because it was important to the rulers, however, it might lead them to take measures to increase revenues, by raising taxes or expanding agricultural production or additional conquests.

Temples, royal courts, and wealthy and powerful elite also managed production of key crafts locally. For example, temples had their own craftspeople, supported by rations from general revenues. In other cases royal or imperial regimes, instead of maintaining substantial numbers of craftspeople or artisans on rations, obtained and allocated raw materials to craftspeople, and in effect contracted the supply of a quantity of finished product with a credit note worth a certain amount of supplies from royal storehouses. But since such production was managed by officers of the king, and not independent entrepreneurs, this was not yet "commerce" in the early modern sense.

The "Black-Headed Ones"

Economic support of rulers and their officers, the heads of the temples, and the supporting artisans and other servants in the cities required (at least) ten people farming for every person in the cities where the rulers and their supporting artisans and military officers lived. Families, the basic units of production, raised crops to feed themselves as well as to support their superiors with tithes and taxes. Larger or smaller groups of families lived clustered together in villages near the land they worked. Families, as well as village communities, were largely self-sufficient, crafting their own clothes and tools. While there was surely barter within the village community, there was little exchange with the outside world. Rulers interfered very little, except to demand their revenues.

In an agrarian society, of course, economic production depended on working the land. The most basic pattern of land tenure, on which several variations developed, was that families possessed hereditary rights to fields on which they raised a subsistence living for themselves as well as enough to meet their rulers' demands for taxes, tithes, and tribute.

Despite these demands, a certain percentage of peasant families were able to persist on their ancestral lands. Their rights to their family inheritance were protected by time-honored customs that kings and temple officials were supposed to observe, and by restraints on the sale of ancestral land.

Observing the people's customary rights to the land was in the rulers' long-range interest as well, in order to keep their productive base viable on ancestral parcels of land to supply tax and tribute. The Code of Hammurabi, the "Great One" of Babylon, includes some laws that protected people's rights to their ancestral land. The appearance of similar laws in other ancient Near Eastern law codes suggests that these reflect what must have been similar customs in several societies that protected the viability of families on ancestral lands. Also in Mesopotamia over the centuries, often during the first year of their reign, kings issued edicts canceling debts and enslavement for debts so that debt-slaves could return to their lands. These edicts may well have provided propaganda to enhance a king's image at the outset of his reign. But they also attest the persistence of peasants working their ancestral lands.

The customs and "common law" designed to protect people's rights to their land, however, were not sufficient to prevent many from succumbing to rulers' pressures for taxes, tithes, and tribute. Bad weather or a damaged crop, particularly a drought, could spell disaster for producer families. Unable to feed themselves after the rulers had taken their share of the harvest, families had to borrow. After exhausting the tiny reserves of their generous neighbors, they were forced to borrow from the only people who had access to larger surpluses, the officers of the king or temple. Ever eager to take advantage of the misfortune of the poor, the officers charged high rates of interest, which only drove the needy families further into debt when they could not repay the loan plus interest at the next harvest. The result, over several years of inadequate harvests, was that their wealthy creditors seized their children to work off the debt. Many never recovered, as the wealthy creditors took over their lands for default on their debts. A certain percentage of producers thus became mere tenants or sharecroppers, perhaps on the land their ancestors had once possessed as family inheritance.

These poverty-stricken peasants who became debt-slaves or lost control of their land (which they sold for their debts) and their descendants must have provided the tenants or renters on the lands that royal officers acquired by "foreclosing" on indebted peasants. Such tenants were constrained to grow the crops that their "absentee landlords" required, such as high-quality wines and oil and nicely fattened livestock, either for their own consumption or to trade for luxury products.

The tenants who worked on the royal lands generally had fewer rights and were far more dependent than peasants still working their families' ancestral lands. Many, perhaps most, were in effect sharecroppers or renters. Their continuation on the land was contingent on the favor of the king, or more likely some royal manager or official or relative of the king to whom the king had granted the revenues from the land. Their ancestors may well have fallen into debt-slavery. While they were by no means slaves, they could be exploited more heavily than regular peasants since they were direct tenants of the monarchy. Some royal peasants, however, appear to have had or gained rights on the land similar to those of traditional peasants. The land was transmitted by inheritance. And while the tenants could lease their land (which was also presumably still royal land) for debts, it was not alienable (i.e., they could not sell it permanently).

The peasants subordinate to the great temples and their priest-managers would presumably have stood in similar relation to their rulers. In earlier centuries they may have held hereditary rights to ancestral land, with a temple having a claim to a portion of their produce and labor. By becoming indebted to the priest-managers of the temple who had control of surplus resources, however, a large number of them had also become debt-slaves, lost control of their land, and become tenants or renters of the temple managers.

The general trend in ancient Near Eastern societies was for the peasant producers to lose their economic rights to land, as well as the fruits of their labor, to the wealthy and powerful. That kings, in their public propaganda, posed as the defenders of the poor peasants, "the widow and the orphan," suggests that the rulers at the very top recognized the problem. The periodic royal edicts of release of debts and debt-slaves and peasants' return to their land (land reform, in modern terms) indicates that they took concrete measures, however temporary and inadequate, to preserve their economic base. In the overall political-economic structure, the royal or temple officials' principal means of enhancing their own power and prestige was by heavier exploitation of "the black-headed ones" subject to their influence, bringing the latter more fully under their control. They had little or no incentive to protect the larger economic base. Peasant economic rights had a greater chance of being protected by rulers who exerted relatively greater vigilance and power over their officials.

Peasants, who constituted the economic base of temple and monarchy alike, were always vulnerable to the rulers' ambitions and special projects, whether wars of conquest or elaborate building projects. A military buildup or the construction of a new palace required both extra produce and higher demands for labor. In this connection we should also take into account the people's vulnerability to the periodic warfare by which empires waxed and waned. Empires expanded their economic base by conquest, leading to wars between empires. Warring armies devastated peasant villages in their advances and retreats, seizing the people's grain and livestock to feed themselves, or destroying crops to weaken the opposing rulers and armies. Only in times of a lull in warfare and especially in times of weak rulers could the peasants even begin to reclaim the land and regain some of their economic rights.

Religion

After this survey of the economy of ancient Near Eastern societies, the obvious question is why "the black-headed ones" would dutifully render up a sizable portion of their crops when it might leave them with less than enough to survive the year. Why would they join gangs of laborers to help build the palace or tomb of "the great one" who took away their produce so that he and his officers could live in luxury? How did the economic system work so that the vast majority of people living at mere subsistence worked so hard to support a tiny elite that lived in luxury? How could the rulers have channeled all that surplus wealth into decoration and display or mere stockpiles rather than invest it in the improvement of the economy or leave the poverty-stricken and often hungry and desperate producers with more of their harvests so that they might live more humanely?

Two dominating factors made the ancient Near Eastern economy work, despite its gross inequality and crass exploitation of the people. One factor was coercion. The rulers had military forces at their disposal. Imperial regimes looked upon failure to render up their tribute as tantamount to rebellion, and sent their armies on punitive expeditions. At the more local level, rulers and their officers had military or strong-arm gangs to "encourage" the peasants to pay their taxes and tithes. As to why many people did not simply flee their desperate circumstances, it would have been impossible for fugitives to survive in the expanse of desert waste beyond the fertile river valleys. Only in cities near hilly or mountainous country, for example, in Canaan or Syria, could peasants have survived after escaping from their village communities.

Equally or perhaps even more important as a motivating factor making the economic system work was the religious-cultural dimension. As already noted, religion and political-economy were inseparable in the ancient Near East. We also noted that some of the principal economic concepts that we simply assume for modern capitalism are utterly inapplicable to the ancient Near East. Yet so far we have proceeded as if it were possible to analyze the economy in terms of political-economic structure and relations without including the religious factor. But we have now bumped up against the impossibility of explaining how the ancient Near Eastern economic system worked without considering the all-important religious aspect. To do this, however, we also need to reexamine our assumptions about religion and some of our basic religious concepts, such as God/the gods and the separation of religion from politics and economics.

The starting point is to note again that religion and political-economy were inseparable. The "houses of the gods," which we call "temples," were also centers of political-economic power. The figures that modern scholars usually label as chief priests were also the managers (CEOs) of the local economy and were the local political heads as well. Kings were sacred, declared at their coronation to be "the son of god." Taxes were sacred obligations, and tithes were the economic revenues of the houses of the gods.

In order to understand ancient Near Eastern religion as it held together the imperial economic system, however, it is necessary to go a giant step further: to broaden our theology, our concept of God/gods. We usually think of God/gods not just as spiritual realities, but as transcendent above empirical phenomena, as supernatural. We commonly think of ancient Egyptian and Mesopotamian religions as polytheism, in contrast with the monotheism that emerged with the Israelites. But this is simply a pious platitude. It is not even clear that the ancient Near Easterners had a generic concept of the gods. It adds to the confusion not to translate the names of the gods in myths of origins and hymns. The names have meanings. The Akkadian names in the Mesopotamian myth of origin that begins with the words "When on high . . . ," were Sea (*Tiamat*), River (*Apsu*), Sky (*Anu*) = Authority, Irrigation (*Ea*) = Wisdom, Storm (*Enlil*) = Kingship, and so on. These were the personified forces that determined the people's lives. Most of them were natural forces. But some, such as Storm-Kingship and Irrigation-Wisdom, were (also) political and/or economic as well as natural. That is, not only were kings and tithes inseparably political-economic and religious, but the Forces that determined the life of society were also inseparably political-economic and religious—as well as, in most cases, natural-cosmic.

The forces, moreover, were Superhuman Persons who could provide or withhold fertility and productivity. In Mesopotamia, River when benignly disposed could provide water to make the crops grow, but when angry might overflow his banks and destroy villages, cities, and crops. In Syria and Canaan, Lord Storm would send the rain that made for a good harvest, but might withhold the needed rain if angered. Yet, as noted, these forces were not simply natural or cosmic but also social-economic, as best illustrated by Irrigation-Wisdom, which was central to societal life in Mesopotamia. All ancient Near Eastern political-economic-cosmic systems depended on having an incomparably virile executive Force at their apex. In both Syria and Mesopotamia this was Storm-Kingship, who had sufficient forces of violence at his disposal to defeat the counterforces of chaos, thus maintaining cosmic order and its derivative, the sacred political-economic order. In Egypt the executive divine Force at the vortex of the cosmic and the political-economic was none other than Pharaoh.

The people were thus both grateful to the divine forces and extremely fearful of their potential anger and destructiveness. This is what made the economy work. The people did not just worship the Forces but *served* them with their produce and labor. The Forces in their proper balance or relationship, Storm and Sea in the Canaanite city-states or Storm, River, Irrigation, and so on, in Mesopotamia, generated the fertility and productivity from which the people lived. The people were therefore expected, in their gratitude, to bring a portion of their crops to the houses of the Forces as what they owed for their favor. Moreover, because the Forces were also awesomely fearful and easily angered, the people had to appease them with offerings.

The kings and priests were the regents of the divine forces and mediators between the Forces and the people. They received the tithes and offerings on behalf of the Forces. They thus had custody over and power to use the resulting resources for purposes that they determined. One such use was to support military forces, which gave them coercive power over the producers.

Rulers also used resources in impressive ceremonies that awed the people with the power of the divine forces. At the climax of the annual cycle of ceremonies in Babylon was the week-long New Year Festival that included the ritual drama of the origin of the divine Order of civilization imposed by Storm-King's violent victory over the threatening forces of chaos. Rituals reinforcing fear of the divine Forces may well have supported respect for the customs and laws protecting the inalienability of the people's ancestral land. In the hands of the rulers, however, the elaborate festivals and ceremonies became the media of mystification by which the people's fear of the Forces was manipulated to motivate their obedient service in produce and labor.

In these and other religious rituals the kings and priests, as the official mediators with the divine Forces, also interpreted the Forces' will to the people. Their will might include the construction of new irrigation canals in order to ensure greater productivity. It certainly included the construction of the pyramids as the tombs of the divine pharaohs and the huge temple complexes, including the ziggurats in Mesopotamian cities, requiring gangs of laborers numbering in the thousands.

Biblical Stories of the Imperial Economy in Egypt

The ancient Israelites, whose historical experience is reflected in episodes of biblical books, knew about how the rulers of the ancient Near East commandeered the produce, land, and labor of their people. Two stories in particular give vivid pictures, the one of the Pharaoh's control of the agricultural base of the economy, and the other of the forced labor by which the regime managed its massive building projects. The latter brings us full circle to the starting point of this chapter.

Seven Fat Cows and Seven Lean Cows (Gen. 41; 47:13-26)

The narratives toward the end of the book of Genesis set the stage for the Hebrews' breakaway from the sacred political-economic system dominant in the ancient Near East. The ancestors Abraham and Sarah had left Mesopotamia in search of a new land and life in Canaan. In time of famine, however, the sons of Jacob/Israel had gone to Egypt in search of food. There the precocious eleventh son, Joseph, had found a low-level position in the regime of the Pharaoh, from which he was suddenly elevated when he interpreted Pharaoh's dream. Pharaoh had dreamed that seven sleek and fat cows came up out of the Nile. Then seven ugly and thin cows came up out of the Nile and ate up the seven sleek and fat cows (Gen. 41:1–4). None of the wise men at the Egyptian imperial court trained in the interpretation of dreams and omens could interpret Pharaoh's dreams. But the young Hebrew, a servant of the captain of the guard, explained that the dreams were about the future performance of the Egyptian economy. "There will come seven years of great plenty," followed by seven years of famine, "and the famine will consume the land." Therefore the imperial regime should stockpile one-fifth of the produce of the land of Egypt during the seven plenteous years as a reserve against the seven years of famine (41:25–36). Pharaoh was so impressed with this interpretation that he appointed Joseph as "chief operating officer" of his regime to manage the collection and storage of the surplus (41:37–49).

So far this story illustrates how instrumental religion was in economic planning, in this case dreams that come from the gods and their interpretation. The story also illustrates how economic planning and organization were done from the top down. The imperial regime commanded the economy, ordering the people to render up one-fifth of their crops to be stockpiled under the control of the regime, ostensibly in the interests of the whole society.

But the story also shows how the regime took advantage of the situation to tighten its grip on producers and production. When the famine became severe and the people cried to Pharaoh for bread, Joseph, chief operating officer of the imperial regime, engaged in what we today would call systematic extortion. The people had rendered up increased taxes supposedly as insurance against the contingency of drought and famine. But when they cried out to Pharaoh for bread, Joseph demanded that they yield up all their donkeys, horses, and herds of sheep and goats in "exchange" (47:14–19). Pharaoh's regime now controlled what had been the people's livestock. When they again came desperate for grain so that they would not starve, they were forced to agree that they and their land would become servants of Pharaoh. The regime of Pharaoh thus took advantage of the people's desperate circumstances, the threat of starvation, to make permanent its claim to one-fifth of the harvest (47:20–26).

This story thus gives a picture, writ large for the whole society, of the steps by which poor peasants, when hit by famine or other misfortune, fell into debt. Their debts mounted during continuing crises until eventually they were forced to "sell" their land and themselves in order to survive. As the ones who had control of the surpluses, moreover, the king or his officers were in position to take advantage of the people's hunger. If crises continued through several bad harvests, the imperial regime and/or its officials could gain control of people's land and even of their labor as debt-slaves.

Hard Bondage in Egypt (Exod. 1–2)

The implication of the very beginning of the book of Exodus is that the Hebrews, outsiders who had entered the country in time of famine, initially had a special arrangement with the imperial regime in Egypt. Perhaps they had been settled along the frontier (as border guards?) and were not treated as ordinary peasants subject to forced labor. When "a new king arose over Egypt," however, this changed. The new regime took measures to subject them to the same demands as those made on ordinary Egyptians. This seemed sharply oppressive to the Hebrews, as portrayed in the opening paragraph of Exodus:

> They set taskmasters over them to oppress them with forced labor. They built supply cities, Pithom and Rameses, for Pharaoh. . . . The Egyptians . . . made their lives bitter with hard service in mortar and brick and in every kind of field labor. (Exod. 1:11–14)

The pharaoh not only expropriated one-fifth of the people's crops but pressed them into forced labor to construct the storage depots and supply cities where the regime controlled the surplus. But it was precisely by means of forced labor that the pharaohs could also manage the construction of the massive pyramids as monuments to their glory as the heads of the great Egyptian civilization.

Serving the Forces and Serving the Rulers

In the ancient Near Eastern empires from which Israel made its departure, rulers demanded and expropriated a portion of the people's crops. In response to the demands of their rulers, the people were compelled to produce enough to meet those demands as well as to support themselves and to supply labor for the construction of the monuments of civilization.

The rulers' control and management of the resulting revenues gave them power over the producers. This can be seen most clearly in the military. Rulers' expropriation of a portion of every producer's crops gave them control of resources from which they could support professional military forces that gave them coercive power over the producers.

The rulers' power over the people also worked in two other ways. Most important for the whole political-economic system was their maintenance of the religion that motivated the people to render up their produce and labor. It was essential to induce and reinforce the people's belief in and deep fear of the cosmic-civilizational Forces that determined their lives. These Forces provided the fertility and productivity that enabled people to survive and supported the superstructure of civilization. But they could also withhold productivity and destroy houses, crops, and, much worse, the irrigation dikes, terraces, and storehouses on which their complex social-economic life depended. As the mediators between the people and the Forces, the rulers, who also feared the Forces, managed the media of mystification that maintained the belief in and fear of the Forces.

While it may seem ironic to us, with our critical distance, a key aspect of this sacred economic system was that the Forces that the people feared and appeased with their tithes and offerings were in large part the products of the people's labor and produce. Perhaps the best illustration of this is the Force called Irrigation-Wisdom in Mesopotamia. Irrigation as a system of dikes and canals was obviously designed and constructed by the people over several generations. Irrigation, with its clear connotations of wisdom/design/science, became one of the major Forces on which the production and reproduction of society and civilization in Mesopotamia depended, hence important for the people to serve with further labor and produce. Perhaps less obvious to us, Storm-Kingship (or Marduk in the Babylon of Hammurabi) was also the product largely of the people's labor and produce. That is, the imperial monarchy was utterly dependent on the produce of the people to support the military by which it conquered and maintained the empire and on the labor of the people for the construction of the monuments by which it maintained the earthly rule corresponding to the rule of the cosmos by Storm-Kingship.

Finally, the rulers and their officials also used the power they held to control the people's produce and thus augmented their power by taking advantage of the people's economic poverty and vulnerability. According to sacred custom and religiously reinforced "common law," the people supposedly had certain ancestral rights to land. Presumably partly to keep their economic base viable, some rulers did take measures to enforce those rights. But the persistent pattern was that both rulers and their officials who had control of grain and other staples in official storehouses made loans at high rates of interest to desperate peasants, who fell seriously into debt. Their creditors could exploit their indebtedness to take control of their lands and often their labor, reducing them to tenants. All people were servants of the divine cosmic-civilizational Forces and, in effect, of their rulers as well, who were the regents of the forces. But a substantial percentage of the people were reduced to being the servants of the rulers and their officials in a more complete way.

This was the service of the divine Forces and the rulers from which the Hebrews withdrew to begin an experiment with an alternative society in which the people no longer bowed down and served the Forces of civilization, but served a transcendent Force of freedom, who insisted upon justice in relations with other people, not hard labor.

Study Questions

1. School textbooks and museum displays tend to glamorize the "wonders" of ancient civilizations. How glamorous were those "wonders" for the ordinary people?

2. How did the wealthy and powerful (rulers and their officers) gradually increase their control over the people's land and labor? That is, how did they turn the produce of people's labor into power over the people?

3. How did fear and service of the divine Powers lead to the people's loss of control over their land and labor (the basis of their livelihood)?

4. Did the people have any ways to defend their right to the basis of their livelihood?

5. Is the story of Joseph and the seven fat cows and seven lean cows included in the book of Genesis to glamorize Joseph, or for some other purpose?

Chapter Two

Covenant Society
and Economic Rights

The Covenant that God made with the people of Israel on Mount Sinai, mediated by Moses, stands at the center of the Hebrew Bible (the Christian "Old Testament"). In the books of the Pentateuch (or Torah = "Teaching"), Israel is encamped at Sinai from Exodus 19 though the beginning of Numbers 10.* The second half of the book of Exodus, the whole book of Leviticus, and the first part of Numbers consist of the Covenant itself (Exod. 20; Deut. 5), extensive lists of covenantal laws and teaching, and ceremonial enactment of the covenant with Yahweh (Exod. 24). The whole book of Deuteronomy has a covenantal structure and consists of covenantal teaching. God's promise to Abraham, often called a covenant, plays a prominent role in the narrative of Genesis. But the bulk of the Pentateuch consists of covenant making, covenantal law codes, and covenantal teaching all related to God's giving of the Covenant through Moses on Mount Sinai. Moreover, the covenantal laws and teachings in these books cover not only religious observances but most aspects of social, political, and economic life as well.

The Mosaic Covenant is also the central theme in the books of the Deuteronomistic History, from Joshua through 2 Kings. These books repeatedly evaluate the actions of the people in the period before the formation of monarchy and the acts of the kings of Israel and Judah according to the criteria of the Covenant. They declare that the kings of Israel and Judah were conquered by foreign empires because they had violated the provisions of the Covenant. The great Israelite prophets

*Read the principal texts of the Covenant and covenant renewal in Exodus 20, Deuteronomy 5, and Joshua 24 and consult those texts as you read the discussion in this chapter.

17

such as Amos, Hosea, Isaiah, Micah, and Jeremiah regularly pronounce God's/Yahweh's indictment of the kings and their officers for having oppressed their people in violation of the covenantal commandments. The principal concern in the formation of the books of the Hebrew Bible after the destruction of Jerusalem and the Temple by the Babylonians in 587 was apparently that the people must learn from this historical disaster. They must now be scrupulous in observance of their Covenant with God.

In modern societies, Christians and Jews have usually understood the Bible as concerned with religious life. The "separation of church and state" in the U.S. Constitution has reinforced this. In effect the churches agreed not to interfere seriously in political affairs and the state not to interfere in matters of faith and church governance. The Bible, however, is concerned with all of life. In ancient Israel religion and political-economic life were inseparable. God was concerned with all aspects of life.

The political aspect of the biblical concern for all aspects of civil life was at least tacitly acknowledged in the Declaration of Independence: it was "self-evident, that all men [albeit free European males] are . . . endowed by their Creator with certain unalienable Rights, that among these are Life, Liberty, and the pursuit of Happiness." "The pursuit of Happiness" suggests that the Declaration included the economic aspect. Historians are clear that Jefferson and the other "founding fathers" were paraphrasing the words of Scottish philosopher John Locke, who had stated explicitly that the God-endowed rights included "life, liberty, and property." But when the founders came finally to make some of the God-given rights explicit in the first ten amendments to the Constitution, they focused on political rights.

If we look more carefully at the Covenant and its teaching in the Bible, however, it becomes evident that God's concern focuses on the social-economic welfare of the people, free of exploitation and oppression by those who managed to consolidate political-economic power in their own hands.

As noted in the introduction, many of the people who fled England to the New World understood their escape across the Atlantic as a new exodus. They also understood their settlements in Plymouth, Boston, and elsewhere in New England as new covenantal communities. A few generations later, in that same tradition, many understood the Revolutionary War as a new exodus and the U.S. Constitution as a new covenant. To reverse the analogy, the exodus of the Hebrews from bondage in Egypt was the very prototype of a people gaining its independence. And Israel's covenant with Yahweh was the ancient equivalent of a people forming a constitution to guide its operations as a society.

In the anticolonial struggles following World War II, many African and Asian peoples gained their independence and formed constitutions for the governance of their society. Most of them, however, simply accepted the prevailing economic system of international corporate capitalism, just as the newly independent United States had accepted the entrepreneurial capitalism only then beginning to develop. Since economic life ("hard labor") was inseparable from the dominant imperial political order in the ancient Near East (see chapter 1), however, Israel had to include economics in its "declaration of independence" and covenantal "constitution."

The Structure of God's Covenant with the People of Israel

Jewish and Christian teaching has long focused on the ten commandments as rules for leading a pious and moral personal life. The principles enunciated in the ten commandments have gone far toward making societal life as civil as it has been. The ten commandments, however, were part of the broader Mosaic Covenant that provided the guiding principles for the political-economic as well as religious life of ancient Israel. To understand just how foundational the Covenant was for the people of Israel we must understand its broader structure and its serious implications for social-economic life.

Christians and Jews have gotten into the habit of reading and interpreting their Scriptures one verse (or one week's lesson) at a time. As we know from the U.S. Constitution or a business contract or a health insurance policy, each particular statement or provision is part of a much larger and more comprehensive document in which the component parts have an overall structure. Similarly we will be better able to appreciate the more comprehensive meaning of the Covenant as a whole by understanding its overall structure. That will enable us to discern the implications of the particular component parts, including those of particular commandments, in ways that will not appear by focusing on one verse at a time.

The overall structure of the Mosaic Covenant as it stands now in the books of Exodus, Deuteronomy, and Joshua may have been a secondary development. Some of the fundamental principles involved may have developed earlier from the common life of the people—just as many of the basic principles of the English common law that governs social-economic life in the United Kingdom and United States developed in the common life of the people. But we might as well take advantage of the clarity that gradually emerged about the broader structure of the Covenant here in chapter 2, and then move to particular covenantal principles and mechanisms operative in the social economic life of ancient Israel in chapter 3.

The broader structure of the Mosaic Covenant in the biblical texts is parallel to that of international treaties that may have been known to early Israel and were certainly known by the time of the prophets. It was not until modern biblical interpreters studied those treaties that they discerned more clearly the structure of the Covenant Yahweh made with the people on Sinai and the more extensive covenantal teaching, as in the book of Deuteronomy. Hittite and other ancient Near Eastern kings made treaties with their vassal kings as a way of governing their empires. A similar international political form was prominent in the Assyrian Empire that dominated the ancient Near East, including Israel and Judah, at the time of the prophets Amos, Hosea, Isaiah, and Micah. Somewhat as the newly independent peoples, for example, of Nigeria adapted the British parliamentary system, so the ancient Israelites adapted the Hittite and Assyrian treaty form in framing the Mosaic Covenant.

While the sequence and emphasis varies somewhat from treaty to treaty, the basic structure consisted of three components, each of which had an important function in the overall treaty and the maintenance of the imperial order. (1) Naming himself as sovereign, the great king who gives the treaty recites the ways in which he (and his ancestors/predecessors) have rescued or protected the vassal king(s). (2) The king then lays out what he requires of the vassals, demands that fall into two main groups: (a) requirements of exclusive loyalty (you shall have no king other than me), and (b) regulations of the relations between the vassals (you shall not raid each other's territory or goods). (3) Finally, evidently in lieu of maintaining a standing army to enforce the demands in step 2, the great king has the vassals enact three ceremonies: (a) recite the treaty on a regular basis as a reminder; (b) call all the gods of the great king's society and of their own societies as witnesses to the treaty; and (c) declare blessings and curses that last into several generations on the vassals themselves if they keep or fail to observe the king's demands.

When we read the Covenant making in Exodus 20 and Deuteronomy 5, the Covenant renewal in Joshua 24, and the covenantal materials in Deuteronomy, the structure that informs all of these texts emerges more clearly. In the original making of the Covenant in Exodus 20 (repeated in Deut. 5) the giver of the Covenant (1), declaring his name, "I am Yahweh your God," narrates briefly his deliverance of the people from slavery in Egypt (Exod. 20:2; Deut. 5:6). (2) Then he declares ten commandments that the people are to observe (see Table 1, p. 22). (a) The first two insist on exclusive loyalty (You shall have no gods other than me, etc., Exod. 20:3, 4–5a; Deut. 5:7, 8–9a). (b) The last six deal with the relations among Israelites (Exod. 20:12–17; Deut. 5:16–21). The commandments about wrongful use of the name of Yahweh and observance of the Sabbath (Exod. 20:7, 8–11; Deut. 5:11, 12–14) pertain to both exclusive loyalty and relations among Israelites. Less clearly evident in the giving of the covenant in Exodus 20 and Deuteronomy 5 is (3) the provision for ceremonies of enforcement. They include no mention of (a) regular reading, although of course renewals of the covenant, as in Joshua 24, were regular occurrences. Insofar as Yahweh was to be the exclusive God of Israel, then (b) calling the gods as witnesses to the Covenant would have been inappropriate. While not appearing as a separate step, (c) the calling down of "blessings and curses" "to the third and fourth—and thousandth—generations" are presupposed in the expansion of the second commandment (Exod. 20:5b–6; Deut. 5:9b–10).

The Covenant structure is mostly explicit and partly implicit in the covenant renewal led by Joshua (Josh. 24). Again the ceremony begins (1) with the naming of the giver of the covenant and a much longer account of Yahweh's deliverance of the people over a period of generations (Josh. 24:2–13). Then Joshua, now in the place of Moses as the mediator, (2a) has the people declare their exclusive loyalty to Yahweh, putting away other gods (24:14–18, 23–24), the point of one group of the king's demands in the treaty structure, and the thrust of the first two commandments in the Covenant (Exod. 20:3, 4–5a). The rest of Yahweh's demands (2b), regarding relations among the people, are presumably contained in the "statutes and ordinances" that Joshua "wrote in the book of the torah of God" (Josh. 24:25–26a). The regular reading of the Covenant (3a) is being explicitly enacted in the covenant renewal itself and implicitly expected in the writing of the statutes in the book of teaching. Despite the fact that Israel could not appeal to other gods as witnesses, even the calling of witnesses (3b) is explicit in the covenant renewal, in two forms. Joshua declares to the people, "You are witnesses against yourselves" (24:22), and he erects a large stone that "has heard the words of Yahweh and serves as a witness against us" (24:26–27). Less prominently, but nevertheless present in the background, (3c) the blessings and curses are presupposed in the reminder that Yahweh is "a jealous God" who would not forgive transgressions of his statutes (24:19).

Table 1: The Numbering of the Ten Commandments in Various Religious Traditions*

	Jewish	Reformed Church Eastern Orthodox	Roman Catholic Anglican, Lutheran
Exodus 20:2 Deuteronomy 5:6	1st	Prologue	1st
Exod 20:3 Deut 5:7	2nd	1st	1st
Exod 20:4-6 Deut 5:8-10	2nd	2nd	1st
Exod 20:7 Deut 5:11	3rd	3rd	2nd
Exod 20:8-11 Deut 5:12-15	4th	4th	3rd
Exod 20:12 Deut 5:16	5th	5th	4th
Exod 20:13 Deut 5:17	6th	6th	5th
Exod 20:14 Deut 5:18	7th	7th	6th
Exod 20:15 Deut 5:19	8th	8th	7th
Exod 20:16 Deut 5:20	9th	9th	8th
Exod 20:17 Deut 5:21	10th	10th	9th & 10th†

* The discussion in this book follows the numbering of the Reformed and Eastern Orthodox traditions.
† Following the version in Deut 5:21, the 9th and 10th commandments in the Roman Catholic and Lutheran traditions refer, respectively, to coveting the wife and the goods of the neighbor.

The book of Deuteronomy is not only full of covenantal laws and teachings, but its overall structure is that of the Covenant. The first chapters serve as (1) a reminder of God's deliverance of the people. The bulk of the book (Deut. 6–26) consists of (2) expansions on one or another of the ten commandments and/or of covenantal laws. Finally (3c) Deuteronomy 27–28 contain a long list of blessings and curses as a motivating sanction reinforcing self-enforcement of Yahweh's covenant demands.

The overall structure of the Covenant in its three basic interrelated components can be seen at a glance in Table 2.

Table 2

Structure of the Covenant	Exodus 20	Deuteronomy 5	Joshua 24
1. Declaration of deliverance	20:2	5:6	24:2–13
2. Principles of social policy			
a. Exclusive loyalty to Yahweh	20:3–11	5:7–15	24:14–16, 21
b. Relations among Israelites	20:12–17	5:16–21	24:25
3. Motivation/enforcement			
a. Renewal and recitation			24:1–28
b. Witnesses against selves			24:22, 27
c. Blessings and curses	20:5a–6	5:9–10	24:19–20

Implications of the Covenant's Structure and Its Components

Yahweh's Deliverance of the People

The most striking feature of the Covenant is that it establishes a relationship between the people and Yahweh that is inseparably political-economic and (almost by definition) religious. It was patterned after international treaties that were also inseparably political-economic-religious, enforced by the gods and ceremonial blessings and curses. But in Israel's adaptation of the treaty patterns into its Covenant, the king who gives the "treaty" is the transcendent God, Yahweh. Or, to restate that, in the Covenant Yahweh is literally the king of Israel. In delivering the Hebrews from bondage in Egypt Yahweh has established a political-economic relationship with them. In Egypt and the rest of the ancient Near East, the people were bound into servitude to their king(s), in agricultural produce that supported the ruling establishment and in forced labor to build temples, palaces, and fortresses. When Yahweh delivers the Hebrews from bondage in Egypt it is a political liberation from subjection but also an economic emancipation from such servitude.

Insofar as the first several commandments demand exclusive loyalty to Yahweh, they also prohibit human kingship. Moses mediates the giving of the Covenant. But he is given no institutionally established power over the people, as a king. Rather the Covenant is a direct relationship between God and the people. Or more precisely, the Covenant assumes and establishes a direct relationship between each constituent family of Israel as "vassal kings" of the Great King as well as between the people as a whole and God. The Covenant also establishes a relationship among the constituent families of Israel focused on their common exclusive loyalty to God.

The statement of Yahweh's deliverance of the people establishes the presupposition for the demands in the second component of the Covenant. The political-economic-religious liberation from servitude to the imperial kings of the ancient Near East and their gods is necessary before a different kind of society can be established. But the deliverance also establishes the basis of the new society in another sense. Since Yahweh has liberated them, the people are now not only grateful to God but obligated to God. This is their prime motivation to keep the commandments God gives them. In theological terms, Gospel precedes Law. Indeed, keeping the commandments is the appropriate response to the proclamation of the gospel of deliverance.

This integral political-economic-religious relationship between deliverance and commandments/laws can be seen in one of the key terms used repeatedly in covenantal connections. The Hebrew verb *shaphat* means "to deliver/liberate/establish justice for." Yahweh *shaphat* (has "delivered") the people. Yahweh is the divine "liberator" of the people (just as the figures such as Deborah or Gideon inspired by "the Spirit of Yahweh" are "liberators," not just "judges," of the people). Reminded of Yahweh's liberation, people would be motivated to obey the *mishpatim* given by Yahweh, that is, the "principles of liberation," the "statutes and ordinances" that detail the way that Israel can maintain its freedom from bondage to human kings.

Yahweh's Requirements of the People: The Ten Commandments

The ten commandments then address key aspects of the people's relationship established with Yahweh, who is their deliverer. This relationship is economic as well as political. The first commandment stipulates in simple, absolute terms the exclusive loyalty to Yahweh that, by implication, excludes servitude to any other god of any society in the ancient Near East. The second commandment is a specification of what this exclusive loyalty means in economic terms. This commandment has often been understood in terms of a prohibition of the worship of idols, which in turn have been understood as empirical images or figurines of the gods. But "idols" was the Israelite critical, polemical, and belittling term for the gods of ancient Near Eastern rulers. As suggested in the wording of the second commandment (Exod. 20:4–5a), those "gods" were the personified, divinized, heavenly, earthly, and subearthly forces, such as River, Irrigation-Wisdom, and Storm-Kingship, that determined life in those ancient Near Eastern civilizations (as discussed in chapter 1).

The point of the second commandment is that, having been liberated from service to those divinized heavenly and earthly forces with their produce and labor, the Israelites were not to revert to serving such gods. There is no implication that those gods do not exist. On the contrary, it is necessary to prohibit reverting to serving them precisely because the people would want the feeling of security provided by the forces that generated productivity (fertility). Because of the uncertainty about the natural forces, the people would still find security and satisfaction appeasing the forces of productivity with tithes and offerings given to their immediate empirical representations in statues and monuments. Good reason, then, to have a commandment that forbade the people from again yielding up a portion of their harvest and labor to the divine Forces because of their fear and insecurity.

The commandment to observe the Sabbath day has a similar economic focus, to relieve the people of the unrelenting labor usually required in service of the gods of ancient Near Eastern civilizations. Feeding families in addition to raising enough for the tithes and offerings demanded by the divine forces and the tribute demanded by imperial regimes required intensive labor on the land. Rulers also required forced labor for construction projects. The Covenant institutionalized every seventh day as a day of rest from labor. In Exodus 20:8–11 it is grounded in the creation by Yahweh. In Deuteronomy 5:12–15 it is grounded in Yahweh's liberation of the people from servitude in Egypt, that is, the reminder that provided the very presupposition of this and the other commandments. (In the next chapter we will see several other economic implications of the principle implicit in this commandment.)

The commandments to "honor your father and mother" and "not commit adultery" protect the integrity and continuity of the family, within and without. This was of fundamental importance since the transgenerational family was the basic form of society, along with the village, which was a community of such families. As we shall discuss more fully in the next chapter, the land was allotted to families as their ancestral inheritance from which they derived their living. The family was the fundamental unit of production, reproduction, and socialization, as well as the fundamental unit in the relation of the people with Yahweh.

It was therefore essential to guard the integrity and continuity of Israelite families according to their ancestral lineages (no adultery) and to ensure cooperation, care, and continuity within the family (honor the elder generation who might become less or nonproductive). As the fundamental building block of ancient Israelite society, the family had at its center an economic function that was the essential basis of the individual, family, and community life of the people and its continuation.

The commandment not to murder protects the integrity of each person's life as of special concern to God. The older translation, "You shall not kill," is too general. In going to war, supposedly only to defend themselves when attacked and not to subject other peoples, the Israelites killed others. They also executed those who violated one or another of the ten commandments, as we will see in the next chapter. But the integrity of each person's life is singled out as one of Yahweh's basic principles. As with the family as a whole, the integrity of each person's life had an economic aspect inseparable from personal and familial roles. The loss of a murdered family member could mean ruin for a family that would no longer have the labor necessary to produce a subsistence living from its ancestral fields. "You shall not murder" evidently applied even to cases of negligence. This can be seen in particular laws of the Covenant Code that immediately follows the giving of the covenant in Exodus 21–23. If an ox gored someone to death, the ox was killed. If the ox had gored someone else previously, then both the ox and the owner were executed. The damage done was severe and, illustrating how serious the homicide was, the penalties were severe.

While the other commandments have economic aspects and implications, the last three are devoted primarily to the economic livelihood of the constituent families of Israel as a people. As with the previous three, the eighth and ninth are brief, simple prohibitions. They give no context or indication of circumstances and implications. It is natural for modern readers to apply them to their own life circumstances. We thus tend to take stealing as the theft of movable goods, such as shoplifting or mugging or, in a more sophisticated vein, embezzlement or tax fraud. We think of false witness as simple lying or as committing perjury when speaking as a witness in court. With no context indicated in the prohibitions of stealing and false witness, however, it is necessary for us to use our informed historical imagination to understand the circumstances to which the commandments applied. Since the tenth commandment offers a short list of objects not to be "coveted," we begin with it.

The tenth commandment has usually been understood to prohibit the subjective desire for another's wife, property, and so on. This is suggested by the standard translation, "you shall not *covet. . . .*" Some scholarly interpreters have found this in the text of Exodus 20 and Deuteronomy 5 itself. They note that the first nine commandments prohibit capital offenses (punishable by death), all of which are concrete actions. They take the tenth commandment as prohibiting the motive that could lead to concrete antisocial actions such as theft or adultery. The separation of "your neighbor's wife" from "your neighbor's house and field" in the Deuteronomic version (5:21) has surely contributed to this reading, as if the coveting pertained to adultery in the first clause and to stealing in the second clause.

In the historical context of ancient Israelite society, however, the tenth commandment, like the other nine, referred to an offense that was concrete. The Hebrew term that has been translated with "covet" (*hamad*) referred to the objective as well as the subjective, "to seize or steal" as well as "to desire." It was also often followed by verbs of seizure, suggesting that it led to and involved taking possession. It should therefore be translated with a compound phrase, "you shall not covet-and-seize." "House," the principal object that is "coveted-and-seized" in Exodus 20:17, referred to far more than a dwelling in Hebrew and other ancient Near Eastern languages. It meant rather the whole *household*, including the dwelling, the family, the family's ancestral lands, and any personnel, draft animals, and goods that belonged to the family/household. As if to specify the basis of the agricultural economy, the land from which the family made a living, "house and field" became a standard formula, often specified further with the addition of "menservants, maidservants, oxen, asses, and everything belonging to" the (head of) household. The list in both Exodus 20:17 and Deuteronomy 5:21 is thus a standard formula for the agrarian household that was the fundamental social form, the basic unit of production and consumption, in ancient Israel.

Several passages in the prophets give us a sense of what was involved, as we shall see more closely in chapter 5. Micah, for example, brings an indictment against the powerful wealthy because

> They covet fields, and seize them;
> houses, and take them away;
> they oppress householder and house,
> people and their inheritance.
> (Mic. 2:2)

Isaiah complains, in parallel phrases (5:8), that those who take advantage of people in difficult economic straits thus "join house to house" and "add field to field." If we want to understand how such "coveting-and-seizing" of houses and fields could happen, we need go no further than the story about Joseph's interpretation and implementation of Pharaoh's dream about the seven fat and seven lean cows. Pharaoh's chief minister had exploited the peasants' desperation during a period of famine to get them in debt and take control of their draft animals and eventually their fields as well.

If we now read "You shall not steal" in the context of the relatively simple agricultural village society of ancient Israel we can better imagine what was meant. We can take a few cues from particular laws in the Covenant Code in Exodus 21–23 that immediately follows the giving of the covenant in Exodus 20. Courtyards and houses in the village were not locked. Fields were not fenced; boundaries were marked only by stones. A family's ox or donkey was not guarded by a security system. Thus theft pertained to such extremely valuable, essential items such as a draft animal that could be slaughtered or sold, leaving a family without the ability to plow its fields for years, or standing crops that could be grazed over, leaving the family's livelihood diminished or destroyed (see Exod. 22:1, 5). "You shall not steal" pertained to actions, even inadvertent acts, that could ruin a neighbor family economically.

The ninth commandment, "you shall not bear false witness," like the prohibitions of stealing and coveting-and-seizing, also pertained to social-economic interactions between families, especially heads of households. The large amount of informal borrowing and lending of goods and draft animals in a village community led to many disputes and conflicts. It seems clear that such cases were handled by courts of elders in the villages. In a situation with no local sheriff or detectives, the resolution of disputes or cases of theft, for example, depended completely on witnesses. Short of such courts, however, the prohibition of false witness also applied to the spread of false rumors and other malicious speech, again as illustrated in laws contained in the Covenant Code (Exod. 21–23; e.g., 23:1–3).

Motivation and Enforcement

Insofar as Yahweh is not only Israel's God but literally its exclusive king, so that there can be no human king, early Israel in effect had no government. With regard to its governance by a transcendent God, early Israel was a theocracy. But with regard to the human historical level, it was an anarchy. While inspired ad hoc leadership such as Deborah or Gideon

(Judg. 4–5, 7–8) emerged in crisis situations, early Israel did not have even local, much less society-wide, magistrates and police. In these circumstances, the Covenant provided for what has to be termed spiritual/religious motivation to keep and enforce the ten commandments and their application in "statutes and ordinances."

The second giving of the covenant in Deuteronomy 5 and the covenant renewal ceremony in Joshua 24 indicate that the Covenant was not just something that happened in the dim and distant past on Sinai. "Yahweh made a covenant with us at Horeb [= Sinai]. Not [just] with our ancestors did Yahweh make this covenant, but with us, who are all of us here alive today" (Deut. 5:2–3). These texts and other repeated references to the writing down of the Covenant and the covenantal laws and torah/teaching in a book, its deposit in the Ark of the Covenant or in inscription on stones, and its *regular recitation* in the hearing of the people all attest to the Covenant as a set of principles very much in the people's individual and collective minds (e.g., Exod. 24:3–8; Deut. 31:24–30). Repeated hearing of the covenantal torah and statutes supposedly had the effect of the people internalizing them, so that they would be "written on their heart," informing their social-economic interaction.

Since Israel is to serve only the one God, the calling of all gods as witnesses in the ancient Near Eastern treaties is transformed into the Israelites *witnessing against themselves* that they "have chosen Yahweh as their God, to serve him." This further reinforces the internalization of "the ten words" of the Covenant. The effect of the witnessing along with the regular recitation was to instill the Covenant and covenantal teachings in the consciousness of the Israelites so that their social-economic interactions would be informed by a covenantal disposition. This may well be the predecessor of what is called the "conscience" in modern Western societies.

The ceremonial *blessings and curses,* of which we see only a residue in Exodus 20:5b–6 but have a full list in Deuteronomy 27–28, provided a third device to motivate the Israelites to observe the guiding principles of the ten commandments of the Covenant. That they extend into the indefinite future or multiple generations (Exod. 20:5b–6) shows that they are rhetorical ceremonial devices to instill "the fear of God" into the people regarding the outcome of their observance or nonobservance. That they go together with the covenantal commandments and other covenantal laws can be seen in the direct correspondences of many of the curses in Deuteronomy 27:15–26 to particular commandments: "Cursed be anyone who makes an idol or casts an image" (27:15); "Cursed be anyone who strikes down a neighbor in secret" (27:24). That a concern for economic well-being lies at the heart of the Covenant can be seen in matters mentioned in the matching blessings and curses in Deuteronomy 28:3–6, 16–19. If the people observe the commandments, then they will be blessed in their agricultural productivity ("the fruit of your ground, . . . livestock, . . . cattle, . . . flock"; their "basket and kneading bowl") and their reproductivity that the productivity makes possible ("the fruit of your womb"). Disobedience will bring just the opposite in the economic basis of their lives.

The Covenant and the Economic Rights of the People

During debates over the ratification of the U.S. Constitution, its advocates compared it to the Covenant of ancient Israel. They hailed the Covenant as well as the Constitution as a model of civil government, indeed a model for other peoples. Considerable research into sermons preached in churches and speeches delivered in State legislatures would be required to know more precisely what they had in mind. Some basic points at least seem clear. For example, leaders of the thirteen States, having just fought for their independence from a king whose rule they compared to the oppression of Pharaoh, greatly appreciated that Israel's Covenant eliminated a human monarchy. Since God was the true ruler of Israel, there could be no human king. And as a transcendent King concerned to aid the people in gaining and maintaining their freedom, God not only did not take "taxation without representation"—God took no tribute at all, and prohibited service of any other god with tribute and forced labor.

Historians and political scientists often point out that the founding fathers who wrote the Declaration of Independence and formulated the Constitution found precedence in Israel's covenant with God for the political rights that they were so concerned to protect. Thinking in the eighteenth-century terms of "natural rights," Thomas Jefferson and his contemporaries believe that "all men" have "from their Creator" all sorts of rights, innumerable rights, some of which people are not even aware of. Mentioned in the Declaration of Independence, these rights were merely presupposed in the Constitution. Then almost as an afterthought, they thought it best to list some of the key rights in the first ten amendments to the Constitution, the Bill of Rights. As suggested by rights listed in the Bill of Rights, the concern of the United States focused on *political* rights. This is what the American ancestors found in the Covenant. The concern for political rights has guided the public interest in and appropriation of the covenant ever since.

Careful examination of the key covenantal texts such as Exodus 20 and Deuteronomy 5, however, finds that if anything the emphasis is on economic matters, the basis of and inseparable from the other functions of the family as the fundamental form of society. Perhaps this can appear clearer in terms familiar to the ordinary language of public affairs if we consider what lies behind Jefferson's famous phrase in the Declaration of Independence: that among the inalienable rights with which people are endowed by the Creator are "life, liberty, and the pursuit of happiness." Behind Jefferson's phrase is the far more concrete "life, liberty, and *property*," of John Locke, which in a largely agricultural society meant the basis of a livelihood working one's land. If we then turn our focus back to God's Covenant with Israel, what it aims to do, built on the foundation of the freedom gained in the exodus from hard servitude under the Pharaoh in Egypt, is to maintain the newly won "liberty" of the Israelites and then to protect their "life" and their "property." "You shall not murder" pertains to "life." The last three commandments all guard the integrity of a family's "property."

If we extend this analysis in terms of the people's rights, then we can recognize that each of the last six or seven commandments serves to protect people's rights in a particular, key area of societal life. "You shall not murder" protects the integrity of life. "You shall not commit adultery" protects the integrity of marriage and the family. "Honor your father and mother" protects the rights of the elderly to a decent living even when they become nonproductive. "Remember the Sabbath" protects people's humanity against exploitation of their labor. "You shall not steal, you shall not bear false witness, and you shall not covet-and-seize" protect people's inalienable right to their property, the resources from which they make a decent living. Every one of those rights, however, is basically economic or has an important economic aspect. In the ordinary terms of public discussion it seems clear that in the context of the Covenant the ten commandments were fundamental principles of social policy intended to protect people's rights, rights that were basically economic. The first three commandments also protect people's economic rights directly or indirectly insofar as they insist that Yahweh is the exclusive God and ruler of the society. This excludes subjection to and service of any human king and service of any other god with produce and labor.

With the implications of the Covenant in mind we can look further at some of the laws and mechanisms aimed at making covenantal economics work and at realizing the economic rights and well-being of the people.

Study Questions

1. What did the ten commandments have to do with Israelite families making a living?

2. How might the Hebrews' servitude (forced labor and field labor) to the Pharaoh and other gods in Egypt have led to the (God's) formulation of the ten commandments as ("constitutional") principles of social-economic interaction for Israelite society?

3. How might reading Exodus 20, especially the ten commandments, have led John Locke or Thomas Jefferson to conclude that "all people are endowed by their Creator with certain unalienable rights," among which are "life, liberty, and property (the pursuit of happiness)"?

4. Why would presidential candidates Theodore Roosevelt and William Jennings Bryan have been on solid biblical ground when they charged that huge corporations were violating the ten commandments, such as "you shall not covet" and "you shall not steal"?

Chapter Three

Mutual Support and the Protection of Economic Rights

How did the Covenant work in Israelite society? How did the covenantal principles of social-economic relations apply to the concrete social-economic structure of the society and social-economic interaction? While the Covenant continued to operate, especially in village communities, after the monarchy was established, we focus on early Israel before the kings consolidated their power.

To gain a sense of the workings of the Covenant in society we need to know the concrete circumstances and patterns of early Israel. In the last several decades many scholarly interpreters have become skeptical about the historical reliability of biblical accounts of the origins of the people of Israel. The biblical accounts as we have them may reflect a later time and may present an exaggerated and idealized picture of the exodus led by Moses, the takeover of the land of Canaan led by Joshua, and the struggle against the Philistines led by the first kings, Saul and David. At most the biblical accounts include some reworked memories of early Israel and its heroic deliverers such as Deborah and Gideon (Judg. 5; 7–8). Historical hints that can be gleaned from those memories, however, are now supplemented and confirmed by recent archaeological surveys of new settlements in the central highlands of Canaan/Palestine. On the basis of this combination of evidence we can, with some confidence, reconstruct the shape of early Israelite society.

Early Israel in the Hill Country

Into the thirteenth century BCE (the time of Joshua), two empires ruled the area of Syria-Palestine, the Egyptians in the south and the Hittites of

Asia Minor in the north. As their control of the area weakened, the kings and warriors of the city-states in Canaan and southern Syria began to lose control of the villagers on whose produce they had relied. Fortified inland cities such as Megiddo and Hazor were destroyed. The stories of the guerrilla warfare led by Joshua against the cities of Ai and Hazor may well contain memories of such attacks (Josh. 8; 11:1–9). Large numbers of uprooted people, free from the grip of their previous rulers, sought new livelihood, evidently many of them in the hill country out of the reach of city-based warriors and tax collectors.

In the last few decades archaeologists have discovered the remains of a network of about 250 villages in the central highlands of Canaan, all established in the span of a few generations around 1200 BCE. These village communities were almost all fairly small, with only a hundred or a few hundred people. They were usually located on ridges or hilltops that were still forested at that time. Many were positioned on the eastern slopes of the highlands, so that the fertile land they cultivated was close to good pastureland for livestock.

The archaeological findings indicate that these people lived a simple hand-to-mouth existence. Each year they grew barely enough food to survive. Their pottery was coarse and basic, mainly cooking pots and storage jars, with no specially decorated vessels. Houses were built of unworked fieldstones, and were all similar in size. There were no large buildings, much less palaces, storehouses, or temples. These findings suggest that there was little social stratification, no significant differences in economic resources and social standing. Also archaeologists found no imported pottery, no jewelry or other luxury items, and no other items that might indicate trade, even between villages. These highland village communities would thus appear to have been basically self-sufficient, with a subsistence economy based on growing grain.

The inhabitants of these highland villages appear to have been the first Israelites. The people who established these villages were evidently mostly indigenous inhabitants of Canaan who had moved up into the highlands, not some ethnically identifiable group from outside Canaan. The archaeological evidence, however, does not go very far in indicating their cultural identity. Their graves were simple, the dead interred without offerings. No religious shrines were found among the remains. An identity that could be termed "Israelite" would only gradually have emerged. Meanwhile, however, the villagers had to work out their social-economic relations. In that connection, many believe that these villagers were the people among whom the principles of the Covenant between

Yahweh and Israel originated, and who attempted to make them work in their village communities.

The Moral Economy of Peasant Societies

The ideal life for ancient Israelite farmers was living in peace, every family "under its own vine and fig tree." The trouble was that their own rulers or foreign imperial armies regularly seized their crops and even their land and houses. They sometimes dreamed about a future utopia in the fantastic terms of God's creating "new heavens and a new earth." But what that symbolized for them (see Isa. 65:17–25) may seem mundane to those who live in the lap of comparative luxury. Their hope was to be able, one day, to build houses and actually inhabit them, instead of being expelled when a powerful creditor seized the house for debts owed. They hoped to plant vineyards and actually eat their fruit, instead of the crop being seized to repay interest on loans at exorbitant rates of interest (25–100 percent). The life they longed for was simply being able not to labor in vain but to enjoy the fruits of their own labor (Isa. 65:21–23).

The Situation of Peasants

The situation of Israelite peasants in the hill country of Palestine, both before and during the monarchy, was like that of peasants everywhere. It was difficult to eke out a subsistence living. The standard focus of modern neoclassical economics, the maximization of profit, is utterly inapplicable to the ancient Israelites. They did not raise crops for market, since there was no market. The problem around which peasant life revolved was raising enough to sustain the family until the next harvest.

While the family was the fundamental unit of production and consumption, ancient Israelite family life was embedded in the communal life of villages. Families relied heavily on the cooperation and mutual support of other families in their village community. All participated actively in the community social and cultural life. Subsistence thus had a moral-social dimension inseparable from the physiological one of obtaining sufficient caloric intake. Each family needed a certain level of resources for ceremonial and social obligation in maintaining their place as an integral member of the village community. Falling below that level meant a loss of standing in the community as well as the risk of starvation. Analysis and discussion of economics is thus inseparable from that of religion and culture.

Many studies of peasant societies have pointed out that concern about subsistence accounts for a number of social-economic arrangements. Peasant societies developed an array of social-economic mechanisms that assured the requisite minimum to the families of a village community. They figured out how to buffer the periodic difficulties of obtaining enough with various forms of reciprocity and cooperation. Such sharing and cooperation in effect spread the risk of bad years across the families of a village (somewhat similar to the way home or health insurance or Social Security spreads the risk across a large pool of insured). These mechanisms cannot be romanticized, for they do not necessarily attest egalitarian social arrangements. But they do manifest a fundamental value that is increasingly threatened by the premium placed on privatization and maximization of profits in a consumer-capitalist society: all members of society are entitled to an adequate living out of the available resources within the village. The cooperative arrangements of sharing resources, mutual aid, and the spreading of risk among villagers in agricultural societies have been called "the moral economy of the peasant" by the distinguished anthropologist James C. Scott.[1]

Mechanisms of the Moral Economy

Even when they are subject to rulers and overlords, such as feudal lords, kings, or aristocratic priesthoods, peasant villages constitute semi-independent local communities. When they had a degree of control over their own community affairs, peasants around the world chose to develop arrangements and mechanisms to protect their weakest families against social-economic ruin due to droughts and other natural or social-political contingencies. Some peasantries in Southeast Asia kept a large percentage of their villages' territories as communal lands that would be redistributed in part on the basis of need. Until enclosure movements, European villages had commons, communal pastures for cattle and often communal woodlands, available to all community families. Standard across many peasant societies are social pressures on the better-off families to share their resources with their less fortunate neighbors and to sponsor community celebrations and projects. Such redistributive mechanisms may be modest in scope but nonetheless provide some minimal insurance against dearth for the poorest villagers.

1. James C. Scott, *The Moral Economy of the Peasant: Rebellion and Subsistence in Southeast Asia* (New Haven: Yale University Press, 1976).

This economy is *moral* insofar as all village families are guaranteed an economic subsistence, so long as the villagers themselves still control the resources to make it possible. This is egalitarian in a sense. But although it may become radical in its effect on overreaching rulers, it is conservative within the village. The fundamental value is that all families should have a place, hence a living, not that all should be equal. The moral economy of peasants thus strives to keep each household intact, in possession of the means of subsistence (its land), so that it does not become vulnerable to exploitation by outside power-holders. Keeping individual families intact on their own land also enhances the ability of the other families in the community as a whole to keep control of the resources on which their lives depend. These protective practices by village communities are what distinguish the traditional agrarian economy from the modern market economy. "It is the absence of the threat of *individual* starvation which makes primitive society, in a sense, more human than market economy, and at the same time less economic."[2]

Motivations: How the Mechanisms Worked

It may well seem baffling to competitive individualistic Westerners that the mechanisms to keep failing families viable on their land could ever work. What motivated one neighbor hovering just above subsistence to help a neighbor in danger of going under? The motivations for activating the mechanisms of the moral economy were various. One was clearly mutuality or reciprocity in the face of common threats. When a peasant family helped a neighbor family it thereby had a reciprocal claim on help in the future. The families understood that they were spreading the risk among them across a span of years. Another motive was social pressure and potential or actual gossip or envy. Studies of peasant villages often comment on such informal social controls that lead neighbor to aid neighbor. The position of the better-off is legitimate only to the extent that they use their surplus resources to aid the poor. There is sometimes even a certain communal pride that the community is able to feed and protect its member families. It is surely significant that the protective power that villages generated for their poor was strongest in those areas where villages remained most autonomous and cohesive, and not yet weakened by the pressures of outside rulers or "development."

2. Karl Polanyi, *The Great Transformation* (1944; repr. Boston: Beacon, 1957), 163–64.

The desire for subsistence security grew out of the chronic needs of families, but it was experienced socially as a pattern of moral rights and expectations. Such moral rights and expectations were often rooted in religion, as the commands of the gods. Failure to respond to the neighbor's need would result in divine displeasure. This is precisely what we find in the village-based moral economy of ancient Israel.

Measures of Assistance and Mutual Support

The Israelites developed a number of interrelated principles and mechanisms by which they attempted to keep each constituent family in its village communities economically viable. Information about these comes mainly from the three principal covenantal collections of laws in the Pentateuch: the Covenant Code embedded in the original making of the covenant in Exodus 21–23, the so-called Holiness Code in Leviticus 17–26, and the laws and legal teachings in Deuteronomy 12–26. References in the historical and prophetic books often confirm the existence and operation of these mechanisms.

These covenantal "law codes" contain customs and laws that derived from customary practices of the people. In many cases this Israelite common law is similar to common law in the codes of other ancient Near Eastern peoples. It is significant that all of these Israelite law codes are understood as covenantal and are framed as specific legal applications of the covenant, both as collections with their own integrity and in their current setting in the Torah.

Except in the most systematically organized section on the jubilee year in Leviticus 25, however, the practices that protected families threatened by poverty appear in different places in the collections of laws that are abstracted from everyday life. In order to discern how they overlapped and worked together in village life, we will proceed systematically, from the more general measures to aid the poor to the more drastic measures designed to aid people in desperate straits.

Two principles lay at the basis of the moral economy of early Israelite village communities. First, *the land belonged to Yahweh and was, in effect, leased to Israelite families for their use.* As the biblical narrative tells it, after liberating the people from servitude to the imperial system in Egypt, Yahweh had given the land into the possession of the constituent Israelite clans or village communities (schematic distribution of land in Josh. 13–21). In village communities the land was further divided into individual families' possession of households and fields. There was no such thing as private property—far less so than in American society, where many only reluctantly acknowledge that the lots (allotments) and houses that they "own" also belong partly to towns and cities and states that also have a claim on them, in the form of property taxes to be used for the common welfare (roads, public safety, schools, etc.).

The second principle underlying all of the principles developed to keep families viable was that *the land allotted to each family was inalienable*, could not be permanently sold or taken away. As Yahweh declared: "The land shall not be sold in perpetuity, for the land is mine; with me you are but aliens and tenants" (Lev. 25:23). In the covenant made following the liberation from the ancient Near Eastern system of servitude, each Israelite family was provided with and guaranteed inalienable possession of a God-given right to land, which was the means of making a living in an agricultural society. The Hebrew Bible exhibits no case of and no provision for an Israelite voluntarily selling land outside his family. These principles underlie all of the mechanisms and programs devised by Israelite covenantal society for the mutual support of its constituent families.

Given the difficult circumstances in which the people were attempting to eke out a living on marginal land, the contingencies of drought and crop failure, damage to crops, or injury or death of a draft animal or family member on whose labor the crops depended, some would inevitably be left without enough. Like many other peasant societies, therefore, Israel evolved certain customary practices, framed as laws in biblical law codes, to aid the poor. We can examine these according to the severity of the economic difficulties they helped with and according to the fundamental social-economic values they exemplified.

Israel's covenantal law codes include laws requiring practices that might provide food to supplement poor families' own inadequate harvest. These measures were rooted in and dependent on the spirit of sharing in the local community.

Gleaning, which could be done at harvest every year, was the most important of these measures.

> When you reap the harvest of your land, you shall not reap to the very edges of your field, or gather the gleanings of your harvest. You shall not strip your vineyard bare, or gather the fallen grapes of your vineyard; you shall leave them for the poor and the [resident] alien: I am Yahweh your God. (Lev. 19:9–10; 23:22)

When you reap your harvest in your field and forget a sheaf in the field, you shall not go back to get it; it shall be left for the [resident] alien, the orphan, and the widow, so that Yahweh your God may bless you in all your undertakings. When you beat your olive trees, do not strip what is left; it shall be for the alien, the orphan, and the widow.

When you gather the grapes of your vineyard, do not glean what is left; it shall be for the [resident] alien, the orphan, and the widow. Remember that you were a slave in the land of Egypt; therefore I am commanding you to do this. (Deut. 24:19–22)

In both cases these laws are framed as part of the statutes of the covenant, and the people are motivated to keep them by the reminder of their ancestors' struggles in Egypt, from which Yahweh had delivered them.

"The [resident] alien, the orphan, and the widow" (and later, as in the Psalms, "the widows and the orphans") were the poorest of the poor, the most dire cases of those in need of support. They also serve as symbols of the need of the poor generally. Orphans and widows had been left without a complete family that provided labor and support. "Resident aliens," many of them probably refugees from oppressive conditions under nearby kings, would not (yet) have had their own allotment of land on which they could make a living. Covenantal laws include them as members of the society, for example in the harvest festival celebrating the people's freedom from hard bondage (Deut. 26:1–11). Specific laws forbid depriving aliens of justice and command the people not to oppress resident aliens, or abuse widows and orphans, since they themselves were once aliens in the land of Egypt (Deut. 24:14–18; Exod. 22:21–24).

A similar but less reliable form of aid for those with insufficient food was what the land produced by itself during the *sabbatical fallow years.*

For six years you shall sow your land [field] and gather its yield; but the seventh year you shall let it rest and lie fallow, so that the poor of your people may eat; and what they leave the wild animals may eat. You shall do the same with your vineyard, and with your olive orchard. (Exod. 23:10–11)

Fields would produce crops even when not plowed, planted, and cultivated. This early statement about the sabbatical fallow year in the Covenant Code presents it as a form of aid for the destitute. In early Israelite practice, reflected in Exodus 23:10–11, it is highly unlikely that the observance of the fallow year was coordinated across the whole society (as in the later formulation in Lev. 25:2–7). Rather each family would have followed its own sequence of sabbatical fallow years in which produce was to be available to the poor. Such a staggering of observance of the sabbatical fallow year would thus have provided supplementary food on a more regular basis in each village.

A similar device to aid the needy was a tithe every third year to be stored in the villages as a supply of surplus food for the resident aliens, orphans, widows, and the Levites (who had no allotment of land; Deut. 14:28–29). This may have been a later device added to tide the poor over between sabbatical years, once the observance of sabbatical fallow year was regularized across the society (under the monarchy?).

Supplementary food from gleaning and sabbatical fallow years, however, did not suffice to make up for harvests inadequate to feed poor families due to drought and other damage to crops and later to taxes and tithes taken by rulers. Families who faced starvation were forced to borrow. Israelite covenantal law codes were vigorous in encouraging liberal *lending* to neighbors. The taking of *interest*, moreover, was strictly *forbidden*. Again these measures were rooted in the strong spirit of sharing and cooperation generated in village communities. But loans potentially led to serious problems of mounting debts that were difficult to pay off.

Borrowing and *lending* were essential in a village-based subsistence economy. Covenantal law included strong exhortation to Israelites to lend generously to those in difficult circumstances.

> If there is among you anyone in need, a member of your community in any of your towns within the land that Yahweh your God is giving you, do not be hard-hearted or tight-fisted toward your needy neighbor. You should rather open your hand, willingly lending enough to meet the need, whatever it may be. (Deut. 15:7–8)

Modern Bible translations give a misleading impression about what was involved in such borrowing and lending in ancient Israel by rendering the Hebrew term(s) for "goods" as "money." But money as coinage was not even invented yet (and only in royal courts and temples would value have taken the form of precious metals in storage or decor). Borrowing and lending in the local community involved such major items as draft animals and, mainly, food (the staples grain, grapes/wine, and olives/oil), and seed grain. Lending therefore involved considerable risk, for lender as well as borrower. A draft animal might be injured. Israelite communities developed laws to deal with just such contingencies, like the one included in the Covenant Code:

> When someone borrows an animal from another and it is injured or dies, the owner not being present, full restitution shall be made. If the owner was present, there shall be no restitution; if it was hired, only the hiring fee is due. (Exod. 22:14–15)

Lenders had to reckon with the possibility that, since they themselves had little or no surplus as a cushion, they too might run out of food before the next harvest, or the next harvest might be poor. It was thus important to reinforce the custom of cooperation and mutual aid among villagers with covenantal exhortation such as Deuteronomy 15:7–8.

Perhaps the most difficult covenantal principle to understand for modern Westerners who live under capitalism, which runs on interest charged on loans, is the *prohibition of interest*. Covenantal laws against charging interest upheld the principle of not taking advantage of another's misfortune, of not gaining benefit from other people's need. It seems highly likely that taking interest was understood as a prime example of violating the commandment not to covet-and-seize, perhaps also of the commandment against stealing. The wording of this principle reflects the experience of having been charged interest by wealthy creditors (subsequently, under the monarchy, or previously, while in Egypt or in one of the Canaanite city-states).

> You shall not charge interest on loans to another Israelite. (Deut. 23:19)

> If any of your kin fall into difficulty. . . . Do not take interest in advance or otherwise make a profit from them, but fear your God; let them live with you. You shall not lend them your [goods] at interest taken in advance, or provide them food at a profit. (Lev. 25:35–37)

The earlier parallel in the Covenant Code is followed immediately by an exhortation regarding the collateral for a loan, which was merely symbolic, a ritual gesture.

> If you lend [goods] to my people, to the poor among you, you shall not deal with them as a creditor; you shall not exact interest from them. If you take your neighbor's cloak in pawn, you shall

restore it before the sun goes down; for it may be your neighbor's only clothing to use as cover; in what else shall that person sleep? And if your neighbor cries out to me, I will listen, for I am compassionate. (Exod. 22:25–27)

A well-worn cloak would have been of dubious value to the lender. It would have been cruel for the creditor to have kept the cloak, which also served as a covering during the cool nights in the hill country of Canaan. Israelite villagers were to share generously what little they had with those in need, without taking advantage of their misfortune. Demand for interest on loans would only have made it more difficult for needy families to climb out of the hole of debt into which they were slipping.

Closely related to lending without interest were laws requiring honest, consistent weights and measures used in measuring out loans of grain and oil (Deut. 25:13–15; Lev. 19:35–36). Like the prohibition of interest, such laws were specifications of the commandments against coveting and stealing. Making loans in short measures while then using long measures was a way of bypassing the prohibition on interest and a typical way of defrauding a needy neighbor.

Measures Addressed to Mounting Debts and Disintegration of Families

Borrowing and lending were about the only way that peasant village communities with limited resources could have enabled desperate families to survive disastrous harvests. Repeated borrowing and lending, however, set up more serious difficulties between creditor and debtor families. The rise of kings dramatically exacerbated the problem. Facing demands for taxes and offerings to support court and temple, ever larger numbers of families had to borrow in order to survive until the next harvest, when the cycle repeated itself over again. Officers of the kings, who had control over large quantities of grain and other goods in storehouses, exploited the situation to expand their own income by charging exorbitant rates of (supposedly prohibited) interest on loans. This made desperate villagers economically vulnerable to those who also wielded political power.

Israelite villagers, like others in the ancient Near East, attempted to deal with indebtedness by means of arrangements between debtor and creditor families. The first major step taken to deal with debts was designed to keep the impoverished family viable on its land, but at the expense of one or more family members. A family heavily in debt sent a son or a daughter to work off the debt as a full-time servant in the creditor household. This debt-slavery was somewhat similar to the indentured servitude common in the settlement of the English colony of Virginia—an arrangement far short of the chattel slavery to which millions of Africans were subjected later in U.S. history.

In extreme cases of indebtedness, the family might be forced to sell its ancestral land. As the laws were formulated, of course, this was understood as selling the control and use of the land. This may have meant that members of the indebted family shifted to a status of paid laborers on their land (like sharecroppers), now controlled by the creditor, or that they were forced off the land altogether into the status of debt-slaves or that of landless day laborers. As poor families' indebtedness increased and they could not recover by working off the loans, they thus became ever more vulnerable to exploitation by the better-off families and later by the wealthy and powerful officers of the king.

Israelite society thus required ways to apply and implement the principles of Israel's Covenant with Yahweh that aimed to protect people's inalienable right to their ancestral lands. The Israelite law codes and other sources include various covenantal laws and mechanisms of social-economic polity that protected the economic rights of all to an adequate living. These laws and mechanisms functioned to prevent the better-off from taking undue advantage of the vulnerable poor. The steps taken to protect poverty-stricken people's social-economic rights escalated with the difficult straits of mounting debts, debt-slavery, and loss of land. The mechanisms are all based on the assumption that people have a right to an adequate living free of debts and slavery, and that their family inheritance of land is inalienable.

With debt-slavery as the principal means by which a family repaid a serious level of debt, covenantal laws extended *minimal protection to those who became debt-slaves.* For example, if a slave master destroyed the eye or knocked out a tooth of a male or female debt-slave, "the slave shall be let go, a free person," to compensate (Exod. 21:26–27). A slave master who killed a debt-slave would be punished (how is unclear; Exod. 21:20). Although they were allowed to buy slaves from other peoples, Israelites were sharply forbidden to treat debt-slaves under their power as slaves or to sell them into chattel slavery (presumably to foreigners; Lev. 25:39).

More serious mechanisms were necessary, however, to deal with debt-slavery, the debts that led to debt-slavery, and the loss of land to which heavy debts might lead. These mechanisms were integral parts of covenantal economics and of the ways that Israel was to maintain itself as a people in covenant with Yahweh. Four different but interrelated mechanisms are mentioned in one or more of the covenantal law codes and elsewhere in Hebrew biblical texts: the cancellation of debts every seven years, the release of debt-slaves every seven years, the right of redemption of land by the next of kin, and the jubilee year proclamation of liberty in which displaced persons returned to their ancestral inheritance of land. References elsewhere in biblical texts indicate that the first three mechanisms were practiced in Israelite society, and are not merely utopian ideals (Jer. 32; 34; Neh. 10:31).

Cancellation of Debts

The Mosaic covenantal law in Deuteronomy 15:1–2 gives instructions on implementation of what was evidently a regular proclamation of "Yahweh's remission" in Israelite society prior to the composition of the Deuteronomic code.

> Every seventh year you shall grant a remission of debts. And this is the manner of the remission: every creditor shall remit the claim that is held against a neighbor, not exacting it of a neighbor who is a member of the community, because Yahweh's remission has been proclaimed.

In Israelite covenantal society "Yahweh's proclamation" of the remission of debts was patterned after the ancient Near Eastern king's proclamation of freedom from debts (see the Code of Hammurabi §117). As the true but transcendent divine king of Israelite society, Yahweh had declared, as part of the covenant, its statutes, and mechanisms, that debts were to be remitted every seven years. The seventh year, whatever else its grounding and meaning, brought this mechanism under the umbrella of keeping the Sabbath commanded in the original making and renewal of the covenant.

The instruction given for the remission indicates explicitly that this was not a mere moratorium or postponement, but a cancellation of debts. Every creditor was to remit the claim held against the debtor, and not exact it against any member of the Israelite community (15:2). The ensuing exhortation in 15:3–6 seems to address a less than rigorous observance of Yahweh's proclamation of remission during the monarchy. It emphasizes the importance of the cancellation of debts as a commandment in the covenant given by Yahweh, and appeals to the blessings (and by implication, the curses) as motivation. It also makes the point of Yahweh's remission bluntly explicit: "There will thus be no one in need among you."

Release of Debt-slaves

If a member of your community, whether a Hebrew man or a Hebrew woman, sells himself or herself to you and works for you six years, in the seventh year you shall set that person free. And when you send a male slave out from you a free person, you shall not send him out empty-handed. Provide liberally out of your flock, your threshing floor, and your wine press, thus giving to him some of the bounty with which Yahweh your God has blessed you. Remember that you were a servant in the land of Egypt, and Yahweh your God redeemed you; for this reason I lay this command upon you today. (Deut. 15:12–15)

Like the cancellation of debts, the release of debt-slaves was to be carried out every seventh year. The years of servitude and the seventh-year release pertained to each case, and was not (yet) a coordinated schedule applicable across the society, in contrast to the jubilee legislation (Lev. 25:8–10). It is assumed that the debt-slave will return to the family land (as also in Lev. 25:41), where it will be difficult to get a new start. This must be the reason for the insistence on not sending the male out "empty-handed," as he (presumably) resumes his role as head of household. As in much covenantal legislation, the reminder that Yahweh had liberated the Israelites from servitude in Egypt forms the basis for the demand and its observance (see also Lev. 25:42).

The earlier laws in the Covenant Code (Exod. 21:1–6, 7–11) address particular contingencies of debt-slavery. Daughters sent out as debt-slaves were presumed to be taken into the creditor family as a wife for the head of the family (or his son). If he does not honor her standard marital status and rights, including food and clothing, however, then "she shall go out without debt, without payment of money" (21:7–11). If a male debt-slave became attached to a wife and children within the extended household, he could choose to become a slave for life (21:4–7). The later legislation in the Holiness Code, however, declared that the children, along with the debt-slaves, "shall be free . . . [and] go back to their own family and return to their ancestral property" (Lev. 25:41).

Right of Redemption

Some families became trapped in such severe poverty that they resorted to the sale of (the use of) their ancestral land. To deal with this loss of the very basis of a family's livelihood Israelite society maintained the right of redemption by the next of kin.

> If anyone of your kin falls into difficulty and sells a piece of property [land], then the next of kin shall come and redeem what the relative has sold. If the person has no one to redeem it, but then prospers and finds sufficient means to do so, the years since its sale shall be computed and the difference shall be refunded to the person to whom it was sold, and the property shall be returned. (Lev. 25:25–27)

It is not difficult to detect the inalienability of the family's inheritance of land underneath this formulation. What was sold was not the land so much as the use of the land to produce crops. Underlying this formulation may be also the assumption that a family's land is part of the land allotted to a clan or a whole village. The next of kin would have been ensuring that the land remained in the control of the clan or village, which would presumably have returned its use to the (heirs of the original) family. We know that such redemption of land was practiced because of Jeremiah's redemption of his cousin's land (Jer. 32)—which he turns into a prophetic sign that the covenantal people has a future on the land, despite the impending doom of Jerusalem. The exception that is made for "dwelling houses in a walled city" (Lev. 25:29–34) points to the purpose of the redemption: to restore the agricultural land of village families (and clans) to their intended use for productivity that supports family and village life.

Jubilee Release of Debt-slaves and Return to the Land

The legislation in the Holiness Code sets the release of debt-slaves and the right of redemption into the frame of yet another mechanism, the jubilee year. On the day of atonement

> you shall have the trumpet sounded throughout all your land. And . . . you shall proclaim liberty throughout the land to all its inhabitants. It shall be a jubilee for you: you shall return, every one of you, to your property and every one of you to your family. (Lev. 25:9–10)

It is not clear how the jubilee release and return was related to the sabbatical release of debts and debt-slaves and the right of redemption of land by the next of kin. It is mentioned in connection with keeping tribal land intact. It is unclear, however, whether the jubilee was ever practiced, or was more of a utopian ideal that articulated the principles on which the others were based. As stated explicitly in Leviticus 25:23: "The land shall not be sold in perpetuity, for the land is mine [God's]." Since God had given the land to his "tenants" for their use, it is the inalienable possession of Israelite families. Yet while the Holiness Code (Lev. 25) appears to be an independent formulation directed to a particular situation, it incorporates and restates most of the Israelite covenantal mechanisms designed to protect the rights of Israelite families to an adequate living on their inalienable land.

Covenantal Protection of People's Economic Rights

At the center of God's Covenant with Israel are principles that protect the people's economic as well as political rights. The Covenant as elaborated in the principal covenantal law codes in the Pentateuch then includes a number of laws, arrangements, and mechanisms that worked to ensure the realization of those economic rights. Two fundamental principles underlay these laws and mechanisms that supported people's economic viability. One is that the land ultimately belongs to Yahweh and was given to Israelite families. That is, people had a God-given right to (and basis for) the economic resources for an adequate living. The second and closely related principle was that their family inheritance of land was inalienable. That is, the God-given resources for people's economic livelihood were inalienable.

As a kind of insurance against the contingencies of inadequate harvests and the resulting hunger and starvation, the Covenant included provisions for economic support from the resources of the community. Families in the village were commanded to leave gleanings in their fields and orchards and the crops that grew without cultivation during sabbatical fallow years as food to supplement the inadequate crops of the needy families. This sharing of resources among the families of a village community was grounded in the understanding that the land, which ultimately belonged to God, was given to the community as a whole as well as parceled out to each family as the basis for their collective as well as their familial livelihood. The sharing and cooperation that enabled needy families to remain economically viable was the result of commitment to communal values represented in the Covenant with God.

That is, in Israel's Covenant the society or body politic, in its constituent communities, is charged with responsibility for guaranteeing the economic rights of the members of the society to an adequate living. When, because of whatever natural or historical contingencies, some people fall short of an adequate living, the surplus resources of the communities of the society are to be made available as aid to those in need. This is grounded in the understanding that the resources available to society in one respect are divided into the property of citizens, but in other respects belong to the society as a whole and its constituent communities. Some resources are communal, and an important use of communal resources is to supply a safety net for those who become needy because of various contingencies.

The Covenant also provides mechanisms by which community members are to respond to the more dire straits into which people may come because of their poverty. They are to respond to neighbors' needs by lending to them liberally. In this connection they are not to take advantage of the neighbor's misfortune by charging interest. Then if fellow Israelites, out of desperate poverty, fall heavily into debt, become debt-slaves, and even lose their land, better-off people are to cancel debts and release debt-slaves every seven years, and allow the next of kin to redeem their land. That is, members of society are responsible for sharing their resources liberally with those in serious need. Moreover, if the poor then come into impossible debt and dehumanizing dependency because of the debts, even losing all resources for an adequate living, to which they have a right, those debts are to be cancelled, the debtors released from dehumanizing dependency, and/or a redemption of the resources for an adequate living is to be made possible.

Study Questions

1. What is the basic purpose or concern of the "moral economy" in peasant societies?
2. How does the biblical principle of people's inalienable right to the basis of a livelihood (their land and labor) differ from and at points conflict with the modern Western concept of "private property"?
3. What was the relationship between individual families' basis of livelihood and the village community's commitment to keeping all families economically viable?
4. How do covenantal mechanisms such as cancellation of debts help protect the economic rights implied in covenantal commandments such as "you shall not covet" or "you shall not steal" or "honor your father and mother"?

Chapter Four

The Monarchy and Economic Centralization

Early Israel made an intentional break with the sacred political economy of the imperial civilizations of Egypt and Babylon. According to the account in Exodus, having experienced hard labor under an imperial monarchy, the Israelites valued their new-found freedom under their God. Their king was now literally to be Yahweh, who had delivered them from that bondage. Their divine King's demands, in the covenantal commandments, were exclusive loyalty to God/Yahweh and nonexploitative economic relations among the families of Israel so that no one would gain the political-economic power to become king. The story of Gideon serves as a historical reminder that God was literally the (exclusive) king of covenantal Israel. In their enthusiasm over his charismatic leadership against the Midianites, the Israelites asked Gideon to become their king. But Gideon knew his covenantal principles. "I will not rule over you, and my son will not rule over you; Yahweh will rule over you" (Judg. 8:22–23).

Readers of biblical history are thus prepared for the dilemma that faces the Israelites, who cannot muster enough military power, with their ad hoc peasant militias, to fend off the raids by the Philistines armed with superior weapons of iron. Desperate to defend their independence, they approach Samuel, last of the liberators and first of the prophets, asking him to "appoint for us a king to govern us, like other nations." Samuel's sense of having been rejected was exceeded only by Yahweh's: "They have not [just] rejected you, but they have rejected me from being king over them" (1 Sam. 8:7).

The Economic Structure of the Monarchy

Yahweh tells Samuel to listen to fearful Israelites ready to relinquish their liberty to gain security, but tells him to "solemnly warn them" about what a king would do as he consolidated power. Samuel's warning outlines the basic structure of political-economy headed by an ancient Near Eastern monarchy.

> These will be the ways of the king who will reign over you:
> He will take your sons and appoint them to his chariots and to be his horsemen, and to run before his chariots;
> and he will appoint for himself commanders of thousands and commanders of fifties,
> and some to plow his ground and to reap his harvest,
> and to make his implements of war and the equipment of his chariots.
> He will take your daughters to be perfumers and cooks and bakers.
> He will take the best of your fields and vineyards and olive orchards and give them to his courtiers.
> He will take one-tenth of your grain and of your vineyards and give it to his officers and his courtiers.
> He will take your male and female servants, and the best of your cattle and donkeys, and put them to his work.
> He will take one-tenth of your flocks
> and you shall be his servants. (1 Sam. 8:11–17, author's trans.)

The primary concern of a monarchy was not the defense of its subjects, but its own security—vis-à-vis its own subjects as well as attack from outside. For this it required a professional military establishment. Central were the chariot forces and cavalry and bodyguards that protected the king and his entourage. In addition, trained officers were necessary to lead the standing army. All this required the ancient equivalent of a military-industrial complex to manufacture chariots and other implements of war. Economic resources were required to support this professional military establishment, especially agricultural labor. While "sons" were drafted into the army, "daughters" were drafted as servants in the royal service.

Economic support for the officers of the regime and the attendants at court took three interrelated forms, as in other ancient Near Eastern monarchies. One was taxation, tithes on the staple products from which the producers themselves lived: grain, grapes, flocks. The second was agricultural lands expropriated from the producers and granted to officers, along with the dependent peasants attached to the land, as the basis of their economic support. The third was corvée or "forced labor" of the people's draft animals, servants, and their own labor for agricultural work in the fields and construction projects. Under a monarchy, the people were the economic servants as well as the political subjects of the king.

Since archaeological excavations now show that Jerusalem did not become a significant city until the eighth century, it seems unlikely that Solomon established the grand imperial monarchy proudly portrayed in 1 Kings 4–10. That portrayal, however, does provide us a fuller sense of how a monarchy exploited its subjects' produce and labor to construct and maintain its institutions of power and privilege. The list of the king's "high officials" at the outset (1 Kgs. 4:1–6) provides an outline of the basic structure of monarchic rule, revenue, and religious legitimation. Heading the royal bureaucracy were two secretaries and a recorder. There were heads of the several "departments": the army, the "officials" (in charge of revenue?), provisioning and managing the palace (court and officers), and "forced labor." Judging from the listing of four different "priests" in three of the nine items listed, conduct of the official religion and its media of mystification must have been particularly important.

The collection of agricultural produce from the village producers was organized by districts. The account of "Solomon's provision for one day" is obviously exaggerated, but it gives a sense of the lavish court life and support for the army and royal officers. The many elaborate construction projects of the monarchy, the royal "house" (palace), the "house" for Yahweh (royal temple), "houses" for the king's wives, and military fortresses, required resources in three interrelated forms (1 Kgs. 5; 6–7; 9). To pay for building materials (and building expertise) brought from Lebanon, Solomon had to provide large quantities of agricultural products produced by his subjects (5:7–12). Additional produce, presumably from taxation, was necessary to feed the construction workers. Transporting the timber and stones and the actual construction required the forced labor of tens of thousands, taking them away from agricultural labor (5:13–18). When agricultural produce did not suffice to pay for the timber and precious metals involved in the construction projects, Solomon simply ceded to Hiram, king of Tyre, twenty villages in northern Galilee along the frontier, along with their people. Even the people, along with their lands, were resources at the disposal of a king in dealings with another king.

As is evident in this exchange of agricultural produce and even producers for building materiel, this was not "international trade" in the modern sense. Accounts of Solomon's "trade missions" (1 Kgs. 10) confirm that trade was carried out not by independent merchants in an international "market economy." Instead it consisted of expeditions mounted by the monarchy to obtain the luxury products, such as spices and precious metals, for their own lavish lifestyle. The acquisition of precious metals such as gold, which was transformed into elaborate decor for palace and temple, was the form taken by the economic "surplus" generated by an ancient Near Eastern monarchy.

The resources that Solomon exchanged for building materials and gold as well as those that supported his extensive military forces and the officials of his regime all came from the producers working the land, the basis of the economy. As indicated in Samuel's warning, these revenues took the three forms of taxes on villagers' produce, the produce of royal lands expropriated from the producers, and forced labor. The fundamental structure of the economy thus consisted of a monarchy extracting produce and labor from villagers by means of its officials to support the institutions of its rule.

Some of the key concepts of modern economics do not apply to the economy of the Israelite monarchy, as noted in chapter 1. It was not a market economy. There was no market. There was no money. Trade was mainly for luxury goods and was managed by the monarchy. There was no private property. As in other economic systems, people had only partial power over their own labor. Not only did the village community have a claim on (the produce of) land and labor; much more ominously the king had a substantial claim on (the produce of) local land and labor. This system was understood in corporate terms. The king as the representative of the whole had a claim on its resources. In a more general way, this arrangement was understood and expressed in religious terms familiar from the imperial civilizations of the ancient Near East. The land belonged to God. The people, as tenants and servants of God, in gratitude and appeasement, were expected to render up tithes and offerings and labor to the gods. The king and/or the priests, as the chief servants of God, received and exercised custody over the tithes and offerings and labor of the people, the ordinary servants of the gods.

The Centrality of Religion in the Monarchic Economy

The Israelite monarchy was sacred, like those in ancient Near Eastern imperial civilizations. In Mesopotamian empires and Canaanite city-states, the warrior executive among the cosmic-civilizational Forces that determined the people's lives was usually Lord Storm (Enlil, Marduk, Baal), who maintained cosmic-civilizational order, including productivity of the land, with his heavenly armies. The Israelite monarchies adapted this imperial ideology to legitimate the relationship between God, king, and people. They transformed Yahweh from the Force that had liberated people from bondage in Egypt into the force that established and maintained the order of the universe forever. Several enthronement psalms celebrate God's enthronement over the cosmos in language taken over from neighboring ancient Near Eastern monarchies.

> Yahweh is King!
> The cosmos is firmly established;
> it shall never be moved. . . .
> Let the heavens be glad, and let the earth rejoice;
> Let Sea roar, and all that fills it.
>
> (Ps. 96:10–11)

In one psalm Yahweh closely resembles Lord Storm (Baal) of contemporary Canaanite monarchies.

> The voice of Yahweh flashes forth flames of fire. . . .
> Yahweh sits enthroned over the flood;
> Yahweh sits enthroned as king forever.
>
> (Ps. 29:7, 10)

The royal psalms then represented the warrior king as the "(only) son" of the imperial warrior God, his regent on earth, and mediator of the cosmic order. In a psalm that was probably part of the liturgy for the king's coronation the king himself declared:

> I will tell of the decree of Yahweh:
> He said to me, "You are my son; today I have begotten you.
> Ask of me, and I will make the nations your heritage,
>   and the ends of the earth your possession.
> You shall break them with a rod of iron,
>   and dash them in pieces like a potter's vessel."
>
> (Ps. 2:7–9)

In another royal psalm, the king is invested with authority as priest as well as king, and is even declared to be the source of fertility in his realm.

> Yahweh sends out from Zion your mighty scepter.
> Rule in the midst of your foes.
> Your people will offer themselves willingly
>   on the day you lead your forces on the holy mountains.
> From the womb of the morning, the dew of your youth will come
>   to you.
> Yahweh has sworn and will not change his mind,
> "You are a priest forever according to the order of Melchizedek."
>
> (Ps. 110:2–4)

Mediation of the society's relationship with God was therefore the principal function of the monarchy, and the central religious institution was the "house of Yahweh." For the monarchy in Jerusalem, the royal temple on Mount Zion was represented as the cosmic mountain where Yahweh dwells.

> Great is Yahweh and greatly to be praised in the city of our God.
> His holy mountain, beautiful in elevation, is the joy of all the earth,
> Mount Zion, in the far north, the city of the great King.
> Within its citadels God has shown himself a sure defense.
>
> (Ps. 48:1–3)

The narrative of Solomon's kingship (see especially 1 Kgs. 5–8) displays the elaborate lengths and cost to which kings went in building, decorating, and maintaining temples and sacrifices to God. The people's obligation was to render taxes and offerings to Yahweh as the God who maintained order and to the king, his son, whom God had invested with sovereignty and fertility. The extensive and prolonged forced labor and huge quantity of agricultural produce necessary to build, decorate, and maintain the Temple, according to the narrative in 1 Kings, illustrates how central the house of Yahweh was to the monarchic economy.

Another way in which the monarchy sought to make itself legitimate was to install the ark of the covenant, symbol of God's presence as well as of the covenant, in the temple in Jerusalem. According to the account in 1 Kings 8, Solomon had "the ark of the covenant of Yahweh," which also symbolized that Yahweh could not be bound to a particular sacred location, brought up to "its place in the inner sanctuary of the house [temple], in the most holy place." This move, however, was also a subordination of the ark and the covenant to the new monarchic order symbolized by "the house of Yahweh." Although the poles were, awkwardly, a little too long, nevertheless neither they nor the ark could be seen from the outside. Out of sight, out of mind, at least for the monarchy.

As Yahweh stated to Samuel, however, the monarchy stood in opposition to the Mosaic Covenant, in which Israel declared exclusive loyalty to God as their king precisely as a way of avoiding falling back into bondage to a human king. Kings and their officials must have been acutely aware of this. Perhaps as a way of blunting the contradiction of the Mosaic Covenant involved in its consolidation of power, the monarchy in Jerusalem came up with a new "Davidic" covenant (2 Sam. 7:4–17). Yahweh had made the Covenant on Sinai directly with the people of Israel. In the covenant only with David, Yahweh promises that the dynasty of David will reign over Israel forever. In contrast with the Mosaic Covenant in which God's blessing is conditional on Israel's obedience to the commandments, God's promise to David is unconditional. In the Davidic covenant the monarchy asserted that the king was not subject to the Mosaic Covenant. Even if David's successors violated its principles, they could not lose God's favor. With this promise of God's unconditional authorization and blessing, the Davidic dynasty was guaranteed to be secure forever.

Political Domination and Economic Exploitation

The elaborate religious ceremonies in which Yahweh was now praised as the force that had permanently established the cosmic meteorological and economic order surely lent an aura of sacredness and inevitability to the monarchic economy. What made the monarchic economy work in more concrete terms—of the producers yielding up the tithes and other revenues necessary to fund the monarchy and its institutions—was a combination of coercive political power and exploitative economic power. The first is evident in the accounts of the rise of the monarchy. The second comes strongly to the fore in the protests of the "classical" prophets of the eighth century BCE. Coercive political-military power continued to be important in the later generations of the monarchy, although more in intimidation than in action. Economic exploitation became more and more important as the economic demands of the monarchy undermined the viability of families and their mutual support in village communities.

It would be naive to imagine that the kings of Israel and Judah maintained a professional army of infantry, cavalry, chariot forces, along with military fortresses at points around the country merely to defend the peasantry. They functioned also as a coercive instrument to intimidate the peasantry into submission to the political domination and economic demands of the monarchy. In the accounts of the rise of David to power, he was indeed acclaimed *messiah* first by the people of Judah and then the elders of all Israel (2 Sam. 2:1–4; 5:1–5). But he already had his own mercenary army, which he used to capture the non-Israelite town of Jerusalem as his new capital (5:6–9). Far more ominously, when all Israel revolted against his rule, he used his mercenary troops to conquer the Israelites, now as his subjects. A powerful professional military, including chariot forces, stationed in fortresses and strongholds at points around the country, was always essential to a monarchy's maintenance of its power.

Of course, the basic structure of the monarchic economy seriously compromised the economic viability of Israelite families. It also reduced the ability of village communities to come to the aid of their needy constituent households. Rendering tithes to the monarchy and temple made it far more likely that households already living at the subsistence level would have to borrow in order to feed themselves. But their neighbors, who were also expected to render up tithes to the monarchy, were now less able to respond to their need. This left an increasing number of village families vulnerable to those with access to resources, usually outsiders.

It is precisely in this connection that the structure of the monarchic economy, as represented in Samuel's warning, does not even begin to suggest how it operated—almost always to the detriment of peasant producers. Samuel's warning does not elaborate, for example, on how the king would take the tithes of produce from the people and give it to his officers and courtiers, or what the latter might do with that produce. For this we need to look more carefully at passages in the eighth-century prophets from the perspective of the dominant ancient Near Eastern economic structure for clues regarding the dynamics of official revenue collection and peasant debts.

What the prophets are protesting has been obscured by projection of modern Western assumptions onto biblical texts. Until recently, most biblical interpreters have simply assumed a market economy, as in early modern Europe. But there was no market in the ancient Near East. Standard translations of the Bible often reflect the assumptions of a market economy and are thus misleading. Terms such as "buying" and "selling," for example, may obscure transactions that were more like trading or loaning.

Most biblical interpreters have also understood the prophets as addressing their oracles to the people of Israel or of Judah generally. This may be the impression given in some of the later materials added to the anthologies of prophecies under the names of Amos, Hosea, Isaiah, and Micah. The prophetic oracles that critical analysis has judged are likely to come from the prophets themselves, however, are addressed more specifically to the kings and the officers of the monarchy. In many cases this is stated explicitly, in unambiguous terms. These prophets indict "the rulers of the house of Jacob and chiefs of the house of Israel," "the elders and princes of the people," and "those who store up violence in their strongholds" on "Mount Samaria" (Mic. 3:9; Isa. 3:13–15; Hos. 5:10; Amos 3:9–11; 4:1–3). It is those same rulers and chiefs, elders and princes, who lounge on "beds of ivory" in their "great houses" and "houses of hewn stone," who sally forth with horses and chariots from their strongholds, and who "issue decrees" and "write statutes" (Amos 3:13–15; 5:11; 6:4–7; Mic. 5:10–15; Isa. 10:1).

These were precisely the kings and their officers who took the tithes of the people's produce as the resources from which they lived in luxury. According to the ideology of monarchic economics, the people owed their tithes to the king or to God and the king, his son. The officers of the monarchy were the ones who presided over the collection and storage of the goods. Their positions of political power also gave them expandable economic power over the producers. They used their control over resources gathered from the people to then enhance their own position at the expense of the people.

The prophets' general charge against the rulers and officers is that they oppress the people. But they also specify the oppression. "They covet fields, and seize them; houses, and take them away," says Micah (2:1–2), and thus "oppress householder and house, people and their inheritance." Micah's contemporary Isaiah confirms these practices: they "join house to house, add field to field," until they alone live in the land (Isa. 5:8). The rulers and officers were taking control of the land-and-houses that were the ancestral inheritances of Israelite householders.

We already have a fairly clear idea of how they managed to take control of people's land and houses from examination in the previous chapter of how peasant debts were dealt with in ancient Israelite society. Having to render up a significant portion of their produce to the king or God in taxes left families all the more vulnerable to falling into debt. With neighbors also having less of a cushion to come to their aid, poor families were vulnerable to those who had control over surplus resources, the officers who collected and stored the tithes. Being outsiders, these officers were insulated against social pressures to observe the prohibition of interest. Having to borrow at high rates of interest left the indebted peasant families ever more deeply in a hole. As debts mounted, many had no choice but to "sell" or relinquish control of their land, their family inheritance, to their creditors, the officers of the monarchy. It seems likely that this is the connection in which Hosea charges that "the princes of Judah have become like those who remove the landmark" (Hos. 5:10), the boundary stone of a family's inheritance, as they "add field to field."

Amos and Micah, in parallel indictments, confirm how the ruling elite were exploiting the people. The principal way that they could get the people and their lands under their control was to exploit their need for loans. According to Amos they could not wait for religious holidays such as the new moon and Sabbath to be over so that they could "sell grain" and "offer wheat for sale," that is, make additional loans (the standard translation may be anachronistic). Taking further advantage of the desperate peasants, they manipulated the weights and measures by which the loans and interest were calculated, making the ephah small and the shekel great, and deceiving the borrowers with "false balances" (Amos 8:4–7) or "wicked scales and dishonest weights" (Mic. 6:10–11). Having gotten the poor peasants hopelessly into debts that they could never repay, they then would not only be in possession of "garments taken in pledge" but also "sell/buy the righteous for silver, and the needy for a pair of sandals" (Amos 2:6–8; 8:6).

In these indictments Amos uses rhetorically a number of symbols connected with the process of borrowing and lending. The "garment taken in pledge" was the symbolic "collateral" or pledge from the debtor that he would repay the loan (to be returned before nightfall, in Exod. 22:26–27). The "silver" was probably the equivalent value of the loan (or loan with interest) that the debtor owed. The "sandals" were probably another symbolic pledge or a symbol used in an oath to repay the loan. What the officers were doing is sending family members into debt-slavery because of their debts. The greedy officers were even so crass as to take "the sweepings of wheat," the gleanings, from the fields of the people whom they were pulling under their own control (Amos 8:6).

The prophetic protests indicate further what the rulers and officers were doing with the lands that they were taking control of and the heavily indebted peasants who had become economically dependent on them, perhaps as debt-slaves. They were building mansions for themselves, "grand houses" and "houses of hewn stone" (Amos 3:15; 5:11). Such houses required builders and artisans accomplished in dressing the stones and the corresponding fine work for the interior decor. Their "houses of ivory" and "beds of ivory" (3:15; 6:4) required long-distance import of such luxury goods from Africa, for which they presumably traded agricultural products derived from their debtors, in repayment of loans with interest. Fine dining on "lambs from the flock and calves from the stall"—in contrast to peasants, who usually could not afford to eat meat—required land and servants to raise the livestock in the desired way. "Drinking wine from bowls, and anointing themselves with the finest oils" (6:6) required imports paid for with other agricultural produce, and/or the development of specialized vineyards and olive orchards (see Amos 5:11; Isa. 5:1–8). An obvious step would have been to devote some of the lands they had taken control of to especially fine grapes and olives from which they could have their wines and fine oils made, again by a staff of tenant farmers and/or debt-slaves.

As the officers were augmenting their own wealth by expanding and specializing production on the lands they came to control via the debt mechanism, so the monarchy itself gradually took control of more and more of "the best of the fields and vineyards and olive orchards" (1 Sam. 8:14). In this way the monarchy could augment its economic and thus its military power. King Uzziah, who died just as Isaiah began his prophesying, evidently mounted an extensive program of economic development on land he had come to control and in newly developed marginal lands as well. "He built towers in the wilderness and hewed out many cisterns, for he had large herds, both in the Shephelah and in the plain, and he had farmers and vinedressers in the hills and in the fertile lands" (2 Chr. 26:10). Those "farmers and vinedressers" must have come from the ranks of those who had fallen into debt-slavery and/or lost control of their ancestral lands. On the basis of this economic expansion, Uzziah was able to expand his army and bolster his fortifications (2 Chr. 26:9, 11–15).

The prophets thus indicate how the monarchic economy in Israel and Judah gave the king and his officials prerogatives and power that further exacerbated the exploitation of the agricultural producers that formed its basis. Although the king stood at the center or head of the sacred political economy, he could not exercise complete control of the whole. Officers in charge of revenue collection and storehouses in given districts easily expanded their power as well as wealth primarily by using loans and peasant debts to gain control of land and labor, the very basis of power in an agrarian economy.

Because the strength of the realm as a whole depended on economically viable families and villages of producers, however, the king had an interest in protecting them from the worst depredations of rapacious royal officials. Although there were other motives, this may have been one of the purposes of proclamations by the Mesopotamian kings of the release of debts and return of people to their ancestral lands in which some have found the background of the jubilee year in Israel. The monarchy of Judah, like that of other ancient Near Eastern societies, developed an ideology of the king as the defender of the poor, symbolized in the widow and the orphan. Kings, however, did not often live up to the ideal.

The Monarchy's Suppression of Economic Rights

The monarchies in ancient Israel and Judah basically became typical ancient Near Eastern imperial economies. The king, as regent of God, ostensibly to maintain security and order, claimed a portion of the produce of the land and labor of peasant families and villages. With the revenues extracted from the peasantry and even by the expropriation of their ancestral lands, the monarchy built and maintained its principal institutions: the royal palaces, the temple and priesthood, the professional military. It supported its officers from tax revenues and by assigning them the revenues from particular villages.

The officers thus became increasingly wealthy and powerful from the resources taken from the peasantry by the monarchy. But the people were often left without sufficient produce to support themselves, even at a subsistence level. Taking advantage of the desperate peasants, the wealthy and powerful, in direct violation of the covenantal principles (especially those against coveting and stealing) made loans to the people at high rates of interest in order to take control of their labor and land, the basis of their livelihood. With their increasing wealth the powerful established an increasingly lavish lifestyle in mansions of hewn stone and ivory. Their exploitation of the peasants, who sank increasingly into debt, debt-slavery, and dependency on the power of the wealthy, threatened the viability of the very economic base on which the monarchy and their own position of power and privilege depended.

To justify and mystify the great divide between the people and the wealthy and powerful, the monarchy changed the focal Israelite ideology. It replaced the story of how God established the people in liberty and justice with hymns of praise to a God-and-monarchy that maintained the order in which the powerful ruled and any protest or challenge was defined as a threat to the sacred economy of the divine cosmos. The monarchy installed its own covenant with God, claiming that the head of state was not subject to the covenantal principles (2 Sam. 7).

Clearly, however, the monarchic economy of ancient Judah and Israel, again like that of the ancient Near Eastern empires generally, was fundamentally unstable, at risk of effectively destroying its own base of productive households and village communities. It was clearly inherently exploitative and oppressive of the very families on which it depended. At the end of the narratives of particular kings' reigns, the books of 1 and 2 Kings evaluate their policies and actions. Only a few "did what was right in the sight of Yahweh." Most of them "did what was evil in the sight of Yahweh." The criteria of these evaluations in the Deuteronomistic History clearly derive from the Mosaic covenant.

Study Questions

1. In what ways does the centralization of economic power in the monarchy stand in conflict with the overall Mosaic Covenant and with particular commandments?
2. How did the wealthy and powerful manipulate/exploit the people's economic vulnerability to gain ever more control of their land and labor (the basis of their livelihood)?
3. How did the wealthy and powerful use religion, including anxiety about social-economic disorder, to legitimate their centralization of economic power?
4. How do the prophets' indictments of the wealthy and powerful on the basis of key covenantal commandments make clearer that the commandments are about economic rights?

Chapter Five

Prophetic Condemnation of Economic Exploitation

The monarchy consolidated political-economic power by gaining more and more control over land and labor, seeking religious legitimation in the unconditional Davidic covenant. But this did not displace the Mosaic covenant as the set of principles and mechanisms that informed social-economic values and interaction in village communities. The Mosaic covenant had become solidly rooted in the popular culture of village life. As it was cultivated orally in village communities, the people were regularly reminded that Yahweh, the exclusive God and King of Israel, had established justice for (*shaphat*) the people in delivering them from exploitation by centralized power, and then demanded that they observe principles of justice (*mishpatim*), principles of mutual respect for one another's rights in nonexploitative economic relations.

For several generations in northern Israel, as ambitious kings began to make higher demands on their labor and produce and expropriate their land, the people were able to resist, even to fight back against the encroachment on their rights. Bands of prophets, inspired by the Spirit of Yahweh, often led such struggles. Once the monarchy consolidated power and the people could no longer mount widespread resistance, individual prophets still made public pronouncements of Yahweh's condemnations of kings and their officers for their abuse of the people in violation of covenantal commandments. Events in international relations seemed to confirm the pronouncements of the prophets. Israel and then Judah were devastated by foreign imperial armies because the kings had not been obedient to the covenant and its principles.

Prophetic Protest and Popular Resistance

Despite the weakening of the economic viability of Israelite families in the monarchic economy, the Covenant and its principles persisted among the people. As the early kings were pressing to establish their power, the people fought back, evidently when the royal abuses became intolerable to their covenantal moral economy.

Included in 1 Kings are stories of how the Israelite people resisted the monarchy's exploitation of the people's labor and land. After the death of Solomon, when his son came to Shechem to receive what he thought would be a pro-forma acclamation as king by the Israelites, the people made their recognition contingent on his reduction of his father's demands for forced labor (1 Kgs. 12). When Rehoboam refused to reduce the forced labor, the Israelites revolted, forming a more popular monarchy in the north that operated for a few generations by what might be called the covenantal consent of the governed. When King Ahab moved to consolidate royal power, however, large numbers of prophets associated with the prophet Elijah led at least some of the Israelite peasants in what must have been local revolts against the monarchy (1 Kgs. 17–19). The smoldering revolt eventually gained enough strength, under the leadership of Elijah's pro-tégé Elisha and the "messiahed" Jehu, to topple Ahab's son.

The story of Naboth's vineyard is a good indication of how the monarchy's violation of the people's rights supposedly protected by the Covenant evoked prophetic condemnation and may have led to the people's resistance. The story dramatically portrays the fundamental conflict between royal prerogative and power and the people's most fundamental economic right according to covenantal principles, the inalienability of their family inheritance. King Ahab was the son and successor of Omri, who first successfully consolidated the power of the monarchy in the northern kingdom of Israel. Omri controlled sufficient resources to construct the new capital city, Samaria, and to establish a dynasty with his son Ahab married to the Tyrian princess Jezebel. In the large town of Jezreel in the fertile plain between Samaria and Galilee, Naboth had a vineyard that was adjacent to the local palace of King Ahab. That he had a palace in Jezreel suggests that the king had already been gained control of lands and buildings at significant places around the realm.

> Ahab said to Naboth, "Give me your vineyard, so that I may have it
> for a vegetable garden, because it is near my house; I will give you a
> better vineyard for it; or, if it seems good to you, I will give you its

value in money." But Naboth said to Ahab: "Yahweh forbid that I should give you my ancestral inheritance." (1 Kgs. 21:2–3)

Whereupon Ahab simply sulked. Naboth appeals to his God-given right to his ancestral inheritance as inalienable. That was fundamental to covenantal law. Was Ahab simply ignoring or was he prepared to violate Naboth's right of ancestral inheritance guaranteed in the covenant? Or was he acting on the assumption that as king he had certain prerogatives that overrode covenantal law?

From her background in the royal court at Tyre, Jezebel evidently assumed that as king Ahab had prerogatives and power to enforce them: "Do you not now rule Israel?" she asked Ahab, and proceeded to use the power that the monarchy had gained to manipulate affairs in the towns and villages. By customary practice in covenantal Israel the elders of a town or village were the guardians of justice. The monarchy had gained some sort of leverage or influence over the elders of Jezreel. Jezebel was thus able to get the local elders to frame Naboth on charges of cursing God and the king, violations of the covenantal law that still governed local affairs (Lev. 24:14–16; Exod. 22:28). Naboth was convicted on the basis of the testimony of two false witnesses and executed by stoning, whereupon Ahab took possession of his vineyard. Royal prerogatives and power rode roughshod over the covenantal rights of Naboth and his heirs to the family inheritance.

The prophet Elijah pronounced the judgment of Yahweh against Ahab because he had "killed and also taken possession." Ahab's monarchy had not only ridden roughshod over the right of ancestral inheritance, but had also violated the covenantal commandments against coveting, false witness, stealing, and murder. The story of Naboth's vineyard reveals a struggle between two different economic systems: the covenantal communitarian protection of people's rights to an adequate livelihood, on the one hand, and the ancient Near Eastern tributary economy, on the other. Abuses such as King Ahab's expropriation of Naboth's ancestral land were evidently a factor that led to popular resistance and to the revolt led by Jehu, whose anointing as "messiah" by Elisha was understood to have been the implementation of Yahweh's charge to the prophet Elijah (1 Kgs. 19; 2 Kgs. 9:1–26).

Prophetic Condemnation of Centralized Economic Power

At the time of Elijah and Elisha, the Israelite people could still mount effective resistance (if we trust the narrative in 1 Kgs. 17–19 and 2 Kgs.

1–9). After further consolidation of monarchic power, however, resistance was evidently reduced to pronouncements of God's condemnation by the classical prophets.

The Israelite prophets provide dramatic examples of how religion was inseparable from politics and economics, of how the height of spiritual experience was directly related to the concrete political-economic circumstances of the people. The story of Elijah's commission to anoint Jehu is a breakthrough of an intensely personal, intimate, spiritual experience of the Divine. The purpose of the experience, however, is fully political-economic, to foment a revolt by anointing Jehu (making him messiah) to lead the people. Similarly the subsequent prophets such as Amos, Isaiah, and Jeremiah, like Elijah's contemporary Micaiah ben Imlah (1 Kgs. 22), experienced being caught up spiritually into the heavenly court of Yahweh. There they eavesdropped on the proceedings of God's court of covenantal justice, where cases were being brought against the kings and God pronounced sentence. The prophets' role was then to proclaim Yahweh's indictment and sentence publicly, often directly to the face of the kings. This is why the prophets introduce their pronouncements with the phrase: "the word [oracle] of Yahweh."

The very center of the classical prophets' message was God's condemnation of the rulers and their officers for violating the Covenant by oppressing the people. This cannot be stated clearly enough and strongly enough. Yes, their prophetic oracles were protests against the rulers' exploitation of the poor. But they were far more than protests. Their oracles were pronouncements of God's condemnation of the rulers. God's condemnation entailed violent punishment, indeed destruction of their mansions, strongholds, fancy vineyards, and life of luxury that was irrevocable, inevitable. The criteria that the prophets applied were covenantal. The crimes for which the rulers were indicted and sentenced were violations of the commandments and principles of the Mosaic Covenant.

In broad general terms, the prophets charged the rulers and officers with brutal oppression of the poor, in violation of the covenantal principles given to protect them. The prophets' language is blunt and sharp, often filled with mockery or sarcasm. The rulers have "oppressed the poor, crushed the needy," "trampled the needy," and "ruined the poor" (Amos 4:1; 5:11; 8:4). Micah condemned the rulers for the brutality of their oppression, the opposite of the justice required by the Covenant, and Isaiah was almost as sharp in his condemnation.

> Yahweh comes in judgment
>   against the elders of his people and their officials.
> "It is you who devour the vineyard;
>   the spoil of the poor is in your houses!
> What do you mean by crushing my people,
>   by grinding the face of the poor?"
>
> (Isa. 3:14–15)

At points the prophets refer to the Covenant, directly or indirectly. Hosea gives a virtual recitation of the Decalogue, summarizing the basic point of the first four commandments, which is loyalty to Yahweh, and listing all but one of the rest, as measures of the "knowledge of God," which is a code phrase for practice of the Covenant. Yahweh indicts the rulers of the land because "there is no faithfulness or loyalty, and no knowledge of God in the land. Swearing, lying, and murder, and stealing and adultery break out" (Hos. 4:1–2). Isaiah pronounces woes against those who "deprive the innocent of their rights," having "rejected the instruction (*torah*) of Yahweh of hosts" (Isa. 5:22–24). Rulers have "transgressed laws, violated the statutes, broken the everlasting Covenant; therefore a curse devours the earth" (24:5–6). In place of the covenantal statutes, they "make iniquitous decrees" and "write oppressive statutes, to turn aside the needy from justice and to rob the poor . . . of their right" (10:1–2).

Besides being the general criteria of divine condemnation of the oppression inherent in the monarchic economic structure and its functioning, covenantal commandments are the criteria for specific indictments of the powerful rulers and officers.

> Alas for those who devise wickedness
>   and evil deeds on their beds!
> When the morning dawns, they perform it,
>   because it is in their power.
> *They covet fields, and seize them;*
>   *houses, and take them away.*
> *They oppress householder and house,*
>   people and their inheritance.
> Therefore thus says Yahweh: . . .
> On that day they shall . . . wail with bitter lamentation, and say,
> "We are utterly ruined;
> Yahweh alters *the inheritance of my people.* . . .

Among our captors he parcels out *our fields*."
Therefore you will have no one to *cast the line by lot*
    in the assembly of Yahweh.

(Mic. 2:1–5; italics added)

As can be seen in the italicized words, the powerful are indicted for violation of the commandments against coveting and stealing. They have seized or stolen the very fields and houses, the ancestral inheritance of families, that the covenantal commandments are supposed to protect. Note also how, in Yahweh's courtroom, the punishment fits the crime, as the fields/inheritance of the powerful, who have seized the inheritance of their fellow Israelites, are parceled out to their captors. Just as they have denied the rights of householders to their inheritance and the periodic redistribution of land in the village assembly, so they will be denied any rights to distribution of land in the assembly of Yahweh.

In several of the particular prophetic oracles, the princes and other officers are indicted for specific violations of covenantal principles or mechanisms aimed at protecting the people from exploitation of their poverty. The practices of the powerful in "selling the righteous for silver and the needy for a pair of sandals," taking possession of their pledges (garments), manipulating the measures, weights, and balances in the transaction of loans, and so on, and expropriating even the gleanings from the fields are all violations of principles included in the covenantal law codes (Amos 2:6–8; 8:4–6).

The juridical parable in Isaiah 5:1–10, Yahweh's "love song" for his beloved, is one of the most artfully crafted oracles in the Hebrew Bible. The love song tells of Yahweh's devoted acts of benevolence for his vineyard, but then calls "the ruler of Jerusalem and man of Judah" to witness against themselves as they hear God's condemnation for having produced bloodshed and anguish instead of covenantal justice and righteousness.[1]

Let me sing for my beloved my love-song concerning his vineyard:
My beloved had a vineyard on a very fertile hill.
He dug it and cleared it of stones,
    and planted it with choice vines;
he built a watchtower in the midst of it,
    and hewed out a wine vat in it;

---

1. My adaptation of the NRSV translation, following Marvin Chaney, "Whose Sour Grapes? The Addressees of Isaiah 5:1–7 in Light of Political Economy," *Semeia* 87 (1999): 105–22.

he expected it to yield grapes,
　but it yielded wild grapes.
And now, ruler(s) of Jerusalem and man (king) of Judah,
judge between me and my vineyard.
What more was there to do for my vineyard that I have not done in it?
When I expected it to yield grapes, why did it yield wild grapes?
And now I will tell you what I will do to my vineyard.
I will remove its hedge, and it shall be devoured;
I will break down its wall, and it shall be trampled down.
I will make it a waste; it shall not be pruned or hoed,
　and it shall be overgrown with briers and thorns;
I will also command the clouds that they rain no rain upon it.
For the vineyard of Yahweh of hosts is the [ruling] house of Israel,
　and the man of Judah is his pleasant planting.
He expected *mishpat* (covenantal justice), but saw *mispah* (bloodshed);
　tsedaqah (righteousness), but heard *tse'aqah* (a cry).

(Isa. 5:1–7)

This artfully crafted prophecy of judgment focuses on what would have been the prized possession of a king or royal officer luxuriating in a lavish lifestyle, a vineyard that produced fine wine suited to the royal table, well pruned and cultivated and protected by hedges and walls. Chances are, however, that, as with Naboth's vineyard, such a vineyard carefully designed and cultivated to produce premium wine had involved expropriation of peasants' ancestral land and exploitation of the labor of people forced off their land. Measured by covenantal criteria, that was the very opposite of justice. The people were uttering anguished cries of distress to juridical authorities for legal redress, which the king and his officers were ignoring. But Yahweh was hearing their cry.

The divine sentence of the next stanza, in which the punishment fits the crime, states explicitly that indeed the king had built his prize vineyard by taking control of the people's houses and fields, supposedly the God-given and inalienable basis of their livelihood. The "woe" with which it begins suggests that a covenantal curse is being enacted.

Woe to you who join house to house, who add field to field,
　until there is room for no one but you,
　　and you are left to live alone in the midst of the land!
Yahweh of hosts has sworn in my hearing:

Surely many houses shall be desolate,
large and beautiful houses, without inhabitants.
For ten acres of vineyard shall yield but one bath [gallon of wine],
and a homer [bushel] of seed shall yield a mere ephah [jar of grain].
(Isa. 5:8–10)

Reform or Radical Condemnation?

The fall of the monarchy in northern Israel to the Assyrian Empire in the late eighth century BCE shocked observers in the southern kingdom of Judah. Followers of the earlier prophets who collected their oracles of judgment added prophetic exhortations that urged the kings and high officials of Judah to do justice, according to covenantal criteria, in order to avoid a disaster similar to that in the northern kingdom. Again some of these prophetic exhortations are blunt and pointed.

Listen, you heads of Jacob and rulers of the house of Israel!
Should you not know justice?—you who hate the good and love
the evil,
who tear the skin off my people, and the flesh off their bones;
who eat the flesh of my people, flay their skin off them,
break their bones in pieces,
and chop them up like meat in a kettle, like flesh in a caldron.
(Mic. 3:1–3)

This prophetic preaching of reform also includes sharp condemnations of the elaborate offerings to God in the temples and other religious ceremonies in which the sacred nature of the monarchic economy was expressed. If, as critical interpreters think, these prophecies belong to a secondary layer in these books, then their prophetic composers surely grasped the same covenantal condemnation of the monarchic economy. Through the prophet God declares clearly to the monarchy that runs the temple,

I hate, I despise your festivals,
and take no delight in your solemn assemblies.
Even though you offer me your burnt offerings and grain offerings,
I will not accept them;
and the offerings of well-being of your fatted animals
I will not look upon. . . .

But let justice roll down like waters,
    and righteousness like an ever-flowing stream.
           (Amos 5:21–24)

Similarly, with a more sarcastic tone,

Hear the word of Yahweh, you rulers of Sodom. . . . Gomorrah! . . .
I have had enough of burnt offerings of rams
    and the fat of fed beasts;
I do not delight in the blood of bulls, or of lambs, or of goats. . . .
When you stretch out your hands, . . .
    I will not listen;
your hands are full of blood. . . .
Cease to do evil, learn to do good;
  Seek justice, rescue the oppressed.

                          (Isa. 1:10–17)

Such prophecies not only demystify a sacralized system, but condemn the central function of the Temple in the sacral, monarchic, political economy.

Toward the end of the monarchy in Judah a number of signs appear that some officers of the monarchy believed that it should take covenantal principles seriously, at least to some degree. The kings' very attempts to silence the prophets indicate that they were apprehensive about their pronouncements. The fall of the kingdom of Israel in the north to the Assyrian armies in the late eighth century seemed to confirm what prophets such as Amos and Hosea had prophesied: the rulers of Samaria had been punished for violation of Covenant principles.

This had a serious effect on scribes and advisers in the monarchy in Judah. A substantial consensus has emerged in biblical studies that the predecessor of our book of Deuteronomy originated as a second book of law, an updated covenantal book, in form and substance, calling for a reform of the monarchy along covenantal lines. This was the book of covenantal teaching (*torah*) "found" in the temple at the time of King Josiah, and the basis of the reform over which he presided (2 Kgs. 22:8, 11; 23:2, 21).

Jeremiah reports and interprets an incident under King Zedekiah during the last years of the monarchy that reveals its ambivalent attitude toward the Covenant. The monarchy ordinarily did not take the Covenant seriously enough to pay any attention to its principles. Yet when it was threatened by foreign conquest, the monarchy was suddenly ready to believe that God's anger could be appeased by suddenly implementing one of its key mechanisms. As the Babylonian armies besieged Jerusalem, King Zedekiah "made a covenant with all the people in Jerusalem to make a proclamation of liberty to them—that all should set free their Hebrew slaves, male and female, so that no one should hold another Judean in slavery. . . . They obeyed and set them free" (Jer. 34:8–10). As soon as the danger had passed, however, "they turned around and took back the male and female slaves they had set free" (34:11). Jeremiah's interpretation may reflect a wider opinion among Judeans that this "covenant" of liberty for slaves was a belated implementation of the Sabbath release of slaves, which Jeremiah says was a covenant made with the ancestors when they came out of the house of slavery in Egypt.

A century or so after Amos and Isaiah, just prior to the Babylonian destruction of the monarchy and its temple in Jerusalem, the prophet Jeremiah again pronounced God's condemnation of the monarchy on the basis of covenantal principles. In a series of oracles he pronounced woes against the presumptuous king (Jehoiakim) for having conscripted forced labor to expand his palace.

> Woe to him who builds his house by unrighteousness,
>   and his upper rooms by injustice;
> who makes his neighbors work for nothing,
>   and does not give them their wages.
>
> (Jer. 22:13)

What may be his best-known oracle is God's condemnation of the temple explicitly because the rulers, believing their position guaranteed by God's protective presence in the temple, violate the commandments of the covenant with impunity (Jer. 7; cf. Jer. 26). Jeremiah's prophecy appears to be an escalation over the oracles of earlier prophets. The indictments of Amos, Isaiah, and Micah focused on rulers' practices that violated one commandment or another. Jeremiah's indictment lists most of the commandments together, suggesting that the Temple, along with the practices of the monarchy, are in violation of the whole covenant.

> Will you steal, murder, commit adultery, swear falsely, make offerings to Baal, and go after other gods that you have not known, and then come and stand before me in this house, which is called by my name, and say "We are safe!"—only to go on doing all these abominations? (Jer 7:9–10)

Earlier prophets condemned particular kings and their regimes. Jeremiah's prophecy that Yahweh is about to destroy the Temple condemns a major institution of the monarchy, as well as the monarchy itself, for systematic violation of the principles of the Covenant.

If we are not careful we may miss the significant difference between the prophetic exhortations to the monarchy to cease its previous abuses of the rights of the people and to begin practicing justice, on the one hand, and Jeremiah's unconditional condemnation of the dominant institutions of the centralized system for having violated the principles of the covenant as a whole, on the other. The difference is between a reformist position and a more radical conclusion. The reformists believed that it was possible to stay with the centralized political-economic system but to check its abuses so as to achieve greater justice. The more radical, such as Jeremiah, had concluded that God had condemned the centralized system as hopelessly contrary to the principles of the Covenant.

Covenantal Checks or Covenantal Co-optation?

Jeremiah and other prophets had warned that the Judean monarchy would be destroyed because of its violation of the Covenant. After the Babylonian conquest and deportation of the ruling families, groups of priests and scribes came to view the fall of Jerusalem as God's just punishment for breaking the Covenant. To restore the relationship with God and avoid another disastrous punishment, priestly and scribal groups focused on the keeping of covenantal laws and teachings. Their efforts can be seen in the books of the Pentateuch and the history books to which they gave definitive shape under the priestly aristocracy and rebuilt Temple that headed Judean society under the Persian Empire (sixth to fourth century BCE).

The covenantal law codes that they edited and the covenantal books of the Pentateuch that they put together attempted to provide checks on the violation of people's economic rights by those who wielded power in the temple-state economy. God's giving of the Covenant and the Covenant Code are placed at the crucial point in the history of Israel's origins immediately after the exodus from bondage in Egypt, as the condition for the future blessing of God. The Holiness Code included in the book of Leviticus is a vigorous re-presentation of covenantal commandments and their applications. The book of Deuteronomy gives a central place to laws about the basic covenantal mechanisms aimed at protecting families' economic viability. All of this covenantal legislation presumably strengthened the hands of the scribal staff and advisers of the temple-state in attempting to check abuses of people's economic rights by priestly aristocrats.

Law codes and covenantal books could lay out principles of justice, but there were no effective checks on the abuse of power by the wealthy and powerful heads of the temple-state. The memoirs of Nehemiah, the Persian governor sent to stabilize affairs in the Judean temple-state, which served also as a local administrative arm of the Persian Empire, offer us a window onto the problems that emerged repeatedly. There was "a great outcry of the people":

> We are having to pledge our fields, our vineyards, and our houses in order to get grain during the famine. . . . We are having to borrow [money?] on our fields and vineyards to pay the king's tax. : . . We are forcing our sons and daughters to be slaves, and some of our daughters have been ravished; we are powerless, and our fields and vineyards now belong to others. (Neh. 5:1–5)

In response Nehemiah enforces the covenantal mechanisms that protect the people's rights.

> Let us stop this taking of interest. Restore to them, this very day, their fields, their vineyards, their olive orchards, and their houses, and the interest on money, grain, wine, and oil that you have been exacting from them. (Neh 5:10-11)

Nehemiah called the priests and made them take an oath to do as they promised, and "shook out the fold of his garment" as a symbolic (covenantal) curse to enforce the oath. For subsequent generations of scribes and priests in Jerusalem, the repetition of covenantal laws and teachings in the books of the Torah presumably provided a basis on which they could at least attempt to mitigate the worst abuses of the people's rights by the priestly aristocrats.

In a somewhat similar way, the books of 1 and 2 Kings provided a history of the monarchy in which kings are praised or condemned for whether or not they observed the covenantal principles. This provided positive and negative examples for those in positions of power in Judea.

All of these texts, however, were only attempts to block abuses within the monarchic or second temple economy, not challenges to it. They were attempts at reform within the system, and precisely in posing as reforms of the system, they served to legitimate it. Deuteronomy, for example, offered laws to check the predatory practices of officials, but it also legislated the further centralization of economic resources and power. It required the centralized celebration of all major religious festivals in Jerusalem, which secured an enhanced and regularized flow of the people's resources to the Jerusalem Temple in offerings and other resources spent at festivals (Deut. 12–14). Deuteronomic laws also checked and compromised the function of village courts (see, e.g., Deut. 17:8–13). The book of Exodus, by inserting requirements of centralization of festivals into the covenant making at Sinai, gave the authority of the Mosaic Covenant to the very centralizing reforms that in effect violated it. Similarly, while the Holiness Code in Leviticus 17–26 may have checked injustice by officials, the other legislation in Leviticus sanctioned the centralization of economic resources and power in the Temple and priesthood. What is more, all of these laws of centralization of festivals in Jerusalem further sacralized the economy, making all forms of official expropriation of people's produce into tithes and offerings that are due to God and the priesthood.

Finally, the replacement of the monarchy by the temple-state introduced yet another dimension of the economic system. Besides constituting the command center of the economy in Judah, the temple-state served as an administrative arm of the Persian and later the Hellenistic and Roman imperial regimes. This was an ominous change in the overall structure of the Judean political-economic system, although Hebrew biblical books barely acknowledge it. The priestly aristocracy, ostensibly the representatives of the people to God and of God to the people, now owed their positions of power and privilege to an imperial regime. The aristocracy that ruled Judah was now itself under the control of an imperial power that it could hardly influence, much less effectively check. Besides the tithes and offerings for the Temple and priesthood, Judean producers were required to render up tribute to the empire. The priestly aristocracy who controlled and lived from the Temple economy were also responsible for collecting the tribute demanded by the empire.

A few late oracles in the prophetic books do, however, articulate the people's yearning and hopes for a time in the future when they would finally be free, when every family would live under its own vine and fig tree. The people yearned for a time when God would create "new heavens and a new earth" so that they could build their houses and then be able actually to live in them, and plant vineyards and be able to eat their fruit (Isa. 65:18–25).

Conclusion

Even after the monarchic centralization of power, the Mosaic Covenant and its principles and mechanisms were still strong in Israelite society, especially in village communities. In northern Israel in particular, villagers resisted the monarchy's expropriations of their resources. With the leadership of the groups of prophets around Elijah and Elisha they even mounted local revolts. Once the monarchies had consolidated power in both Israel in the north and Judah in the south, individual prophets pronounced God's condemnation of the monarchy and its officials for having violated the covenant commandments. Although the prophets and people could no longer mount serious resistance, the prophets asserted the covenantal principles that articulated the people's God-given economic rights in a public way that gained some resonance even in ruling circles.

Thus asserted in public in the face of the rulers and officials, the covenantal principles gained further resonance as a convincing explanation of the Babylonian destruction of Jerusalem. The scribes advising the priestly aristocracy that replaced the monarchy then included the covenant and covenantal laws in the books of the Pentateuch written to guide and authorize the temple-state. The covenantal laws were thus available as checks on abuses within the system. But the books of the Pentateuch also required the centralization of economic resources in the Temple economy. Almost unnoticed in the Pentateuch, however, was the new imperial dimension in the economy, with the priestly aristocracy now serving the interests of the imperial regime as well as their own, at the expense of the Judean peasantry.

Study Questions

1. In 1776 thirteen colonies appealed to the inalienable rights with which their Creator had endowed them in their "Declaration of Independence" from the centralization of power; to what principles did the ancient Israelites appeal in their "declaration of independence" from the centralization of power?
2. The prophets are often referred to as calling for "reform"; but aren't they delivering more of an indictment and condemnation not just of the abuse of power but of the centralization of power that is no longer "regulated" (restrained) by covenantal principles?
3. The law codes in Exodus, Leviticus, and Deuteronomy were, in effect, reformist attempts to apply covenantal principles to cen-

tralized power in books designed to support that very centralization; but isn't this a basic contradiction?

4. How could the biblical laws be effectively applied to those who
   held power in Judea when the latter owed their position to those
   holding even more (imperial) power?

Chapter Six

The Roman Imperial Economy in Jesus' Time

The people Jesus addressed were poor.

> Blessed are you who are poor, . . . blessed are you who are hungry. (Luke 6:20–21)

The prayer he taught his disciples focused on the most basic economic problems for dirt-poor farmers, enough food to stay alive and spiraling debts:

> Give us our daily bread. . . . Cancel our debts . . . (Luke 11:2–4)

Nor does he mince any words about the rich.

> Woe to you who are rich. . . . (Luke 6:24)

> It is easier for a camel to go through the eye of a needle than for someone who is rich to enter the kingdom of God. (Mark 10:25)

He tells a wealthy man who eagerly desires to have eternal life to give all that he has to the poor (Mark 10:21).

We may not think of Jesus as concerned with economic issues. But throughout the Gospel accounts, and particularly in confrontation with the rulers and their scribal representatives, Jesus focuses on the institutions, power relations, and exploitative practices that leave the people poor, in debt, and hungry. He accuses the high priests of robbing the people, like bandits who then seek refuge in the sacred precincts of the Temple (Mark

11:15-17). He accuses their representatives the scribes of "devouring widows' houses" (Mark 12:40). To the crowds of listeners in Galilee he mocks their "king," Herod Antipas, for his life of luxury in his royal palace (Luke 7:25). And he boldly, as well as craftily, answers the Pharisees' attempt at entrapment with the question about whether it is lawful, according to covenantal law, to pay the tribute to the Roman emperor (Mark 12:13–17). His concern covers the whole gamut of economic relations in Galilee and Judea under Roman imperial rule. Obviously, in order to understand Jesus and his mission, we need to know a bit more about what had recently become the Roman imperial economy in Galilee and Judea.

Impact of the Roman Rule

When we move from the books of the Hebrew Bible to the Gospels and Paul's Letters, we jump from life in Judah and Israel under ancient Near Eastern empires to life in Judea and Galilee under the Roman Empire. The story of Jesus' birth in Bethlehem points immediately to who controlled the economy from the top. "In those days a decree went out from Emperor Augustus that all the world should be taxed" (Luke 2:1). About sixty years before Jesus was born, the Romans had conquered Galilee, Judea, and the other districts of Palestine, and laid the people under tribute. The Romans impacted economic relations in Judea and Galilee in three main areas: the devastating effects of their repeated wars of (re-)conquest, their extraction of tribute, and the complications they introduced in their shifting arrangements of client rulers.

As dramatized repeatedly in the accounts of the first-century CE Judean historian Josephus, the Romans consistently practiced a scorched-earth policy: they burned villages and slaughtered or enslaved the inhabitants and crucified any who resisted as a way of terrorizing the remaining populace into acquiescence to Roman domination. Galilee was hit particularly hard repeatedly by Roman armies moving through the district to put down minor insurrections or major revolts. We know from recent massacres in Bosnia, the "shock and awe" invasion of Iraq, and other conflicts that such violence can leave collective social trauma among the people. Among the events Josephus mentions were the Roman warlord Cassius's massacre of thousands in Magdala fifty years before Mary Magdalene's time, and the devastation of Sepphoris, near Nazareth, right around the time Jesus was born. Economic and social recovery in such cases would have been difficult and slow.

After their initial conquest in 63 BCE, the Romans had laid the Galileans and Judeans under tribute, as a punitive humiliation as well as source of revenue. According to Josephus Rome required a quarter of the harvest every second year, that is, roughly 12.5 percent a year (*Ant.* 14.202–203). This was in addition to the tithes and offerings already due to the Temple and high priestly aristocracy, which was charged with collection and delivery of the tribute. Rendering tribute to Caesar as Lord and Savior of the world, of course, was a violation of the second commandment in the covenant, which prohibited bowing down and serving other Lords/gods. But the Romans viewed failure to render to Caesar as tantamount to rebellion, and the high priests and other Roman client rulers in Judea and Galilee, whose own positions depended on Rome's favor, prudently collected and paid the tribute. The issue of the tribute came to the fore particularly in 6 CE and after, when Rome imposed more direct rule through Roman governors. Josephus mentions in passing that there were silos containing grain for the Roman tribute in upper Galilee at the beginning of the great revolt against Rome in 66–70 CE.

After conquering the area, the Romans continued the basic economic structure in which rulers demanded and the peasant producers rendered up tithes, taxes, and tribute—while the rulers and their officers found ways to enhance their income by exploiting the people's need for loans to pay the tithes and tribute. The Romans' changing arrangement of Herodian kings and Jerusalem high priests as client rulers in Judea and Galilee complicated economic relations and exacerbated the situation of the people. For the Roman period we also have at least a bit of information on how the people fought back, partly and perhaps largely in defense of Israelite covenantal traditions. This is the context in which we must understand the mission of Jesus attested in the Gospels.

Herod's Economic Program

The first major step in the complication of the political-economic structure in Palestine came when the Roman warlords, unhappy about rival factions in the Hasmonean high priestly family, installed Herod as "king of the Judeans." Herod's intense economic "development" created the circumstances out of which the social-economic and political conflicts and movements of the next generations flowed.

Herod quickly became the Romans' favorite client king, partly because he kept tight control on Judea and the surrounding districts of his realm, with repressive measures to stifle any dissent. But it was also because he mounted intensive economic "development" in the areas under his rule.

Herod built or lavishly rebuilt fortresses around the countryside that he staffed with garrisons of mercenary troops. He built whole new cities named after Caesar, the seaport city of Caesarea on the Mediterranean coast and Sebaste (= Augustus) in Samaria. He built temples to Caesar in new cities and Roman institutions such as a hippodrome in Jerusalem. His most impressive building project was the massive expansion and rebuilding of the temple complex in Jerusalem, which became one of the wonders of the Roman imperial world. In addition to these adornments of his own realm, Herod became one of the most generous of imperial client rulers in the munificence of his gifts to the imperial family and to major cities of the empire. He also established a lavish court in Jerusalem, with satellite palaces such as atop the impregnable fortress at Masada. The officers to staff the elaborate regime had to be supported in a style commensurate with their importance and with Herod's own grandiose pretensions.

Herod thus had huge expenses. He had to generate revenues far in excess of what the territory he ruled had previously produced. The demands he made on his subjects to meet his extensive expenditures "stimulated" the almost exclusively agricultural economy, but they also threatened to ruin the economic base. To intensify agricultural production Herod surely ratcheted up demands on the tenants of the royal estates in the fertile great plain just south of Galilee. He also extended the areas cultivated into the lands east of the Sea of Galilee that Caesar placed under his control. And he sponsored the cultivation of specialty crops such as balsam in the Jordan Valley, on which the regime had a monopoly.

The peasants in the village communities of Judea and Galilee and other districts Herod ruled, however, constituted the principal economic base from which Herod had to extract more production. He increased demands for royal taxes—on top of the tithes and offerings for the temple and priesthood—and increased the efficiency of tax collection. In Galilee, for example, he established fortress towns on hilltop sites such as Sepphoris and stored grain and other goods taken in taxes in the royal fortresses there. The effects of overtaxation were soon felt in the countryside. The historian Josephus mentions that in order not to destroy the economic base, Herod had to grant temporary tax relief (*Ant.* 15.365).

Governors and High Priests in Judea

As "king of the Judeans" Herod had kept the Temple and high priesthood intact, and used them for his own purposes. He quickly got rid of the remaining members of the previous (Hasmonean) high priestly family, and brought in one after another of his own appointments. By the time Herod died in 4 BCE, the priestly aristocracy in Jerusalem consisted of four extended families. After ten years of unsatisfactory rule in Judea by his son Archelaus, the Romans placed Judea (along with Samaria and Idumea, but not Galilee) under the command of a Roman military governor, who in turn ruled Judea through the high priestly aristocracy. Structurally there were thus still at least two levels of rulers with demands for revenues from the peasantry, the Romans looking for their tribute and the Jerusalem high priesthood for tithes and offerings. The priestly aristocracy was responsible for collecting the tribute as well as managing their own revenues. The Roman governor appointed and deposed the high priest from one or another of those families, while other leading members of the families occupied other offices in the temple-state.

The Temple was the centralized religious institution of Judean society, where the priesthood offered various sacrifices and offerings to God and where the people of Judea and Judeans from the Diaspora communities came on the great pilgrimage festivals, particularly Passover. Jesus and his entourage were among the pilgrims ascending to the Temple Mount on at least one of those festival occasions.

But precisely because of those sacrifices and offerings and festivals, the Temple with its high priestly aristocracy was also the centralized economic institution that dominated the economy of Judea. Revenues of the Temple and priesthood included tithes, offerings, and sacrifices. All priests, regular as well as aristocratic, received a portion of their support from the tithes and offerings. Certain choice cuts of the sacrificial animals were reserved for the priests. Many of the ordinary priests lived in villages outside Jerusalem. But all participated in the Temple sacrifices and offerings during the four weeks of pilgrimage festivals such as Passover and during two other weeks of alternating service. The pilgrimage festivals, during which Judeans (and presumably Galileans as well) were supposed to bring sacrifices and offerings to the Temple, meant considerable additional income for Jerusalem generally as well as for the Temple and priesthood. The flow of resources to Jerusalem and the Temple was compounded as well by the massive reconstruction of the Temple begun by Herod, which was not completed until the early 60s CE. The massive unemployment that resulted when it was completed is a measure of just how central it had been to the economy of Jerusalem—and how much of a drain it had been on resources derived from the peasants of Judea and other districts.

The references to "money changing" in the Temple point to a degree of monetization of the Temple economy. This pertained mainly to Judeans traveling a distance to Jerusalem, who brought coins instead of animals and exchanged money, for example, for Passover sacrifices in the Temple courtyard. But this did not constitute a money economy for Judea in general. As earlier in the ancient Near East, wealth was stored in the Temple in the form of precious metals such as gold and silver, all under the control of the high priesthood. Temple income was further supplemented by the Temple tax expected of all adult males, including those now resident in Diaspora communities. The Temple tax had recently been raised from a third to a half shekel per year.

Temple resources controlled by the high priesthood were evidently also used to support the scribes and the scribal association known as the Pharisees, who served as advisers and assistants to the aristocracy in the operation of the temple-state. One of the functions of the scribes and Pharisees was to know the traditional laws of the temple-state, including the covenantal law codes, and to interpret and apply them, along with laws that were not included in sacred texts, perhaps because they were relatively new. Artisans were also required to serve the needs of the Temple and its operation as well as those of other Jerusalemites. The artisans thus also received at least some of their support, directly or indirectly, from the Temple and high priesthood. While some trade in luxury goods mainly for the Temple and the priestly aristocracy and other wealthy families may have been managed by the Temple officers, there were presumably independent traders who brought goods into Jerusalem.

An important additional source of income for the wealthy priests, Herodian officers still resident in Jerusalem, and other wealthy families was to make loans at hefty rates of interest. It has been reasonably surmised that resources coming into the Temple from Diaspora communities as well as from local revenues created a surplus of funds. High priestly families and others with access to such funds drew upon them to make loans to villagers who were struggling to feed their families after meeting their obligations for tribute, tithes, and offerings. From the interest charged and from foreclosure on loans, well-positioned families increased their wealth. Archaeologists have found a dramatic increase in the construction of mansions in the section of Jerusalem just to the west of the temple complex during the first century.

Herod Antipas in Galilee

When Herod died in 4 BCE the Romans installed his son Antipas as ruler in Galilee (and Perea, east of the Jordan River). Antipas's estimated income from his territories was less than a quarter of what Herod the

Great had derived from his realm. Yet, like his father, he launched massive building programs. He first rebuilt the fortress town of Sepphoris, in western Galilee, as a much larger fortress city. With his pretensions of Hellenistic Roman culture, he built a theater in Sepphoris, his "jewel." In the village of Nazareth only a few miles away, people would have watched the construction of this city. Indeed, a builder such as Joseph, Jesus' father, may have worked in the construction.

Within twenty years Antipas had built a second capital city on the southwest shore of the Sea of Galilee, named Tiberias for the new emperor. To clear the site Antipas had to destroy several villages and displace the villagers, events that would have been known around the shore surely as far as Capernaum, across the Sea of Galilee to the north, where the villagers could have watched the rise of the Roman-style city that was the new capital from which they would be taxed. Tiberias is where Antipas constructed the elaborate "royal palace" to which Jesus was referring (in Luke 7:25) and which Antipas decorated with all sorts of representations that Josephus says were against the traditional Judean laws (*Life* 65–66).

In these huge construction projects Antipas was one of the first Roman client rulers to implement the policy of urbanization, establishing cities as a way of controlling and exploiting the countryside. Contrary to some inflated recent estimates, the population of these cities would have been small, probably not over five thosuand, with the overall population of Galilee, in its "two hundred villages" (Josephus), at no more than a hundred thousand.

Antipas clearly needed to maximize his income from his subjects. It helped that for the first time in history the ruler of Galilee now resided in the area. Antipas's regime could thus mount far more efficient tax collection than previous rulers working from distant Jerusalem. In fact, between them these two capital cities literally had oversight on nearly all of the villages in lower Galilee. It seems that to enhance his income Antipas also developed a rudimentary fishing industry. This is the most convincing hypothesis to account for the combination of the discovery of a 26-foot boat that required a crew to operate it, references to imported "fish sauce" in Roman sources, references in the Gospels to fishing by Galileans, and the Greek name Tarichaeae ("Fishville") for the town of Magdala ("Tower"—of drying fish?). Antipas thus may have launched a commercial enterprise to bolster his income. But this enterprise sponsored by the ruler did not transform Galilee into a market economy.

It has gone almost completely unnoticed in New Testament studies that the Romans' appointment of Antipas as ruler in Galilee meant that Jerusalem rulers no longer had direct jurisdiction in the area. This must have reduced the revenues that the Temple and high priesthood could draw from Galilee in tithes and offerings, after the Hasmonean high priesthood had taken control of the area a century before. We may reasonably doubt whether voluntary tithing had taken hold among the Galilean villagers after only a hundred years under Jerusalem rule. Neither Antipas nor the Romans would have been happy about the Jerusalem high priesthood's active competition for revenues from Galilean villagers. It may be, however, that the high priesthood and its scribal staff developed circuitous devices by which they might extract offerings from Galileans (see discussion of *korban* in chapter 8).

In a pattern that continued from the ancient Near East, officials in the regimes of Antipas's successor, Agrippa II, as ruler of Galilee had "estates beyond the Jordan" (Josephus, *Life* 33). This is surely Josephus's way of referring to lands and villages controlled by the rulers of Galilee that they assigned to their officers. Antipas had probably followed his father in this means of support for his high-ranking staff. These officials would also have used the traditional means of loans to peasants to enhance their income.

Impact of the Roman Imperial Economy on the People

With two and sometimes three layers of rulers simultaneously making demands on them for tithes, taxes, and/or tribute, it is understandable that the Galilean and Judean people were poor, hungry, and in debt. Both Galilean and Judean villagers experienced the same disintegration of family and village life under the Roman imperial economy. But the impact varied according to their different historical backgrounds and the different client rulers that the Romans installed in Judea and Galilee after the death of Herod.

The standard Christian construction of the history of salvation, focusing broadly on the emergence of "Christianity" from "Judaism," has habitually referred to the people living in both Galilee and Judea as "Jews." Only "the Samaritans" have usually been distinguished from "the Jews." Ancient sources such as the histories of Josephus, however, are more precise, referring to "the Judeans," "the Samaritans," and "the Galileans." In sources such as rabbinic literature, the term used to refer to all of them collectively was not "the Jews" (which is a modern English term), but "Israel." Such rabbinic references are among many indications that all of the people living in these different areas were of Israelite heritage.

The Galileans had been brought under Jerusalem rule little more than a century before the time of Jesus. In 104 BCE, during a period of imperial weakness, the Jerusalem high priests had taken control of Galilee and required the Galileans to live according to "the laws of the Judeans." The latter presumably meant primarily the laws governing political-economic relations between the Jerusalem Temple and high priesthood on the one hand and the villagers subject to it on the other. The Samaritans had reason to be resentful about Jerusalem rule since the Hasmonean high priesthood in Jerusalem had destroyed their temple on Mount Gerizim. The Galileans may have been positive about being joined with their Israelite cousins to the south. But they would presumably have been unhappy about having to pay tithes and taxes to Jerusalem, enforced by garrisons of mercenary soldiers in fortresses overlooking their villages.

Evidence for economic circumstances at the time of Jesus, fragmentary as it is, points to another cycle of impoverishment and indebtedness of the peasantry. As in earlier centuries, the fundamental social-economic forms were still the family and the village community. The household was still the fundamental unit of production and consumption. Families consumed most of what they produced and produced virtually all of what they consumed. Clothing and other necessities were produced in the household or in barter with other households. There was little need for trade between villages except for products such as ceramics, which required a supply of clay that few villages had in their vicinity. Families lived in village communities where they cooperated in various ways, such as the construction of houses and maintenance of a community water supply. The form of local governance as well as social coherence was the village assembly (*synagoge* in Greek).

Under the impact of pressures from multiple layers of rulers, however, both families and the village communities began to disintegrate. As mentioned above, Herod had exhausted his economic base of peasant producers to underwrite his massive building programs and other expenses. The effects on the peasant producers was similar to those noted under imperial regimes in the ancient Near East and the monarchies in ancient Israel. Families unable to feed themselves after rendering up tithes and taxes fell into debt, often to Herodian officials who controlled stores of food. With their debts spiraling out of control, the poor gradually lost control of their lands, presumably becoming tenants of Herodian officers or of the king. Both archaeological evidence and passages in Josephus indicate that during Herod's reign more and more of the land in the

Judean hill country became royal estates. Other peasant families would have been threatened with loss of land.

Beginning in 6 CE Judean peasants, already exhausted by the demands for taxes to support Herod's ambitious programs, were required to render tribute to Caesar, again in addition to the tithes and offerings to the Temple. With the priestly aristocrats and wealthy Herodians eager to lend, the people's poverty led to debts, which in turn led to losing control of their land to their wealthy creditors. Land in the Judean hill country moved ever more into the control of Herodian and high priestly families. The prolonged drought and acute famine of the late 40s CE further exacerbated the people's desperate situation.

During Jesus' lifetime in the first three decades of the first century CE, the Galilean people were no longer under Jerusalem jurisdiction, but under the Roman client "king" Antipas (officially a tetrarch). Given Antipas's need for revenue to build his new cities and the increased efficiency with which a ruler resident directly in Galilee could collect taxes, economic pressure on the Galileans must have intensified. Investigations of village life in Galilee in the last decades have generated a more precise picture of economic conditions than previously available.

Archaeologists working without benefit of historical sociology have posited a reciprocal urban-rural exchange, modeled evidently on more commercial, modern economic patterns. Some, for example, have argued that the manufacture of pottery at a few sites in Galilee attests an extensive trade and market economy. Their data, however, are more consistent with manufacturing to meet orders, whether from other villages or from the newly built cities. Although the cities depended on village producers for their livelihood, it is unclear that the cities had anything to offer villagers, who generally strived to be self-sufficient and had no income for anything but the necessities that they produced mostly themselves. The accounts of Josephus, our principal source for urban-rural relations in Galilee, represent "the Galileans" as sharply hostile to the officials of both capital cities. First-century CE Galilee looks rather to have comprised roughly two hundred or so village communities onto which Antipas had imposed the newly built ruling cities of Sepphoris and Tiberias.

An older picture of rural life in Galilee common in New Testament interpretation based on Jesus' parables as slices of life may also be misleading. Several of Jesus' parables—the dishonest steward, the laborers in the vineyard, the wicked tenants, and the unmerciful servant—sketch a picture of large estates owned by absentee landlords, run by their stewards, and worked by tenants and/or day laborers. This raises the crucial issue for assessing the economic circumstances in Galilee, that of the people's land tenure. There were indeed large estates in Palestine, but they do not appear to have been in Galilee. Land in the Judean hill country was being transformed increasingly into large estates during just this period of time, as mentioned above. The great plain, just to the south of Galilee, had long since become royal land. This fertile area, almost certainly farmed by tenants or sharecroppers, was run for the direct income of the ruler in Jerusalem or granted to members of the Herodian family or turned over to colonies of Roman soldiers. As Josephus mentions, some of the Herodian officials in Tiberias had "estates beyond the Jordan" (*Life* 33). These two areas just to the south and east of Galilee may have been the source of Galileans' knowledge of large estates and of the illustrations of economic power relations in Jesus' parables.

These pieces of evidence, along with indications in the Gospels and in early rabbinic traditions, suggest that many, perhaps most, Galileans were still living on their ancestral inheritance of land. The process was only beginning by which land was transformed into large estates under absentee landlords. But that is exactly what Galilean villagers would have been most anxious about. Under pressure for tithes, taxes, and tribute many Galileans had fallen into debt and had long since exhausted the possibility of loans from other villagers, who were also having difficulty meeting their own subsistence needs. Their only recourse was to borrow from outsiders, very likely officials in the cities, who had control of supplies of grain and other staples. They might also supplement their income by hiring out as day laborers in addition to continuing work on their own fields. Along the shore of the Sea of Galilee some could work in the new fishing industry being developed by Herod Antipas. As families and village communities began to disintegrate, villagers found themselves threatened with loss of their land, with the prospect of becoming tenants or completely dependent on day labor. These are precisely the economic circumstances that are conducive to the emergence of popular movements or even, rarely, peasant revolts, judging from studies of similar societies in similar circumstances. In these circumstances hungry and indebted Galilean villagers may well have been receptive to a prophet who taught people to pray for the coming of the kingdom of God, which would mean that they would have sufficient daily bread and a (mutual) cancellation of their debts.

Covenantal Criteria for Criticism and Reform

The covenant and covenantal economic principles were very much alive during this time of worsening circumstances for the Galilean and Judean people. Covenantal law codes continued to be cultivated, and some of the covenantal mechanisms designed to protect the basis of people's livelihood were practiced. Given the division and structural conflict between the priestly aristocracy who lived from tithes and offerings and the peasantry who supplied those revenues to the Temple, it should not be surprising that there were differences between the cultivation of Israelite tradition at the elite level, which included written texts, and the corresponding cultivation of tradition at the popular level, which was strictly oral. While our sources are limited and often indirect, there are clear indications that covenantal tradition and forms concerned with economics continued at both levels.

At the elite level, where scribal circles produced written texts (including the predecessors of our biblical books), there are a number of indications that covenantal economics was still operative in late second temple Judea. The "memoirs" of Nehemiah indicate that the descendants of the Jerusalem elite who had been restored to power in the Jerusalem temple-state had identified with the Covenant. In the lengthy covenant renewal ceremony recounted in Nehemiah 8–9, they interpret their continuing political-economic subjection to imperial kings as due to their having broken the Covenant. Toward the end of their prayer of confession comes a lament: "Here we are, slaves to this day—slaves in the land that you gave to our ancestors to enjoy its fruit. . . . Its rich yield goes to the kings whom you have set over us because of our sins" (9:36–37). The same memoirs recount with evident approval, however, that the Persian governor Nehemiah had to force the predatory "nobles and officials" to implement the covenantal mechanisms designed to protect the producers, to cancel the debts of impoverished peasants and restore to them their ancestral houses and lands (5:1–13).

During the second temple period circles of scribes and priests in the service of the temple-state compiled the various covenantal law codes, as mentioned at the end of the last chapter. The existence of these law codes does not mean they were implemented as public policy and practice. But there is evidence that scribal teachers taught the laws of the covenant to their scribal and priestly students. In the book of Sirach (Ecclesiasticus), composed about 200 BCE, the Jerusalem scribe Ben Sira offers instruction in wisdom, emphasizing obedience to the Covenant and observance of its laws. His instruction is addressed to scribes training to serve as advisers to the priestly aristocracy, on whom they would be economically dependent. It is clear, however, that the powerful and wealthy aristocrats who control the temple-state do not observe the covenantal principles. Ben Sira strikingly admonishes prospective scribes to mitigate the worst effects of the wealthy aristocrats' oppression of the poor, even to "rescue the oppressed from the oppressor" (e.g., 4:1–10). The circle of scribes who produced the Epistle of Enoch (*1 Enoch* 94–104), Ben Sira's contemporaries, turned against the priestly aristocracy precisely because they had severely oppressed the poor. They pronounced what are evidently covenantal woes against the wealthy and powerful, as had Amos and Isaiah before them.

Perhaps partly because scribes such as Ben Sira persistently agitated for observance of the covenant and its laws, at least some of its key covenantal mechanisms became widely practiced during the second temple period. Passing references in our sources, such as Josephus's histories, indicate that the sabbatical fallow year had become regularized into a recognized seven-year cycle. This was factored into the calculation of the tribute to Rome (Josephus, *Ant.* 14.202–3). The sabbatical release of debts had also become regularized and widely accepted as binding on creditors. This is indicated by the famous *prosbul* devised as a bypass of the debt release by the Pharisaic sage Hillel, a somewhat older contemporary of Jesus. By placing loan documents into the hands of a court, creditors could then ignore the year of release. The motive for the device is often explained as the need to make credit available in the last years before the scheduled year of release. The effect over a longer period of time, however, would have been to drive the poor more deeply into debt. What the device of the *prosbul* indicates is that covenantal mechanisms meant to protect the people's economic viability had become so widely accepted as law that those seeking to benefit from making loans to the poor sought ways to bypass their implementation.

Covenantal principles and mechanisms were also cultivated by the people in their village communities. Since the nonliterate ordinary people did not leave written sources—except for the teachings and acts of Jesus that were later written down in the Gospels, an almost unique occurrence in history—we have no direct sources for popular cultivation and practice of covenant principles. Reports about their acts of resistance to exploitation by their rulers, however, indicate that their resistance was rooted in their commitment to covenantal commandments. This grounding of resistance to oppressive treatment in violation of covenantal principles is also evident in the parallel resistance of scribal-intellectual groups.

Covenantal Criteria for Protest and Resistance

Both New Testament interpreters and, to a degree, Jewish historians have portrayed Judaism or Judean society as unified in its loyalty to Temple and Torah (the Law). Our written sources, however, do not attest this picture. Serious dissent periodically emerged among the scribal circles serving the temple-state. Active resistance, by scribal groups as well as among ordinary people, erupted particularly in the decades right around the time of Jesus against both the Romans and their high priestly and Herodian client rulers. Much of this resistance was rooted in the Covenant and covenantal principles. Some of the contents of the books of the Torah/Law did indeed give the Temple grounding in the Scriptures. But insofar as the covenantal principles and teachings were at the center of the Torah, the latter provided the criteria for resistance to the high priesthood as well as the other rulers in command of the Roman imperial economy.

Two particular actions taken by scribal teachers and Pharisees indicate that many of them were opposed to Roman rule and the Roman tribute in particular, evidently on the basis of Mosaic covenantal principles. In the one, as Herod lay dying, two teachers inspired their students to cut down the golden Roman eagle that Herod had erected above the gate of the temple, clearly a violation of the second commandment. In the other, the teacher Judas and the Pharisee Saddok led a group that Josephus calls "the fourth philosophy" in organizing to refuse to pay the tribute to Rome. They based their resistance squarely on the first two commandments of the Covenant. Since the people had God as their exclusive Lord and Master, it was impossible for them to pay tribute to Caesar as lord and master.

Many protests and resistance movements emerged at the popular level. Even our limited evidence indicates that several of these were clearly rooted in Israelite traditions of the exodus and Covenant, even motivated by particular violations of covenant commandments. The celebration of God's liberation of the people from bondage in Egypt at the Passover Festival evidently became an occasion for protest, so much so that the Roman governors sent troops to stand atop the porticoes of the Temple during the celebration of Passover. When Pontius Pilate sent Roman troops through the Judean countryside into Jerusalem carrying their army standards with representations engraved on them, a large number of people protested, baring their necks in readiness to die for covenantal principles. In mid-century a whole series of popular movements formed that focused on a prophet who posed as a new Moses or Joshua calling his followers to a new exodus from oppressive foreign rule or entry into the land where God would drive out or destroy the Roman occupiers, as he had done in the battle of Jericho.

Galileans were particularly adamant about observance of covenantal commandments, judging from several incidents recounted by Josephus, a Jewish historian of the period. Two of these in particular are obviously rooted in popular resentment over economic exploitation. When the emperor Caligula (Gaius; ruled 37–41 CE) ordered his image to be installed in the Temple, large numbers of peasants mounted a strike, refusing to plant their fields (Josephus, *Ant.* 18.261–88; *War* 2.184–203; cf. Philo, *Leg.* 188–249). The presence on their soil of the statue of the emperor violated the covenantal commandments concerning exclusive loyalty to God. Their strike, which meant no harvest from which the Romans could extract their tribute, was a defense of the commandments regarding exclusive loyalty to God. As both the Roman legate of Syria and the Herodian officials in Galilee recognized, Roman punitive action against the strike, which was about to result in no harvest of grain, would only have produced "a harvest of banditry" instead (from hungry peasants fleeing into the hills; *Ant.* 18.273–274).

In the second incident, at the beginning of the great revolt in 66 CE, Galileans attacked and burned the Herodian palace in Tiberias, one of the capital cities in Galilee in which Antipas had installed representations of animals forbidden by "the laws" (Josephus, *Life* 65–66). Popular grievances about economic exploitation again crystallized around violation of the covenantal commandments that called for exclusive loyalty to God.

In the decades after Jesus' ministry and other popular protests and resistance movements, social unrest grew, rooted in the spreading poverty, debts, and despair that Jesus had addressed. When widespread revolt finally erupted in the summer of 66, the rebels in Jerusalem set fire to the public archives in order to destroy the records of debts (Josephus, *War* 2.427). The people knew very well that periodic cancellation of debts was an integral device intended to mitigate poverty and hunger. Jesus of Nazareth was rooted in just such covenantal economic principles: "Your kingdom come. . . . Cancel our debts, as we herewith cancel the debts of our debtors."

What holds the political-economic structure of a society is the people's belief that the holders of power are legitimate. This is what motivates the people to yield up the taxes and offerings needed to support kings in their palaces and high priests in their mansions. In ancient Israel this focused on whether they were approved by God. What the prophets were doing was denying the legitimacy of the kings and their officers, saying that God had condemned them for violating the principles of the Covenant. Alien imperial kingship was utterly illegitimate, except temporarily as punishment for the kings of Judah having broken the covenant. Payment of tribute might be partly hidden, when the high priesthood sent a portion of the revenues to an imperial regime as tribute. But the Roman emperor imposing tribute as lord and savior of the world was a blatant violation of the first and second commandments. Moreover, a client king appointed by Rome was hardly acceptable according to covenantal criteria.

Covenantal principles also became criteria according to which the high priestly aristocracy again and again appeared illegitimate to the people and even to their scribal advisers. Powerful aristocrats repeatedly exploited the people, in violation of covenant laws, as just noted in the memoirs of Nehemiah (5:1–13) and the wisdom teaching of Ben Sira. Most notably, in the decades just before and during Jesus' ministry, the four high priestly families from which the Roman governors appointed the high priest not only collaborated closely with the Romans but became predatory on their own people. In a time of periodic provocations by Roman governors such as Pontius Pilate and popular protests against abuses, the high priestly families never protested or represented the people to the Roman authorities. They exploited the people's need for loans to expand their own wealth, with which they built mansions near the Temple in Jerusalem. According to Josephus's accounts, they even sent gangs of thugs to the village threshing floors at harvest time to expropriate the tithes, depriving the ordinary priests of their share (*Ant.* 20.181, 206–207).

In the decades following the death of Herod, both Judeans and Galileans mounted a number of protests and resistance movements against Roman rule and/or the priestly aristocracy who were maintained in power by the Romans. It is evident that most of those protests and movements were rooted in the Mosaic Covenant and its principles. The mission and message of Jesus of Nazareth and the movement he led belong in just this context.

Study Questions

1. Why would the people of Galilee have responded well to Jesus' proclamation of the kingdom of God, such as the beatitudes ("blessed are the poor, . . . the hungry") and the Lord's Prayer ("give us bread . . . cancel our debts")?

2. How will collapsing the modern Western separation of religion from politics and economics help us to understand how Roman imperial rule worked in Judea and Galilee?
3. How had Roman imperial rule brought intensified economic demands on the Galilean and Judean people?
4. How did payment of the tribute to Caesar place faithful Judeans and Galileans in a double bind (damned if you do and damned if you don't)?
5. When widespread revolt finally erupted after decades of disintegration of family and village life under intensified economic burdens, why did the people focus on setting fire to the records of debts in the archives?

Chapter Seven

Jesus' Renewal of the Covenant

Jesus is keen on the Covenant as well as concerned with economics. In fact, covenant and economics go closely together in his prophetic preaching and teaching. Covenant commandments are at the basis of his sharp criticisms of the high priest and scribes who operate and live from the Temple economy. He accuses the scribes of ignoring "you shall not covet" in "devouring widows' houses" (livings; Mark 12:40). When he blocks operations in the temple courtyard, he accuses the high priests of stealing, like brigands who then flee to their stronghold, in this case the sacred precincts of the Temple (11:15–17). Similarly, when the Pharisees urge Galileans to "devote" (*korban*) some of their land or its produce to the temple, Jesus condemns them for "rejecting the commandment of God, . . . 'Honor your father and your mother'" (7:9–13). And rendering the tribute to Caesar, about which the Pharisees and Herodians attempted to entrap Jesus (12:13–17), flew in the face of the first two commandments.

The petitions for daily bread and cancellation of debts in the Lord's Prayer are covenantal as well as economic (Luke 11:2–4; Matt. 6:9–13). The cancellation of debts every seven years was one of the basic covenantal mechanisms to keep people economically viable on their ancestral land, as explained in chapter 3. The underlying point of all the covenantal commandments and mechanisms was to enable people to have sufficient food day by day, year by year, as discussed in chapters 2 and 3.

Once we begin looking seriously for economic concern and covenantal themes in the teaching of Jesus, we find that they are extensive and prominent. For example, the longest speeches that Jesus gives in both Matthew and Luke are covenant renewal speeches, and the most sustained instruction that Jesus gives in a series of dialogues in the Gospel of Mark is, in effect, yet another long covenant renewal discourse.[1]

A Gospel is not just a bunch of paragraphs strung end to end like a string of beads (a standard view in mid-twentieth-century scholarship), but a sustained, complete story, which has a plot, a point, a message. In the Gospel sources, moreover, Jesus does not utter separate sayings, but gives shorter or longer speeches and engages in dialogues. His particular sayings have meaning in the context of these sustained speeches. The speeches are focused on key issues of concern to Jesus and his audience, such as sending the disciples out on a mission (Mark 6:7–13; Matt. 10; Luke 10:2–16) or making bold confession when arrested by the authorities (Mark 8:34–38; Luke 12:2–12).

The longest speeches Jesus gives—the "Sermon on the Mount" (Matt. 5–7), the sustained series of dialogues in Mark (10:2–45), and the "Sermon on the Plain" (Luke 6:20–49)—are all covenant renewal speeches. We will focus on the Sermon on the Mount in chapter 10, the dialogues in Mark in chapter 8. In this chapter we focus on Jesus' covenant renewal speech that most interpreters believe lies behind both the parallel "Sermons" in Matthew and Luke. Many Gospel scholars believe that this speech and many shorter ones on other issues that appear in Matthew and Luke, but not in Mark, were taken from a common source, called Q (for German *Quelle*, "source"), which they both used in the composition of their respective Gospels. Whether this speech and the rest of Q existed in written form or was simply performed repeatedly by Jesus' followers, its reconstruction gives us access to the basic teaching of Jesus.

Since it may be new to many that covenant renewal that included economic cooperation and sharing was central to Jesus' ministry, it may help to know just how alive covenant renewal was in his society at the time. The discovery of the Dead Sea Scrolls revealed new evidence of just how prominent the covenantal pattern and the covenantal concern with economic justice were in Judean society at the time of Jesus, especially for movements opposed to imperial economic domination.

Covenant Renewal and Covenantal Community at Qumran

Among the many scrolls of ancient documents found at Qumran, near the Dead Sea, were manuscripts of the previously known *Damascus Docu-*

---

1. Scholars have been slow to recognize these speeches. In part, this is because of biblical interpretation's historical bias against the Law and all things Jewish. Also, scholars have paid too much attention to individual verses and not to the larger context of Jesus' sayings.

ment and, more striking, copies of the *Community Rule* of the community at Qumran that hid the scrolls when the Romans attacked a generation or so after Jesus. These documents, which were in effect charters or handbooks for newly formed communities, indicate that the covenantal form as well as covenantal laws were still alive, that a movement could take the form of a covenantal community, and that this renewed covenantal community focused on economic sharing and justice.

First, both of these documents, which were charter instructions for the community's common life, were covenantal not only in content but in form as well, including all three basic components. Early sections of both documents provide lengthy statements of God's deliverance of the people. Both contain laws and regulations for community life. Those in the *Community Rule* are extensive, somewhat as the Covenant Code in Exodus 21–23 extends the covenant principles into a lengthy list of "statutes and ordinances" (1QS 5:1–11:24). Both documents, finally, contain (closing) declarations of long life and God's rewards for those who keep the covenant and retribution for those who do not.

Particularly striking and parallel to Jesus' covenant renewal speech, as we shall see, is the transformation in the function of the blessings and curses. In the original Mosaic covenant structure, blessings and curses were the principal form taken by the motivating sanctions on keeping the principles of social policy. In the Qumran *Community Rule* they have been transformed into a component of the declaration of God's deliverance of the people. The blessings and curses are delivered as part of the covenant renewal ceremony described at the outset of the *Community Rule*. They apply, respectively, to the insiders and outsiders, the community members who keep the covenant and other Judeans who do not. People who must have been discouraged about their continuing subjection to foreign rule and may have been blaming themselves for not having kept the covenant are now hearing that they are receiving God's deliverance in the present and future.

Second, as indicated in these two covenantal community handbooks, the people who had withdrawn into the wilderness at Qumran had formed a new covenantal community. Both the *Community Rule* and the *Damascus Document* articulate this repeatedly. The community itself is often referred to as "the covenant" and its members as "those who hold fast to the covenant." The opening section of the *Community Rule* states the annual ceremony of covenant renewal in which new members were taken into the community. The laws and procedures in the *Community Rule* are clearly for the life of the community, for the community in general or its courts or its council. Christian interpreters previously caricatured the Pharisees as rigorous legalists. The Qumran community considered them rather as "smooth interpreters." The Qumran people themselves were the rigorists, determined to keep the covenantal torah of Moses.

Third, while the Qumran community was rigorous in observing purity regulations in which its priestly and scribal members were steeped, it was every bit as rigorous in its community economic practices. The covenantal declaration of deliverance proclaims "an end for injustice" (1QS 4:18–24). Members of the covenant community are to "practice . . . justice and uprightness and charity and modesty" (1QS 5:4–6). In commitment to the covenant, they "shall love each man his brother as himself; they shall succor the poor, the needy, and the stranger" (CD 6:20–21).[2] As a community of priests, scribes, and others who had broken with the Jerusalem temple authorities, the Qumranites pressed the rigor of covenantal mutuality further than possible in a peasant village. They pooled their resources, their property, which the community then held in common. After a year of probation, member candidates handed over their property and earnings to the congregation. After the second year their property was merged into the common fund. All decisions concerning property and justice were made by the priests and other members of the community who adhered to the covenant (1QS 5:2–4; 6:18–24). So seriously did they take the sharing of goods that lying in matters of property, that is, failure to pool all of one's goods, was grounds for exclusion from the community meal (1QS 6:25). The community of the covenant at Qumran thus practiced covenantal mutuality and cooperation in the most rigorous way, sharing all goods in common.

The *Damascus Document* evidently gave covenantal guidelines for communities of the group that lived in various towns away from the Qumran community itself. These scattered communities also maintained a rigorous economic discipline. Members placed "the earnings of at least two days out of every month into the hands of the guardian and the judges," who used it in economic support of the orphans, the elderly in poor health, the sick, captives, young women who were unattached to a household, and "the poor and needy" generally (CD 14:13–15). They also insisted, with what effect on the actual operations in the temple we can only surmise, that unjustly gained goods could not be offered on the altar—presum-

---

2. Translation of the *Damascus Document* and other Dead Sea Scrolls is from Geza Vermes, *The Complete Dead Sea Scrolls in English* (New York: Penguin, 1997).

ably aimed at oppression of the poor by the wealthy and powerful (CD 16:13–14). They also forbade people to consecrate to the temple the field or the food that belonged to their ancestral households (CD 16:15–17; 4Q266, fr. 8 ii, 2–3). The communities for which the *Damascus Document* was composed thus appear to have attempted to press measures of covenantal economic justice, protection of people's economic rights, onto the society in general.

Jesus' Covenant Renewal Speech

From their parallels in beatitudes at the beginning, the "love your enemies" set of sayings in the middle, and the motivating sayings and double parable at the end, it is clear that the Sermon on the Mount (Matt. 5–7) and the Sermon on the Plain (Luke 6:20–49) followed the same earlier speech of Jesus. This speech, like the other shorter speeches of Jesus parallel in Matthew and Luke, would have been repeatedly recited and heard and resonated in communities of Jesus followers. In the oral tradition of such repeated performances, the wording may vary according to the circumstances and audience, but the basic pattern and gist of the speech remain consistent. On the basis of the parallels in Matthew and Luke, we can reconstruct the basic covenant renewal speech of Jesus, as recited repeatedly by his followers. Since it was almost certainly in poetry, not prose, in both the original Aramaic of Jesus and the Greek of some of the early Jesus movements, I present it in poetic form. I will also give a fairly literal translation, often awkward in English, partly in order to indicate how in Greek the poetic lines were parallel in words and sounds. The numbers in parentheses show where the parallel phrases can be found in Luke 6. The steps in which the speech proceeds are those of the traditional components of the covenantal structure, which I will discuss further.

As an act of communication a speech focuses on a topic or issue and has distinctive terms, phrases, and language appropriate to the topic. In a worship service, words of assurance, dedication of the offering, and sermonic exhortation to lead a faithful life all have distinctive language and tone. Speech on a topic usually fits a certain context, and some of those contexts have deep cultural traditions and audience expectations upon which the speech must draw. A funeral oration or eulogy is delivered at a funeral, not a wedding banquet, for which a toast would be the appropriate speech. A speech often makes an argument and usually has a structure or pattern, which may also be more

The Text of Jesus' Covenant Renewal Speech in Luke [Q] 6:20–49[3]

Step I

(20) Blessed are the poor, for yours is the kingdom of God.

(21) Blessed are those who hunger, for you shall be filled.
Blessed are those who mourn, for you shall laugh.

(22) Blessed are you when they reproach you
and speak evil against you on account of the son of man.

(23) Rejoice and be glad
for your reward is great in heaven.
For so they did to the prophets.

(24) Woe to those who are rich, for you have received your
consolation.

(25) Woe to those who are full, for you shall go hungry.
Woe to those who laugh, for you shall mourn.

(26) Woe when all people speak well of you.
For so they did to the false prophets.

Step II

(27) Love your enemies,
do good to those who hate you.

(28) Bless those who curse you,
pray for those who abuse you.

(29) To the one who strikes you on the cheek, turn also the other.
And from the one who takes your coat, [offer] also the tunic.

(30) To the one who asks from you, give,
And from the one who borrows, do not ask back.

(31) And as you wish that people would do to you, thus do to them.

(32) And if you love those who love you, what credit is that to you?
For even the toll collectors do the same.

(33) And if you do good to those who do good to you, what credit is
that to you?
For even the [other] peoples do the same.

(34) And if you lend to those from whom you hope to receive,
what credit is that to you?
Even lend to. . . [?]

3. My translation, which attends closely to the reconstruction in *The Sayings Gospel Q in Greek and English*, ed. James M. Robinson et al. (Minneapolis: Fortress, 2002), attempts to reflect the poetry of Jesus' speech in Greek text, which in turn reflects the poetic patterns of the underlying Aramaic, as well as to present the speech in its overall covenantal structure. The words enclosed in brackets [ ] indicate places where the reconstruction of the speech from the parallels in Matthew 5–7 and Luke 6:20–49 are uncertain.

(35) But love your enemies, and do good, and lend,
     and your reward will be great.
And you will become sons of your Father,
     for he is kind to the ungrateful and the evil.
(36) Be merciful, as your Father is merciful.

(37) And do not judge, and you will not be judged
     for with the judgment you judge you will be judged,
(38) for with the measure you measure it will be measured to you.
(39) Can a blind person guide a blind person?
     Will not both fall into a pit?
(40) A disciple is not above his teacher,
     but everyone well trained will be like his teacher.
(41) Why do you see the speck in the eye of your brother,
     but the log in your own eye you do not notice?
(42) How [can you say] to your brother,
     "Let me remove the speck from your eye,"
and behold, there is a log in your own eye?
Hypocrite!
Remove first the log from your own eye,
and then you will see [clearly]
to cast out the speck from the eye of your brother.

Step III
(43) There is no sound tree that bears bad fruit,
     nor again a bad tree that bears sound fruit.
(44) For from the fruit a tree is known:
     they do not gather figs from thorns,
          or grapes from a bramble bush.
(45) The good man from the good treasure brings forth good [things].
     The evil man from the evil [treasure] brings forth evil [things].
For from an overflow of the heart speaks the mouth.
(46) Why do you call me "lord, lord,"
     And not do what I tell you?
(47) Everyone who hears my words and does them
(48) is like a man who built his house upon the rock.
     And the rain came down and the river beat upon that house,
     and it did not fall, for it had been founded upon the rock.
(49) And everyone who hears my words, and does not do them,
     is like a man who built his house upon the sand.
And the rain came down and the river beat upon that house,
and it fell, and its fall was great.

or less dictated by long cultural tradition. One might think of U.S. presidents' State of the Union addresses or sermons of preachers at revival meetings.

In order to tune in to what a speech is all about, the listeners, or in our case the readers of translations of the speech centuries later, need to pick up the cues that enable them to understand what the context is, what the speech is about, and more generally to get or catch on to what is happening. Jesus' covenant renewal speech gives distinctive cues right at the outset: "Blessed are you. . . . Blessed are you," and so on, and "Woe to you. . . . Woe to you . . . ," and so on. This combination of blessings and curses immediately suggests that we are in the context of covenant making, except that the blessings and curses come at the beginning of the speech and not at the end the speech as one might have expected from the traditional sequence of the covenant components.

The blessings and woes are followed by a set of admonitions beginning with "Love your enemies." These also cue those familiar with Israelite tradition (or those with good cross-referenced Bibles) into what the speech is all about. The admonitions (in Luke [Q] 6:29) to "do good," "from the one who takes your coat, offer also the tunic," refer directly to the covenantal complex of laws dealing with lending to one's neighbors included in both the Covenant Code (Exod. 22:25–27) and Deuteronomy (24:10–13). The summary of the admonitions (in Luke [Q] 6:35), "love your enemies, and do good, and lend," with its repetition of the covenantal insistence on liberal lending to one's needy neighbors (Exod. 22:25; Deut. 15:7–8), confirms the previous clue that we are listening to covenantal teaching.

When we probe more deeply into Jesus' covenant renewal speech it becomes abundantly clear that the speech is thoroughly covenantal both in structure and in substance. We noted in chapter 2 that the Covenant consisted of three interrelated steps: a declaration of God's deliverance, a statement of principles or commandments governing relations with God and with fellow Israelites, and devices of motivation to observe those principles. In the original covenant and covenant renewal (in Exod. 20; Deut. 5; Josh. 24), the declaration of deliverance focused on the exodus and related events in the past, while the blessings and curses were one of the motivating devices. In the *Community Rule* from Qumran, however, the declaration of deliverance focused on the present and future, with pronouncement of blessings and curses as part of God's present-and-future deliverance. Jesus' covenantal speech has made the same adaption of the traditional form. In this speech the opening blessings clearly extend deliverance in the present and future to the poor, the hungry, and the mournful. Correspondingly the speech pronounces woes on the wealthy and well-fed who presumably thought that they were blessed.

That Jesus' speech begins rather than ends with blessings and curses is surely the key to how it uses the components of the covenant structure to enact a renewal of the Covenant. In the traditional enactments of the Covenant (as in Exod. 20; Deut. 5) the blessings and curses were perhaps the principal mechanism by which the people were motivated to keep the commandments. As noted in the continuing operation of the covenant at the elite level in the Second Temple period, the blessings and curses were used to interpret the people's current situation. In the covenant renewal prayer in Nehemiah 9, the political-economic subjugation was under-stood as God's punishment for having broken the covenantal commandments. The controversy story focused on Jesus' healing of the paralytic, in Mark 2:1–12, indicates how the scribes had encouraged the people to blame themselves for their misfortune. Their paralysis, poverty, subjugation, and other malaise were due to their own or their parents' sin.

In opening the covenant renewal speech with blessings (and curses) Jesus pointedly addresses the people's debilitating belief that their poverty, hunger, and general misery were God's curses for their own sins. By transforming the blessings and curses that had worked to make the people feel hopeless, proclaiming blessings on the poor and hungry but woes against the wealthy, Jesus declares God's new action in the present and future to deliver the people from their oppression. Jesus' speech is thus performative: it *enacts* a renewal of the Covenant.

Having declared God's new action of deliverance, giving the people a new lease on life, Jesus calls the people to embody the justice they are receiving in God's blessings in their social-economic relations with one another, in positive rather than negative imperatives. On the basis of God's new action of deliverance, Jesus insists that the people share their blessings with one another, which is a most fundamental covenantal principle. Matthew's juxtaposition of Jesus' admonitions with the actual covenantal commandments in the Sermon on the Mount (Matt. 5:20–48) transforms them into commandments. In the earlier speech of Jesus, however, the admonitions and examples are more like covenantal teaching in the Mosaic covenantal tradition (as in Deut. 15:1–11).

Jesus' teachings here are richly covenantal in background and allusions. We have just noted what may be the most obviously covenantal admonitions and illustrations. In addition, "neighbor" (or the synonym "brother/sister") was a general term for a fellow Israelite community member. "Enemy" was a traditional term used in covenantal law codes and teaching for a neighbor with whom one had come into conflict. "If you meet your enemy's ox or the ass of one who hates you lying under its burden, you shall refrain from leaving him with it, you shall lift it up" (Exod. 23:4–5; Deut. 22:1–4). In "love your enemies" Jesus is thus creatively transforming the traditional covenantal command to "love your neighbor as yourself" that was included in the Holiness Code (Lev. 19:18). In rounding out the first set of admonitions focused on "doing good and lending," moreover, Jesus offers a version of another traditional covenantal exhortation ("be merciful, as your Father is merciful"), a different form of which had also been included in the Holiness Code ("You shall be holy . . . ," Lev. 19:2). It should be noted that in covenantal tradition, the call to imitate God was closely linked with the Covenant commandments and mechanisms aimed at economic assistance (e.g., Lev. 19:2–4, 9–13).

With the blessings and curses transformed into the declaration of deliverance, as in the Qumran covenant, what provides the motivating device in the speech? In the second covenantal text found at Qumran, the *Damascus Rule*, the rules and regulation for the community were followed by simple declarations of long life for those who keep the Covenant and of retribution for those who do not (CD 7:4–6, 8–10). These declarations carry the substance of the blessings and curses without their explicit form. In the covenantal speech in Q the double parable at the end (Luke 6:46–49) has the same function: the household of those who heed "the words" of Jesus will be secure and stable because it is built "on the rock." The household of those who do not heed "the words" of Jesus will be washed away by troubles. "The words" was a traditional term used for the commandments and laws of the covenant as delivered by Moses. The double parable states the same results of keeping or not keeping the covenantal "words," but without the ominously threatening tone of the blessings and curses.

It is conceivable that the previous lines (6:43–45) also function as part of the motivation to observe Jesus' covenantal teachings. The imagery in the observations is quite fitting for people who are engaged in farming. Even less threatening than the double parable, these observations assure the people that they are essentially good and capable of doing good, and hence should show that goodness in keeping Jesus' teachings.

The Renewal of Covenantal Economics

Blessed Are You Poor

Jesus' covenantal speech, whether or not it had also taken written form, would have been performed in communities of a Jesus movement. The movement had begun with villagers' response to Jesus' mission in Galilee. It is clear from the "mission" speeches in both Luke (Q) 10:2–16 and Mark 6:7–13 that Jesus and his envoys were building a movement village by village, not just calling individual followers. The movement had evidently spread across the frontiers of Galilee into the bilingual villages of Syria. This is suggested by the hostility toward the ruling cities of Tyre and Sidon in the woes at the end of the mission speech in Luke (Q) 10:2–16. Such a spread of the movement into Syrian villages would parallel the Jesus movement that produced and cultivated the Gospel of Mark. Mark portrays Jesus as extending his mission across the frontiers in the villages or "regions" of Tyre, Caesarea Philippi, and the Decapolis—thus writing the movement's spread back into the story of its prophet-founder.

The political-economic circumstances in Galilee were conducive to the emergence of a movement such as Jesus catalyzed. The peasant producers, many or most of them, were still on their ancestral land. Having already suffered under repeated Roman military conquests, however, they were under the demands for tithes to the Temple, for Roman tribute, and for taxes from Herodian rulers now resident in Galilee itself. Families had sunk into debt. Having exhausted the reserves and goodwill of their neighbors, they were forced to borrow at high rates of interest from the wealthy, probably Herodian officials who had control of storehouses. Their own minimal ability to aid their needy neighbors exhausted, village communities were beginning to disintegrate. Although perhaps not as severe as in Galilee, villagers elsewhere in Syria would have come under similar economic pressures following the Roman conquest and imposition of control by Roman client rulers.

Jesus' covenant renewal speech focuses on just these circumstances. The blessings and curses directly address the desperate economic circumstances of the impoverished and discouraged peasantry/villagers: "Blessed are you poor, . . . you who hunger, . . . you who weep." That Jesus focuses here on people's concrete poverty is confirmed by his addressing people who are desperately indebted, hungry, and worried about bare subsistence in some of his other speeches (Luke [Q] 11:2–4; 12:22–31). This is no philosophical discussion of the general human condition of poverty and suffering. Jesus speaks as a prophet, like Moses of old, pronouncing the blessings of God's imminent action of deliverance, the coming of God's direct rule, for Galilean and other villagers. That he also pronounces woes on the wealthy suggests that there is a relationship between the poverty of the poor and the wealth of the wealthy. The latter have been exploiting the former. The fundamental concern of the Covenant, its principles and mechanisms, of course, was for the economic viability of each family in the villages that constituted the people of Israel. The blessings announce God's new action to restore such justice. The woes call down God's condemnation on the wealthy whose actions have brought about the people's poverty and hunger.

Love Your Enemies

The covenantal admonitions and illustrations that begin with "love your enemies" focus on local economic relations. In recent generations these sayings have often been taken as a teaching of nonviolence, even nonresistance to a foreign enemy, such as the Roman armies that had conquered Judea and Galilee. These are the sayings on which pacifists (including myself) who demonstrated against war and for civil rights based our nonviolence. This interpretation, however, takes the sayings by themselves out of the context of the covenantal speech. "Enemies" was a standard term in covenantal teaching for those local neighbors with whom people had come into conflict (and who could sabotage one's crops, Matt. 13:25), not a reference to the Romans. Neither in this speech nor in Matthew's adaptation in the Sermon on the Mount do these admonitions and illustrations concern violence. The slap on the cheek (Luke [Q] 6:29a) is an insult, not a full-fledged physical attack.

The contents of these admonitions and examples clearly indicate the context to which they are addressed. The slap on the cheek is an insult by one villager to another. The seizure of the garment (6:29) concerns lending and borrowing between villagers, as does the begging for a loan and Jesus' exhortation to lend. These admonitions and their illustrations deal with local economic interaction, especially the lending, borrowing, inability to repay a loan, and the social tension and the overt conflicts that result from those economic interactions.

The opening admonitions address just such tensions and conflicts into which local village "enemies" had come under the economic pressures in first-century Galilee. Local tensions were endemic in virtually any peasant society. But they would have been seriously exacerbated as villagers became mutually indebted and unable to repay one another, perhaps because obligated to repay outside creditors first. Still-viable villagers, seeing their neighbors going under, would have become reluctant to help them as outside demands took a toll on their harvests.

The illustrations in 6:29–30 indicate that local borrowing and lending are the source of the social tensions. The reference to the garment taken in pledge would have evoked in the minds of the listeners the whole complex of covenantal laws and provisions regarding borrowing and lending in Israelite tradition: the importance of lending liberally to needy neighbors, but not becoming a creditor by taking interest (e.g., the provisions that appear in Exod. 22:25–27; Deut. 15:7–11; 24:10–13; see again chapter 3 above). Jesus' covenantal demands here stand directly in this tradition, build on it, and renew it.

He is also creatively transforming it, indeed intensifying the covenantal principles. The imperative "Love your enemies" is surely a creative transformation of the traditional covenantal command to "love your neighbor as yourself" (which had been included in the Holiness Code, Lev. 19:18). Jesus is demanding that villagers "love" and "do good" even to those in the community with whom they are in conflict, who may "hate" them. Concretely this means that they must lend to them. He is commanding villagers who are almost certainly poor and perhaps needy themselves to "give to everyone who asks." He even tells debtors to embarrass their creditors into forgiving their debts, albeit with quite a sense of humor. He purposely chooses the example of a creditor calling upon a debtor to pay up, as he comes again to seize the poor man's cloak that he sleeps under at night (supposed to be only symbolic collateral for the loan). Jesus tells the debtor to render up his shirt (undergarment) as well, so that he is standing there stark naked before the now embarrassed creditor and any onlookers. The intensification of covenant demands is also embodied in the rhetorical questions (Luke [Q] 6:32–34). If "even toll collectors" [or Gentiles or sinners] love those who love them, the villagers must do better. Jesus is demanding greater rigor in covenantal economic relations than evident previously in Israelite tradition. But of course the villagers had already received the blessings of the new declaration of deliverance ("yours is the kingdom of God, . . . you shall be filled, etc."), surely a solid basis on which they could regain their commitment to economic sharing and cooperation.

The ensuing exhortation not to judge and condemn one another in 6:37–42 addresses the social tensions that result from the conflicts over borrowing and lending in the village community. Lowering the level of social tension, bickering, and backbiting in the community would obviously better enable villagers to respond to one another's genuine need for economic assistance. Again the speech resonates with and draws upon covenantal tradition, in which commands not to bear grudges and not to take vengeance were closely linked with the principle of "love your neighbor" (as in the Holiness Code, Lev. 19:17–18).

Jesus' covenant renewal speech, building on and intensifying the Israelite covenantal tradition of local sharing and cooperation, thus calls

Galilean and other villagers to revive the sharing and cooperation that helped keep the constituent families of village communities economically viable. Both because of and despite their desperate circumstances of out-side economic pressure from multiple layers of rulers, villagers are to renew their mutual aid so that they can stand in solidarity resisting the disintegrative power of the exploitative rulers.

The economic focus of the speech, along with the Lord's Prayer, the woes against the scribes and Pharisees, and the reassurance about sub-sistence (Luke [Q] 11:2–4; 11:39–52; 12:22–31) indicates that the move-ment Jesus addressed was more than a religious revival. The speech and the movement directly addressed the people's poverty, hunger, debts, and the disintegration of village communities that traditionally were the source of mutual aid in difficult circumstances. The movement that responded to Jesus' mission spread rapidly into rural areas near Gali-lee and far beyond where the consolidation of Roman domination was adversely impacting the peasants' economic viability. Jesus' covenant renewal and other speeches, the Gospel of Mark, and the *Teaching of the Twelve Apostles*, all of which focus on village communities, were addressed to and cultivated in village communities and towns in Syria. Within two generations the movement had spread into rural areas as far away as northern Asia Minor, as indicated in the letters of Pliny, the Roman governor of Pontus-Bithynia. The movement had taken hold in the lives of peasant producers whose religion was inseparable from their concern about debts and daily bread. The very survival and presence of the cov-enant renewal speech as the most prominent of Jesus' speeches indicate that it had resonated with villagers, who responded to the combination of God's new act of deliverance and the intensification of communal efforts at cooperation and mutual aid.

In this connection we should come back around to the final blessing at the beginning of the speech, concerning reproach and persecution (6:22–23). Persecution or repression of those addressed is mentioned several times in other Jesus speeches, and one speech focuses on remaining stead-fast when hauled before a court (Luke 12:2–12). The people addressed see themselves, like their own prophets John the Baptist and Jesus, as belong-ing to the tradition of the prophets who were persecuted and killed by the authorities (Luke [Q] 6:23; Luke 11:49–51; 13:34–35). The blessings on those who are poor, hungry, and in despair address the people's condition before (as well as after) the covenant renewal. The blessing on those who are persecuted addresses what has happened as a result of the renewal. The Jesus movement was not politically and economically innocuous.

Rulers and their representatives in the ancient world rarely intervened in the lives of their subjects except to collect revenues from the threshing floors and to send the military out on punitive expeditions when their subjects failed to render up revenues in timely fashion. They did not maintain surveillance on the people's religious practices (the Gospel of Mark gives a historically false impression in that connection). But a movement that was strengthening local communities' economic solidarity in the face of outsiders' attempts to exploit people's poverty to enhance their own wealth would surely have drawn attention from the authorities, who, in many cases, were also the predatory creditors.

Jesus' Renewal of Covenantal Community

Jesus was concerned directly and in a primary way with economic issues. In teaching people to pray for the coming of the kingdom of God, he focused on the most basic and urgent economic matters: enough food to eat, day by day, and cancellation of the debts that were threatening the basis of their livelihood. The hungry and indebted people Jesus addressed, and among whom his movement(s) spread, were embedded in families and village communities, the basic social forms of any traditional agrarian society. In Israelite society in particular, the Mosaic Covenant had long been the guide for social-economic interaction. The covenant was still very much alive in Jesus' time, or at least some of its mechanisms were still widely observed, as in the officially sanctioned sabbatical years when the land was not planted and harvested.

The Jerusalem rulers of the Galileans, Judeans, and Samaritans who still adhered to Israelite traditions, however, often observed Mosaic covenantal principles only partially. They sought ways, for example, to bypass mechanisms such as the sabbatical release of debts. The Romans' requirement of tribute, along with the taxes and tithes for their client rulers, the Herodian kings and Jerusalem high priestly families, placed unbearable demands on the produce of families and resources of village communities. Under such pressures, village communities began to disintegrate. With families no longer able to aid their neighbors, households became increasingly indebted to outside creditors. Mutual hostility replaced mutual aid in local communities.

In proclaiming the presence of the direct rule of God, Jesus addressed just these circumstances. Not only the Lord's Prayer, but Jesus' Covenant renewal speech as well focuses on the desperate economic situation of the people. Drawing on the Mosaic covenantal form and teachings deeply rooted among Galilean and Judean villagers, Jesus transformed the form in order to revitalize covenantal teaching and practice. He worked directly in village communities, into which he also sent his disciples to extend his mission. To people dispirited about standing under God's curses for having violated the covenant (judging from their life circumstances), he proclaimed God's new act of deliverance: "blessed are the poor/those who hunger, for yours is the kingdom of God." With confidence in God's new act of deliverance, the people had a basis for responding to Jesus' renewal of covenantal principles. If anything, he intensified the covenantal demands for communal cooperation and mutual aid, to love enemies, do good, and lend liberally, despite or perhaps precisely because of the pressures. Thus strengthened by rededication to cooperation and mutual sharing, the village communities would be able all the better to resist the disintegrating pressures placed upon them by the wealthy and powerful rulers.

Study Questions

1. How does it change the way we understand and use the teachings of Jesus to recognize that what the Gospels present, for example in Luke 6:20–49, is not a bunch of separate sayings, but a whole coherent speech that adapts the highly familiar traditional pattern of covenant and covenant making?

2. How does already knowing the structure of the Mosaic Covenant and its basic social-economic concern for the livelihood of families in covenantal communities (chapters 2–3) help us understand Jesus' covenant renewal speech?

3. Why does Jesus first pronounce God's new act of deliverance in offering the kingdom of God to the poor, before he declares new covenantal principles such as "love your enemies, do good, and lend"?

4. How does the *content* of particular sayings in the "love your enemies" set of sayings indicate the *context* of people's lives (i.e., local community social-economic interaction) that Jesus is addressing?

5. How does the renewed covenantal reciprocity and cooperative sharing that Jesus calls for address the disintegration of community life? How might such reciprocity, cooperation, and solidarity help communities to resist the pressures of intensified, multiple demands on their produce?

Chapter Eight

Covenant Renewal and Economic Justice in the Gospel of Mark

If we had any doubts that Jesus and the Gospels were concerned with the Mosaic Covenant and economics, they should disappear quickly as we read the Gospel of Mark.[1] Now that we are learning to read the Gospel of Mark as a whole story in which episodes are integral components of an overall plot, we are also beginning to notice just how prominent the Covenant is.

Mark is far more than a story about individual discipleship. The disciples and their misunderstanding and falling away constitute only a subplot in Mark. The dominant plot in Mark's story focuses on Jesus spearheading the renewal of Israel. Like the prophet Elijah calling Elisha as his protégé, Jesus calls disciples to extend the work of his mission. Then Jesus appoints twelve disciples as representative of the people of Israel. Right after his parables speech (Mark 4) come two similar sequences of episodes reminiscent of Moses and Elijah sequences: a sea crossing, an exorcism, two healings, and a feeding of multitudes in the wilderness (Mark 5–8). The appearance of Moses, the prophet-founder of Israel, and Elijah, the prophet of renewal, on the mountain with Jesus then confirms that Jesus is a prophet like Moses and Elijah.

Moreover, Jesus carries out his renewal of Israel over against the rulers of Israel, the priestly aristocracy appointed by the Romans and the scribes and Pharisees who represent the Jerusalem Temple in confrontation with Jesus. The Gospel story climaxes in Jesus' confrontation with the chief priests in Jerusalem. There he carries out a forcible demonstration

---

1. Read the Gospel of Mark, especially the principal passages discussed here, as you read this chapter.

against the Temple in which he quotes the famous condemnation of the Temple by the prophet Jeremiah.

At the center of Jesus' renewal of Israel over against its rulers is the Mosaic Covenant. In John the Baptist's proclamation of the "baptism of repentance for the forgiveness of sins" (1:4) with which the Gospel opens, the Covenant is the measure of what constitutes sins. The "repentance," the turnaround, is a recommitment to the covenant. Most recognize that the reference to the prophecy to "Prepare the way of the Lord" signals that the "way" of Jesus is a new exodus. But the recitation of that Isaiah prophecy also includes a line from the prophet Malachi, which indicates that the "messenger" is "the messenger of the Covenant." References to the Covenant and quotations from the commandments of the Covenant continue through the story. Most dramatic of all, in his last supper with his disciples before his arrest, trial, and crucifixion, Jesus celebrates a covenantal meal. The term "new," while present in Paul's recitation of the word over the cup (1 Cor. 11:25), is missing from early manuscripts of Mark. In Mark (14:24) Jesus is not instituting a *new* covenant but solemnizing a *renewal* of God's Covenant with Israel. His word over the cup directly alludes to the ceremony on Sinai in which the Covenant was solemnized (Exod. 24:3–8).

Less noticed has been Mark's concern with economics. The covenant renewal at the center of the renewal of Israel is focused on economics, in two interrelated ways. One is the renewal of local community, which parallels Jesus' covenant renewal speech discussed in the last chapter. The other is resistance to, even rejection of, the rulers' claim on the people for tithes and offerings and tribute.

Renewal of Covenantal Community and Economics

In the Gospel of Mark Jesus carries out his mission in village communities. He works mainly in the villages of Galilee. But he extends his mission also to the villages subject to Tyre and Caesarea Philippi to the north and those subject to the cities of the Decapolis to the east (Mark 7:24, 31; 8:27). This suggests that the Gospel itself addresses communities in just such villages and towns.[2] As in the mission speech in Luke 10:2–16, so in the mission speech in Mark 6:7–13 Jesus sends his envoys

2. According to Christian tradition, the Gospel of Mark was addressed to the Christians in Rome. But nothing in the Gospel itself suggests this. See further Richard A. Horsley, *Hearing the Whole Story: The Politics of Plot in Mark's Gospel* (Louisville: Westminster John Knox, 2001), 29–30.

to work in village communities, where they are to stay in households and eat whatever is offered them.

Mark even has Jesus going directly into the *synagogai*, which have been understood in modern terms as religious buildings where "the Jews" went to worship. While archaeologists have uncovered many buildings where people gathered in late antiquity (especially fifth century and on), there is no evidence for them in Galilean villages at the time of Jesus. Like the term *knesset* in rabbinic teachings, *synagogai* in Mark refer to local village assemblies that met once or twice a week for community business as well as prayers. Jesus preaches and does healings and exorcisms in the midst of those village assemblies.

Besides working in villages and their assemblies, Jesus is concerned to revitalize those village communities, which were the fundamental social form in which the people of Israel were embodied. In Mark 10:2-45 Jesus engages in a series of dialogues (10:2–12, 13–16, 17–31, 32–45). These dialogues have some significant common features. The question-ers serve as foils for Jesus' declarations. The first and third dialogues refer directly to covenantal commandments. At a key point in each dia-logue Jesus makes declarations ("whoever . . .") that sound like new cov-enantal laws on major social issues (10:10–11, 14, 29–30, 43–44). These declarations are, in effect, statements of principles designed to govern social relations in the communities of the movement Mark addresses. This sequence of dialogues containing Jesus' declarations thus consti-tute a renewal of covenantal community focused on the four issues of marriage, membership, economics, and political relations. By far the most attention is given to economics. In these four dialogues Jesus thus delivers a covenantal renewal speech as the final step of his ministry in the village communities of Galilee and beyond, before he heads up to Jerusalem to confront the rulers.

Marriage and Family (10:2–12)

The Pharisees' question signals that covenantal teaching is coming. Their question about divorce leads to his declaration about the marriage bond at the center of the family, the fundamental unit of production, consump-tion, and reproduction in any agrarian society. In the original covenant, two of the six commandments on social-economic relations dealt with marriage and the family ("no adultery," "honor father and mother"). As evident in the somewhat later rabbinic discussions, marriage and divorce were matters not merely of marital relations, but of economic rights (especially for the wife-mother) and of inheritance of the ancestral land that constituted the basis of family livelihood.

While modern Christian interpreters pegged the Pharisees as strict legalists, the ancient scribes and priests at Qumran knew them as "smooth interpreters." Like the earlier scribes who formulated the second law in Deuteronomy, they helped loosen the requirements of covenant law to accommodate the contingencies of social-economic life. Lax laws on divorce, like the Deuteronomic provision (Deut. 24:1–4) referred to here (Mark 10:3–4), could enable ambitious men to consolidate their economic power at others' expense (gaining control of land through divorce and remarriage). Jesus rejects the Pharisees' elite version of "what Moses allowed" as "for your hardness of heart," suggesting that it would be cruel to the woman who would be so summarily "put away," in violation of her economic rights. Jesus reframes the issue, shifting the focus from divorce to marriage, which he grounds in the creation. He then, in effect, intensifies the covenantal commandment on adultery (10:10–12). Divorce for the purpose of remarriage, on the initiative of either the husband or the wife, is tantamount to adultery, the violation of God's commandment. Jesus' covenantal declaration against divorce thus reaffirms the economic rights of women in marriage and family as integral members of the fundamental social form of production and consumption.

The Dignity, Respect, and Rights of Members in the Community (10:13–16)

In the second dialogue the foil is the disciples' rejection of the children. This is a repetition of their previous misunderstanding of what Jesus' mission is about. After his second announcement of his death, the disciples had been arguing about which was the greatest. He embraced a child to make his point about acceptance (Mark 9:30–37). The issue in this dialogue must also be understood in the context of the succeeding dialogues in which the desire for wealth and political power are the foils. In imagining what life would be like in the kingdom of God that Jesus was preaching, the only alternative that peasants accustomed to poverty and powerlessness knew about was the luxurious life of their wealthy and powerful rulers in their palaces in Tiberias or Caesarea Philippi or Jerusalem.

To appreciate that concern for children involved economics it may help to remember that in the Hebrew Bible, as in the ancient Near East generally, the king's protection and provision for widows, orphans, and the poor were central to the royal ideology. Moreover, in contrast to the failure of kings to adhere to the ideology of kingship, covenantal exhortation in both Israelite law codes and the prophets stress that God is particularly concerned for the welfare (economic rights) of widows and children.

Modern interpreters tend toward the sentimental in imagining that receiving the kingdom "like a little child" might refer to innocent child-like trust. But "childhood" is an invention of modern Western society. In ancient Galilee and probably any traditional agrarian society, children were merely the human beings with the lowest status. Although they worked in the fields with their elders, they were, in effect, not yet people. For Jesus to declare that "the kingdom of God belongs" to *children* sharpens the agenda of the whole gospel story that the kingdom of God is present for the poor villagers, as opposed to the wealthy and powerful. This statement is the equivalent of the blessings of the kingdom given to the poor in the covenant renewal speech in Q or "blessed are the meek" in Matthew's Sermon on the Mount.

Economics (10:17–31)

The covenantal dialogues in Mark 10 devote most attention to the economics of a renewed Israel. What are usually separated into three paragraphs in English Bibles (Mark 10:17–22, 23–27, 28–31) should be read together as a statement of egalitarian economics for the communities of the Markan movement. The "man" (he is not identified as a "rich young ruler" in Mark) serves as the foil for raising the issue in the first step. If we can summon some sensitivity to peasants' economic situation, which is always marginal, we can immediately catch that the man's question is a dead giveaway. Only someone who is wealthy would be thinking about "eternal life." The peasants that Jesus and the Gospel of Mark addressed would have been focused instead on how they could support their families, even on where the next meal was coming from.

In response to the man's question Jesus makes a point of reciting God's commandments, which also set the fellow up. The audience knows very well that these commandments govern social-economic interactions in the society. "You shall not defraud" is a pointed substitution for "you shall not covet-and-seize." The desire to gain control of another's goods or labor or land would lead the coveter to defraud a needy peasant desperate to work as a wage laborer or to obtain a loan to feed his family (see Deut. 24:14–15). The audience would immediately see through the man's claim that he had observed the commandments. Of course the man cannot do as Jesus says and give his wealth to the poor. He not only has great possessions but is deeply attached to them.

The audience understands how Jesus was leading the man to just this point. The principal way that someone became wealthy in an ancient agrarian society such as Galilee and Judea was to take advantage of vulnerable peasants. As discussed in chapters 3 and 4, such fraud might consist of charging interests on loans, which was forbidden in covenant law, and could easily lead to gaining control of others' labor and/or fields. The first step in the discussion of covenantal economics thus puts forth the negative example of a man who had gained great wealth by defrauding others, by flouting the covenant commands not to covet and not to steal. The point about the importance of observing the covenantal principles guiding economic relations could not be any clearer.

Mark's Jesus, however, keeps hammering away on covenantal economics. The uncomprehending disciples now provide the foil. Jesus moves from the particular case of how extremely difficult it would be for the wealthy to enter the kingdom of God (Mark 10:23), to the more general situation of anyone and everyone (10:24), then back to the case of the wealthy: "It is easier for a camel to go through the eye of a needle than for someone who is rich to enter the kingdom of God" (10:25). This proverb is a case of caustic peasant humor. The hostility of the Israelite peasants to their wealthy rulers and officials is not even veiled. In every one of these parallel declarations, following on the dialogue with the wealthy fellow, the criteria for "entering the kingdom" are the economic principles of the covenant commandments Jesus has just recited. Jesus' declarations bluntly articulate the peasants' resentment of and objection to their exploitation by the wealthy. They state in no uncertain terms that aspiring to personal wealth that comes at the expense of others runs diametrically against the covenantal sharing and cooperation necessary for mutual support and communal solidarity.

The disciples continue as the foil in the third step of the discussion of covenantal economics (10:28–31). Peter articulates the puzzlement of the undiscerning disciples upon hearing Jesus' declaration about "how difficult it is to enter the kingdom of God": "Look, we have left everything and followed you." Surely *we* will be the first to enter! As throughout this section of the Gospel, the disciples represent a fundamental misunderstanding of Jesus' renewal of Israel. As evident in their rejection of the children in the previous dialogue and James and John's request for positions of power in the next dialogue, the disciples represent a desire for position and power in the movement. Peter's outburst sets up Jesus' final declaration on economics, marked with emphasis in the "Truly, I tell you. . . ." The form is similar to the covenantal principles articulated in the previous dialogues, only with the shift from "whoever" to "no one who . . . will not. . . ."

> Truly I tell you, there is no one who has left house or brothers or sisters or mother or father or children or fields, for my sake and for the sake of the good news, who will not receive a hundredfold now in this age—houses, brothers and sisters, mothers and children, and fields, with persecutions—and in the age to come eternal life. (10:29–30)

In order to hear what Jesus is saying here we may need to push out of our heads the standard old scheme of the origins of the early church derived from the early chapters of the book of Acts. In that scheme, the disciples left their households and village communities in response to Jesus' call and, after Jesus' crucifixion and resurrection, founded the new communities in Jerusalem and beyond. But that is not how Mark understands the disciples and the Jesus movements. In the open ending of Mark's Gospel the figure in the empty tomb sends the women (and the disciples and the hearers of the gospel story) back up to Galilee to continue the work of the kingdom of God.

In his response to Peter's outburst (Mark 10:29–31) Jesus envisions *restored households and village communities*. Peter's appeal recalls Jesus' call of his most intimate disciples to "leave" and "follow" at the beginning of the story. But after calling them he sent them to work, preaching the kingdom of God and healing in villages. Here he reassures them that the kingdom of God will mean the restoration of households "now in this age." The last phrase, "and in the age to come eternal life," is a "throwaway line." It refers back to the wealthy man's misguided quest that touched off the discussion of covenantal economics. "Eternal life" is mentioned nowhere else in Mark. Only the rich who defraud the poor are interested in eternal life. Jesus' promise of eternal life is facetious. What mattered to people subject to Roman client rulers and their officials in Tiberias, Tyre, Caesarea Philippi, and Jerusalem was the possibility of rebuilding their family and community life.

Far from fantasizing about never-never land, Jesus is speaking in very concrete terms, of fields and family, the fundamental economic basis and social form of the continuing life of the people. He is speaking, albeit with extreme exaggeration for emphasis ("hundredfold"), about a restoration of the traditional peasant household in village community life *in this age*. He is speaking about the economic renewal that is happening with the coming of God's direct rule. Moreover, Jesus has no illusions about the sudden disappearance of the wealthy and powerful rulers. He knows that to maintain their positions of power and privilege the Roman rulers and their local clients will arrest and even kill those who resist. The renewal of household and community life will be happening with all the trials and tests that participants in the movement will experience at the hands of the rulers, who are still intact. Both earlier and subsequently in the story Jesus warns that participation in the movement will likely evoke repression (4:17; 8:34–38; 13:9–11).

Jesus' declaration about the restoration of households is one of the key indications in the Gospel that the agenda of the Jesus movement was the renewal of Israel in village communities and their constituent households, which were the fundamental economic basis and social forms of life in such a society. This declaration completes the discussion of covenantal economics that began with the recitation of the commandments and the wealthy man as a negative example of violating them. Observance of the egalitarian economic principles of the covenant, where no one seeks to become wealthy by taking advantage of others' circumstances, will result in sufficiency for all in the community, albeit with no illusions about the continuing political power relations in the Roman imperial world.

The discussion of covenantal economics in Mark 10:17–31 parallels Jesus' covenant renewal speech in Luke 6:20–49 as supplemented by the speech about anxiety about economic sufficiency in Luke 12:22–31. In Jesus' earlier covenantal speech, after declaring that the kingdom belongs to the poor and hungry, he insists that they can now renew the traditional covenantal cooperation and mutual assistance in their local communities despite limited resources. Indeed, if they single-mindedly pursue the kingdom of God with such mutual cooperation, then there will be sufficient shelter, clothing, and food for the people in need (Luke 12:22–31). In Mark, after Jesus announces that the kingdom of God is at hand and then manifests its presence in exorcisms and healings, he calls upon the people to observe the covenantal commandments. With the coming of the kingdom of God the people's life will again thrive in the constituent households of their village communities.

Political Relations, Leadership (10:32–45)

Jesus' third announcement, that he will be killed and rise again leads into the fourth dialogue, concerning leadership in the movement (10:32–45). The disciples again are the foil, this time James and John's outrageous request to be seated in positions of political power and honor at Jesus' side, that is, as imperial rulers. This is the very opposite of what Jesus' program of the kingdom of God as renewal of Israel is about. As Jesus says, he does not have the power to elevate the disciples to such positions (10:35–40). Before long in the unfolding of the Gospel story, of course, the two who are elevated to Jesus' right and left hand are the brigands between whom he is torturously crucified (15:25–27). The "baptism" that Jesus is to undergo and the "cup" that he will "drink" are metaphors for his martyrdom (10:38–40; 15:25).

In 10:42–45 Jesus gives instruction about political(-economic) relations in the movement. The later use of the statement in 10:45 about "the son of man" giving "his life as a ransom for many" as a proof text for the vicarious death of Christ, so important to Christian faith, has diverted attention from the point of the instruction in 10:42–45. The statement about the ransom for many serves as a motivating sanction for the principle enunciated in 10:43–44. Significantly, the "ransom" refers to the covenantal mechanism by which those who had fallen into debt-slavery could be ransomed and their land, which had come into another's control, could be redeemed (see Lev. 25:25–28, 47–55, and the discussion in chapter 3).

Pointedly Jesus evokes the images of imperial rulers and "great ones" tyrannically exercising absolute power over their subjects—the very thing that he and his movement(s) oppose. He offers instead the image of the abject "servant" of rulers, except that he relocates the servant's role to his egalitarian movement. He declares yet another covenantal legal principle in the form of "Whoever . . . ," this time in a paradoxical statement. Not only will there be no rulers with political-economic power in his movement, but the leaders will be servants of the movement. This principle in the covenantal renewal powerfully reinforces the previous instruction on economic relations insofar as political power was usually the basis of economic exploitation.

Taken together this sequence of four dialogues featuring Jesus' declarations of principles governing community relations constitutes a covenantal charter for the communities of the "Markan" Jesus movement. The observance of covenantal economic commandments and obligations stands at the center of the renewal of households and village communities.

Familial Community (3:31–35)

As if in anticipation of the covenantal charter later in the story (Mark 10), Jesus declares another covenantal principle (like those in 10:9, 15, 43–44) at the close of the first major step in his mission in Galilee (1:14–3:35): "Whoever does the will of God is my brother and sister and mother" (3:35). Jesus had begun his mission in Galilee with the pronouncement that the kingdom of God is at hand (1:14–15). At the completion of this section of the story in the Beelzebul episode (3:22–27) he argues that the kingdom of God has already prevailed over the kingdom of "the strong man," Satan. Since, in the new declaration of deliverance, the kingdom of God is at hand, it is only appropriate for the people to live under the direct rule of God, to "do the will of God." Those familiar with the parallel clauses in Matthew's version of the Lord's Prayer (6:9–11) will recognize that doing the will of God was synonymous with living (under) the kingdom of God. "Doing the will of God" meant observing the covenantal commands and mechanisms in the social-economic relations of family and village life.

This episode that begins with Jesus' mother and brothers outside has sometimes been misinterpreted as Jesus' rejection of his family. That is an overinterpretation of the rhetorical ploy here and the episode of his rejection in his own "hometown" (6:1–6). In neither of these episodes or in any other does Jesus express hostility to or rejection of family. The episode with the mother and brothers outside is not a call to reject one's family in order to "follow" Jesus or to form a new group. The message is personal, but not individualistic. The members of the family are metaphorical, but they are not spiritual as opposed to this-worldly. The contrast between the crowd that came together and Jesus' mother and brothers standing outside is simply a rhetorical ploy that sets up Jesus' declaration of the covenantal principle. Jesus is calling for people to do the will of God in the social interaction of community life.

Far from replacing the family with a new association, Jesus is extending kinship relations to the whole community (cf. 9:36–37; 10:13–16). Members of movements often express their mutual attachment and solidarity in such kinship terms as "sisters" and "brothers"—without suggesting that they have left or replaced their families. In traditional Israelite covenantal mechanisms, the loyalty and mutual care of kin provided economic protection for individuals and families (as discussed in chapter 3 above). If people in the Markan Jesus movement understood themselves as brothers and sisters and mothers to one another, they might be all the more prepared to take care of one another with the same sense of responsibility that families had traditionally exercised. With some families disintegrating under the economic pressure of taxes, tribute, and debts, the larger community could function as a supportive "family" in just the ways that covenantal teaching called for. Jesus is calling people to operate as "familial" communities to protect those left vulnerable by the economic pressures from multiple layers of rulers.

Covenantal Condemnation of Rulers' Expropriation of the People's Resources

Corresponding to Jesus' renewal of covenantal community and economy in the Gospel of Mark is his rejection of the claims of rulers on the people's resources on the basis of covenantal criteria. As explained in chapter 6 above, Roman imperial rule of Judea and Galilee imposed multiple layers of rulers, all of whom made demands on the peasant producers: tithes and offerings for the Temple and high priests, taxes for the Herodian "kings," and tribute for the Romans. In his dramatic confrontation with the Roman client rulers and their representatives in the Temple, Jesus pronounces God's condemnation of the oppressive economics of the Temple in a prophetic demonstration and declares that it is against the Covenant to render tribute to Caesar. He also charges the scribes and Pharisees with exploiting the people in violation of the Covenant as representatives of the Temple.

Devouring Widows' Houses (12:38–40)

At two different points in Mark's Gospel Jesus charges the scribes and Pharisees with oppressing the people economically in violation of the covenantal commandments. In the older Christian theological picture, the Pharisees were caricatured as "hypocrites" as well as legalists obsessed particularly with purity codes and empty rituals. We now recognize that the scribes in general and the Pharisees as a political faction among the scribes served as advisers and assistants to the priestly aristocracy in the administration of the temple-state. Their training for this service in the temple-state made them thoroughly knowledgeable in the Torah/Law and other elite cultural traditions of the Jerusalem temple-state. Thus Mark's story quite appropriately has them based in Jerusalem and present in the temple courtyard.

The second of Jesus' accusations against the scribes comes at the end of his confrontation with the Jerusalem rulers and their representatives in the Temple. He warns people, "Beware of the scribes, who [among several lesser offenses] . . . devour widows' houses. . . . They will receive the greater condemnation" (12:38–40). Their actions are tantamount to coveting and stealing the widows' livelihood (on behalf of the Temple). In the very next episode a widow proceeds to give "everything she had, all she had to live on," that is, her household and inheritance, to the Temple (12:41-44), thus illustrating Jesus' charge. In the following episode Jesus declares that the Temple in which the scribes are based will be destroyed (13:1–2).

Diverting People's Resources to the Temple (7:1–13)

Jesus' first indictment of "the Pharisees and some of the scribes who had come from Jerusalem" is more developed than the second. It is at the center of one of the most misunderstood episodes in Mark's Gospel. Until recently it was the prime illustration of the Christian theological doctrine that Jesus rejected the Law of Judaism. That in turn was based on a long outmoded picture of "Judaism" and its history. A more precise sketch of the historical situation will help us discern the issue at the center of this episode.

Mark's representation of the Pharisees and scribes as keeping Jesus under surveillance in Galilee is surely not historical. Yet they may have been important actors in the relations between the Jerusalem Temple and the Galilean people. The high priests of the Jerusalem Temple had ruled Judea for centuries. They had taken control of Galilee, however, only about a hundred years before Jesus' birth and required the Galileans to become subject to "the laws of the Judeans." This presumably meant the official laws, perhaps including those in the Pentateuch, that concerned the relationship between the productive peasantry and the Temple and priesthood (i.e., tithes, offerings, etc.). The Galileans, who were presumably descendants of northern Israelites (but not Judeans, who lived in the south), were already well acquainted with the Covenant and covenantal teachings and mechanisms. During the lifetime of Jesus, however, after the Romans imposed Herod Antipas as ruler of Galilee, the Jerusalem Temple and high priesthood no longer had jurisdiction over Galilee. So what business would the Pharisees and scribes, representatives of the Jerusalem Temple and high priests (3:22; 7:1), have had in Galilee?

The first part of the episode in Mark 7 focuses on the Pharisees' charge that Jesus' disciples did not "wash their hands" in accordance with "the tradition of the elders" (7:1–5). This has led many interpreters to believe that the main issue was Jewish purity codes. But the Pharisees' accusation and "the tradition of the elders" are a caricature, the foil that sets up Jesus' countercharge. The Pharisees push their "traditions of the elders," mere human precepts, while abandoning the basic "commandment of God" (7:6–8).

Jesus then restates and intensifies his general charge against the Pharisees and gives an illustration from the most sacred and fundamental of duties in any society, people's care for their aging parents (7:9–13). He thus in effect also changes the subject to covenantal economics. In holding to their tradition the Pharisees reject the commandment of God received on Sinai by Moses, who said, "Honor your father and mother," and in the ensuing covenantal law code, "Whoever speaks evil of father and mother shall surely die" (Exod. 20:12; 21:17). Jesus clearly understands this to mean economic support of the parents. The Pharisees are not allowing people "to do anything for" a father and mother; they are siphoning off "whatever support [the parents] might have had from [their children]."

The particular device in "the tradition of the elders" by which the Pharisees are denying fathers and mothers any economic support from their children is *korban*. For Greek speakers Mark translates this Aramaic term as "an offering [dedicated] to God." For *korban* to have had the effect of depriving parents of needed support from their children, it must have involved the dedication of part of the family land or its produce to the Temple. The Pharisees must have been encouraging Galileans (and perhaps Judeans as well) to dedicate resources (the produce of the land) that were needed locally for support of parents and other such purposes to the support of the Temple. This fits the historical context of the story. No longer having jurisdiction over Galilee, the Jerusalem high priesthood and its representatives could not be very aggressive in demanding payment of tithes and offerings. That would have been in direct competition with Herod Antipas's expectation of tax revenues from the area. The Pharisees, however, devised an alternative way of deriving revenue from Galilee. With the device of *korban* they encouraged Galilean peasants to dedicate to the Temple a portion of their land's produce.

Jesus objects, however, that such dedications to the Temple removed scarce resources from already struggling families with the result that they could no longer care adequately for their aging parents. That violated the fundamental commandment of God given precisely to protect the people's economic rights to an adequate living. Jesus rejects the demands of the Temple and its agents on the basis of the Covenant's protection of the livelihood of the people.

A Sacred Stronghold of Brigands (11:15–19)

The climax of Jesus' renewal of Israel in opposition to the rulers of Israel in Mark's Gospel is his confrontation with the high priests in the

Jerusalem Temple. Mark's story mentions three times that Jesus announced the destruction of the Temple or that he was accused of threatening to destroy it and suggests that this threat was the principal reason for his condemnation and execution (13:1–2; 14:58; 15:29). His confrontation with the Jerusalem rulers began with his prophetic action in the Temple.

Many interpreters and even English Bibles still refer to Jesus' demonstration in the Temple by the traditional phrase "the Cleansing of the Temple." Any cleansing, however, would have been done by the priests properly qualified to conduct the appropriate rituals. Jesus' action in the temple courtyard was a forcible demonstration, overturning the money changers' tables and restraining other activities standard in the Temple. That the activities that Jesus forcibly blocked were economic reminds us that the Temple, while indeed a sacred institution featuring sacrifices to God, was also the central institution of the Judean political economy. The sacrifices, along with the related tithes, were also (directly or indirectly) resources rendered up by Judean producers and constituted part of the economic support of the presiding priesthood.

In Mark's account Jesus indicates what he is doing in a reference to Jeremiah's famous prophecy against the temple: "You have made [the Temple] into a brigands' stronghold" (Mark 11:17). In his prophecy against the Temple (Jer. 7:2–25; 26:1–6) Jeremiah had stated explicitly that the reason that God was about to destroy the Temple was because its heads had consistently engaged in actions directly in violation of the covenant commandments. They had then sought safety in the Temple as a guarantee of God's favor. That was the point of the accusation of having made the Temple into a bandits' stronghold. They had been stealing the people's goods on the presumption of their sacral security. Jesus is repeating Jeremiah's charge in explanation of his prophetic act that symbolized God's destruction of the Temple. That significance of Jesus' action in the Temple is confirmed by his cursing of the fig tree and its withering that frames the episode in Mark's narrative.

Predatory Tenants (12:1–12)

Two episodes later, in the parable of the tenants, Jesus pronounces God's condemnation of the priestly aristocracy that controls the temple. As Mark states explicitly, the high priests realize that the parable was told against them. The parable is ingeniously crafted. The vineyard was a traditional metaphor for the people of Israel; the tenants were those charged with its care and cultivation for the lord of the vineyard, God. The four high priestly families that ruled Judea after the death of King Herod had come to control extensive lands farmed by their tenants. The people listening to Mark's Gospel would have understood the intense hostility of tenants toward their landlords, because they may themselves have been threatened with becoming mere tenants on their own ancestral land.

Considering that the overall plot of Mark's story is the renewal of Israel against its rulers, there is no justification whatever in taking the clause in the "punch line" about "giving the vineyard to others" as a reference to "the Gentiles." But it is quite clear that the "tenants" who the owner will destroy points to the high priests, and that they are to be destroyed because of their greed and violence.

People's Well-being versus Temple Sacrifices (12:28–34)

In the last of Jesus' confrontations in the Temple, one of the scribes, testing his knowledge of Israelite covenantal tradition, asks him which is the most important commandment of all. As he often does in response to challenges from the scribes and Pharisees, Jesus does not accept the question and shifts the focus. There is not one "greatest" commandment, there are two: love God and love your neighbor. Whereupon the scribe must admit that "this is more important than all whole burnt offerings and sacrifices." That is a remarkable admission by one of the scribes, who served (and were economically dependent on) the temple.

Taken out of the context of Jesus' dramatic face-off with the Jerusalem rulers and their representatives, this episode has been interpreted to imply that at least one scribe and Jesus have come to a basic agreement. This scribe, anyhow, was "not far from the kingdom of God." In context, however, the episode makes no suggestion of a reconciliation between Jesus and the scribes. The scribe's question is no less a test of Jesus than that of the Sadducees in the previous episode, where the same verb is used (12:18). Only after Jesus answers well does the scribe address him with respect. The summary statement at the end of the episode, which is also the end of the whole confrontation, indicates that Jesus has confuted this scribe as he had the other challengers: "after that no one dared to ask him any question" (12:34). Shortly after this episode Jesus warns the people, "Beware of the scribes . . . who devour widows' houses."

What many interpreters of this episode miss is that in the two inseparable commandments Jesus is giving a succinct summary of the covenant. He is doing this at the end of his confrontation with the rulers in the Temple as a statement of the basis on which he has pronounced God's condemnation of the ruling institutions of Temple and high priesthood (because of their exploitation of the people). He begins his response to the scribe's challenge with what the scribe himself would surely have answered, reciting the Shema, the basic confession of faith in the one God, a summary of the covenantal commandments requiring exclusive loyalty to God (known in our biblical text in Deut. 6:4–5). But he binds that confession closely with "love your neighbor," which he is thus clearly emphasizing (known in our biblical text in Lev. 19:18), just as the commandments focused on social-economic interaction are inseparably connected with those focused on exclusive loyalty to God (Exod. 20:3–11, 12–17; Deut. 5:7–15, 16–21).

Not only the people, whose economic rights and livelihood were protected by the commandments, but also the earlier generations of priests and scribes who had edited the Holiness Code knew that "love your neighbor" was a summary of those commandments. It functions there as a summary of a whole series of covenantal injunctions to leave crops in the field for the poor to glean, not to steal or deal falsely, not to oppress the neighbor, not to do injustice, and not to slander or witness against one's neighbor (Lev. 19:9–18). The scribe's admission that Jesus' reframing and response to this challenge "is right" indicates not only that Jesus knows his Covenant commandments, but that they are the basis for Jesus' pronouncement of God's condemnation of the exploitative ruling institutions. The Temple and high priests have been violating the commandments, violating their economic rights, in siphoning off the people's resources.

Tribute to Caesar? (12:13–17)

One of the episodes in Jesus' confrontation with the rulers has Pharisees and Herodians attempt to entrap Jesus with the question of whether it is lawful to pay tribute to Caesar. As discussed in chapter 6, requiring subjected peoples to pay tribute was the principal way that Rome, like earlier imperial regimes, extracted economic resources from its empire. The tribute was also a punitive measure, demeaning to conquered peoples. In a temple-state such as that in Jerusalem, the Romans made the priestly aristocracy responsible for gathering the tribute. A quarter of the harvest every two years (= 12.5 percent a year) was thus taken from the people's crops in addition to tithes and offerings for the temple and taxes to Herodian rulers.

Interpreters working from the modern Western assumption of the separation of religion and politics (and economics) have generally misunderstood this episode. The belief that there is no conflict between "worshiping God" and "paying taxes" or even loyalty to the one God and loyalty to the state is anachronistic to ancient Israel and the Roman Empire. For ancient Galileans and Judeans, loyalty to God and tribute to Caesar stood in fundamental, diametrical opposition.

The Pharisees' and Herodians' question was a trap precisely because, as they well knew, it was clearly not lawful to pay tribute to Caesar, according to covenant commandments and covenant laws. The first two commandments, requiring exclusive loyalty to God, meant that Israelites could not serve, with their tithes, offerings, or tribute, any other lord and master. But the Roman state and Caesar, as lord and master, demanded tribute. By the time of Jesus, Caesar was viewed as divine, at least as "the son of (a) god." Given their Israelite heritage, this placed Galileans and Judeans in a conflict that had life-and-death consequences. To maintain exclusive loyalty to the one God as their true, literal lord and master they would have to refuse to pay the tribute to Caesar. But the Romans viewed failure to render up the tribute as tantamount to rebellion, to be met by punitive reconquest more brutal than the original conquest.

This conflict came to a head shortly after Judea was placed under direct Roman rule a little over two decades before Jesus' face-off with the rulers in Jerusalem. Some of the predecessors of the scribes and Pharisees who confronted Jesus, led by the teacher Judas and the Pharisee Saddok, organized a resistance movement, refusing to pay the tribute. According to the Judean historian Josephus, this resistance movement (which he calls the "fourth philosophy among the Judeans") agreed in all things with the other philosophy of the Pharisees—except that they were adamant in their passion for the independence of the people under the rule of God (*Ant.* 18:23). They insisted that it was utterly impossible to render tribute to Caesar since God was their true lord and master.

Jesus skillfully wriggles out of the trap by not answering directly whether the people should pay the tribute. But his response is far from innocuous. Key to his crafty response are the phrases "the things that are Caesar's" and "the things that are God's." Everyone listening knew that "the things that are God's" meant basically everything, and that according to the covenantal commandments nothing belonged to Caesar. Jesus is saying in so many words that the people do not owe Caesar anything, that the tribute is utterly contrary to the people's covenant with God. Jesus is, in effect, restating the first two commandments of the Covenant as applied to the circumstances of living under Roman imperial rule.

It would be going too far to say that the Gospel of Mark is primarily about economics. The Gospel tells a broader story about Jesus' renewal of Israel in opposition to and opposed by the Jerusalem and Roman rulers of Israel. But the renewal of Israel means renewal of family and village community, the fundamental social forms in which Israel was constituted; and central to the renewal of village community are covenantal economic principles. Jesus proclaims that the kingdom (direct rule) of God is at hand. Observance of the covenantal commandments is the way of "entering the kingdom of God." To take advantage of another's economic difficulties would be the very antithesis of life in the kingdom. But with a renewal of covenantal cooperation in local communities will come the restoration of sufficiency in family and community life.

While Mark's Jesus has no illusion that the Jerusalem, Roman, and other authorities will suddenly disappear, he proclaims that they stand under God's judgment. Like the earlier prophets of Israel, such as Amos, Isaiah, or Jeremiah, only more forcibly, Jesus declares God's condemnation of rulers because their economic demands have led to the disintegration of family and community life. Although it is not clear whether Jesus actually encourages refusal to pay the tribute, he clearly declares that the people living according to the Covenant with God do not owe tribute. As in Jesus' covenant renewal speech, however, so in Mark's Gospel Jesus goes well beyond the earlier prophets in his program of renewal of covenantal community. Amos, Micah, and Isaiah, in their indictments of the rulers and their officers for oppressing the people in violation of covenantal principles, had defended the people's economic rights and interests. Jesus, proclaiming God's new act of deliverance in bringing the kingdom directly to the people, works directly with the people in a program of renewing covenantal community in mutual support and cooperation.

Study Questions

1. How does Jesus insist on the rights of women (in the context of the patriarchal family) in Mark 10?

2. How does Jesus use the rich man who seeks eternal life as an (negative) example in addressing his followers in Mark 10? How had the man become rich? How seriously (literally) did Jesus mean that "it is easier for a camel to go through the eye of a needle than for someone who is rich to enter the kingdom of God"?

3. How do Jesus' covenantal dialogues in Mark 10 parallel and reinforce his covenantal speech in Luke 6:20–49 (see chapter 7)?

4. According to Jesus' prophetic condemnations, how have the Romans, the high priests and Temple, the scribes and Pharisees who represent them, all together as a system, violated virtually all of the covenantal commandments?

5. Was Jesus (in Mark) primarily a reformer who strove to clean up the abuses in the system by which the people's resources were drawn upward and to the center (to the Temple and Caesar) or a prophet in the tradition of Amos, Isaiah, Micah, and Jeremiah, who pronounced God's judgment on the very institutions of centralization?

Chapter Nine

The Assemblies of Christ
in the Letters of Paul

The movements that grew up in response to Jesus' mission of renewal expanded rapidly into areas beyond Galilee. What began as a movement of renewal of Israel in its village communities soon established a community in Jerusalem led by the disciples (summarized in the first chapters of Acts). Within a few years the movements spread among Judeans in towns and cities beyond Galilee and Judea, such as Damascus, Caesarea, and Antioch in Syria. As the movements established communities in eastern Mediterranean towns and cities, non-Judean (non-Israelite) people became interested and wanted to join. Paul and his coworkers, such as Prisca and Aquila, were soon establishing fledgling assemblies (*ekklēsiai*) of Christ among non-Israelites in the cities of Greece.

We know very little about most of these new communities. But thanks to the Letters of Paul we have significant information about the assemblies of Christ in several Greek cities. These assemblies were more than just small congregations of a new religion. Like the village communities in Galilee in which Jesus had carried out his mission, the assemblies of Christ were communities with political-economic aspects inseparable from the religious aspect.

There was a dramatic difference between renewing village communities in Galilee or Judea and establishing completely new communities in Greek cities. The village communities were beginning to disintegrate under severe economic pressures, but a communal infrastructure, including the village assembly (*synagōgē*), was still somewhat intact. The people, moreover, were thoroughly grounded in Israelite tradition and had known one another's families for generations. In Philippi or Corinth, Paul, Prisca, and Aquila were starting from scratch to mold a community from a mix of people in a different culture with different personal backgrounds. Very few were of Israelite heritage or had any acquaintance with Israelite tradition. Except for their immediate household network, probably few had known one another before. Most significant economically, members of the assemblies of Christ were city dwellers, not peasants, and were slaves or artisans or underemployed wageworkers, not farmers in an agrarian village. Further, the Greek cities had an economic history different from that of Judea and Galilee in the ancient Near East. It is important to have at least a basic sense of the economic patterns in which they were embedded.

The Roman Imperial Economy in the Greek Cities

The political-economic structure in the Greek cities had some fundamental similarities to what still prevailed in Galilee and Judea under Roman rule. But it also differed in significant ways.

The economy in the Greek cities, like that in Palestine and nearly everywhere in the Roman Empire, was still predominantly agricultural and primarily local. Overland transport of goods was extremely costly. Most cities derived the vast majority of their food and other materials from the immediately surrounding countryside. Peasant or tenant producers raised crops primarily for their own consumption and for whatever portion they were required to pay in taxes or rents to their lords and rulers, not to sell in markets. Trade was mostly in luxury goods for the elite. Some of what may look like trade to modern scholars was extraction and sea transport of resources taken in tribute or taxes from subject peoples for consumption in Rome and other large imperial cities close to the Mediterranean.

The much idealized classical Greek city-state of citizen-farmers who had a voice in the city assembly was a distant memory. In the centuries before the mission of Paul and his coworkers in the mid-first century, much of the land of the Greek cities had come into the hands of a few extremely wealthy families. Since engagement in commerce was not respectable for aristocrats, they invested their wealth in land. They rented their lands to tenants or farmed them with gangs of slaves, thus generating the resources to maintain their lavish households in the cities and villas in the country. Semi-independent villages as self-governing communities had disintegrated as absentee urban magnates consolidated their land into large holdings with villas staffed by tenants and/or slaves.

As the Roman Senate took control of the area, they established close alliances with the wealthy magnates of each city in Greece and Asia Minor.

The popular assemblies of the city-states had gradually lost power to the plutocratic families. The councils, composed of the most wealthy and powerful magnates, held power in each city. The most prominent Roman Senators and warlords established effective patron-client relations with these powerful families. Then under the emperor Augustus this system of patronage relations became the dominant mode of political-economic-religious relationship by which Rome controlled the cities around the Aegean Sea. City and provincial councils and wealthy magnates established temples, shrines, festivals, and Caesarean Games to honor the emperor. In return the emperor granted privileged status to cities and favorable rulings for wealthy magnates. City councils in turn established special local inscriptions or monuments in honor of the wealthy and powerful figures who had funded imperial temples, games, or monuments and brought imperial favor to their cities.

New Testament scholarship has tended to construct a general synthetic picture of the "Hellenistic world" of the Greek cities in which the apostle Paul carried out his mission and early "Gentile Christianity" developed. There were significant variations from city to city, however, in economic as well as cultural life, variations that often resulted from Roman intervention in particular cities. We look briefly at three cities in which Paul and his coworkers established assemblies of Christ.

Philippi was particularly important to the Roman province because of its situation as an outpost along the main overland route linking Rome to the East. After the significant victory of the warlords Antony and Octavian over Cassius and Brutus in the prolonged civil war following the assassination of Julius Caesar, the victors established a Roman colony of discharged veterans at Philippi with allotments of land. Ten years later, in 30 BCE, Octavian established another Roman colony, giving some of Antony's defeated troops allotments of land and civic privileges in Philippi. Thus in addition to the strong Roman influence in Philippi, the descendants of Roman soldiers held economic advantages over the indigenous Thracian population, who had lost ground to the new settlers. The "Philippians" who responded to Paul's mission may well have been among those whose families had been displaced from their lands, which were given to the Roman army veterans eighty or so years earlier.

No Roman colony of veterans was imposed on Thessalonica. Yet for a small provincial capital it had strong diplomatic and economic links with powerful Roman senators. The magnates of the city had carefully cultivated the Roman warlords, shifting allegiances in timely fashion. Once Octavian triumphed over Antony in the Battle of Actium, the wealthy potentates of Thessalonica spared no expense in erecting temples and monuments to honor Augustus. We should remember that what might appear as diplomatic and religious gestures were major economic expenditures. It was precisely these expenditures by the city elite that cemented their relationship with the imperial court, but also secured their own political-economic dominance as the holders of the principal city offices and of much or most of the city's land. We can understand how the message of "another king [alternative emperor] named Jesus" (Acts 17:7) might resonate with the Thessalonians as well as with the nearby Philippians, whose economic rights had been trumped by the overwhelming power of Caesar over the disposition of people and the basis of their livelihood.

Among the cities into which Paul and his coworkers carried their mission, Corinth had the most complex economy and political-economic history. The Romans had purposely provoked a war with the Achaian League of cities, and destroyed the city of Corinth in 146 BCE. A century later Julius Caesar established a Roman colony on the site of the destroyed city, sending army veterans and large numbers of freed slaves and other "riff-raff" among the surplus population of Rome itself. In the following decades, Corinth became one of the principal hubs of shipping in the supply lines to Rome because of its situation at the narrow isthmus between the Aegean Sea and the Adriatic Sea. Its population was a mixture of displaced people from a wide variety of backgrounds.

With regard to the economic circumstances of the people who joined the assemblies of Christ in these cities, a supposed consensus emerged from a few studies that asked about their social status—a category derived from the sociology of modern American society but of questionable application to the Roman Empire. These studies were based largely on passing references and characterizations of people mentioned in 1 Corinthians, such as Stephanas, the head of a household (1 Cor. 1:16; 16:15). They were also based on the modern assumption that there was a spectrum of social-economic status in the cities of the Roman Empire. The conclusion was that the members of the assemblies of Christ were a cross-section of Roman imperial society generally.

What these studies failed to do was to consider the economic level of people in the cities of the Empire. There were indeed different levels of *social* status in the Roman Empire. Slaves were considered virtually subhuman, and subject to severe beating by their masters, who were also presumed to have sexual access to their slaves. Freedmen and freedwomen, because of their servile background, were despised socially by free people, perhaps even more so if they were economically better off. Only the very few who were both wealthy and nobly born held high status and honor. Economically, however, Roman imperial society was sharply divided between the extremely wealthy city and provincial elite and the vast majority of the rest, well over 90 percent, who lived mostly at subsistence or just above or just below subsistence. A small percentage had a somewhat higher level of income, but they did not constitute anything like a middle class. Virtually all of those who joined the assemblies of Christ, including both slaves and those who may have been heads of households, thus would have lived around the subsistence level. There is simply no evidence that any were wealthy.

Surely of more significance, except that we have even less information about it, would have been the economic power relations in which the members of the assemblies were embedded. Slaves were almost completely under the power of their masters. Freedpersons still owed certain services to their former masters. Many artisans would have been dependent on the wealthy who ordered and purchased their products. Day laborers were dependent on those with enough resources to hire help. In Rome itself, as many as half of the populace had been pulled into networks of patron-client relations in which the clients performed services to the wealthy magnates, often Senators or Knights, in return for promises of economic support (that usually did not amount to much). We have no evidence that such patronage networks had spread outward and downward into the Greek cities. Probably some magnates in these cities had networks of clients. Short of more formal patronage networks similar to those in Rome, however, many poor artisans and other workers in the Greek cities were surely dependent on the favor of those who bought their products or services.

The bottom line is that the economy in the Greek cities of the Roman Empire was controlled by the wealthy and powerful families for their own and the empire's benefit. In the Greek cities and often in the countryside surrounding them, there were few remaining social forms such as village communities that provided a supportive network that might cushion the vulnerability of individuals and families to exploitation by the wealthy landowners and leading citizens. Even impoverished citizens might still have certain civil rights, in contrast to slaves and freedpersons. But very few enjoyed any economic rights, and many were dependent in various ways on others for the means by which they could achieve even a subsistence living.

Communities of an Alternative Society

The most helpful thing we can do to understand the assemblies of Christ in such cities as Philippi, Thessalonica, and Corinth would be to drop the term "church" ("house of the Lord"). The term used by Paul, *ekklesia*, ordinarily referred to the *assembly* of citizens in a self-governing city-state, not to a specifically religious group. The very conception and self-understanding of the communities of Christ loyalists was thus not as a religious association but as an alternative political as well as religious body. We should also erase from our minds the fictional picture from the book of Acts of Paul preaching the gospel in public places. Paul and his coworkers such as Prisca and Aquila avoided the marketplace of religious competition (cf. 2 Cor. 2:17) for the more intensive and long-term inter-action of small groups in people's houses ("the assembly in the house of Prisca and Aquila," 1 Cor. 16:19; Rom. 16:5; cf. Phlm. 2)

From Paul's ad hoc letters to particular assemblies we get the sense of small numbers of people meeting regularly in certain members' "houses." References to "the whole assembly" coming together for particular purposes such as the Lord's Supper and discussion (1 Cor. 14:23; cf. 11:18, 20; Rom. 16:23) indicate that at other times smaller "assemblies" met in households. The assembly at Cenchreae in which Phoebe was the principal leader (Rom. 16:1) suggests that a network of smaller household-based communities had spread out from Corinth into the satellite towns and villages. There were evidently similar networks in Macedonia centered around Thessalonica and Philippi. Moreover, these household cells and whole assemblies did not gather for what the Greeks would have recognized as religious rituals such as sacrifices to the gods and libations to ancestors. The picture Paul gives of these assemblies is not of a religious cult but of a nascent social movement made up of a network of cells based in key cities.

When we look more closely at Paul's Letters, particularly 1 Thessalonians and 1 Corinthians, we get the sense that these assemblies were communities of a nascent alternative society that separated itself from the dominant imperial society as much as possible. Paul reminded the Thessalonians, who had recently suffered from attacks by others (the officials?) in their city, "to live quietly, to mind your own affairs, and to work with your hands . . . and be dependent on no one" (1 Thess. 4:11–12). He insisted that the Corinthian assembly conduct its own affairs in independence of "the world" (1 Cor. 5–6). That did not mean cutting off all contact with nonmembers, among whom they were trying to proselytize. But it did mean handling their own disputes, in avoidance of the civil courts and the unjust of the society. Paul's list of outsiders in 5:10 pointedly features the injustices of coveting and theft, two key economic matters covered by key covenantal commandments. In handling their own internal conflicts independent of the established courts, the assemblies of Christ were similar to the covenantal Qumran community and the Matthean communities (see chapter 10). The assemblies stood diametrically opposed to "the world" as communities of "saints." "Saints" did not signify that they claimed to be particularly holy, but that they practiced holiness in their relations with others. They maintained communities of justice.

In their exclusive loyalty to the one God the "members of Christ" could also no longer participate in the sacrifices to the gods (see especially 1 Cor. 10:14–22). Sacrifices were not merely religious rituals but were ceremonies that cemented fundamental forms of social relations in the dominant society. Sacrifices were integral expressions of community life in ancient Greek and Roman cities, at every social level from extended families to city-wide celebrations, including festivals in honor of the emperor. In building their own solidarity over against the networks of power relations by which the imperial society was built up, members of the assemblies of Christ had to withdraw from participation in the ceremonies by which those power relations were maintained.

Paul advocated all of this community discipline and solidarity in the conviction that "the appointed time has grown short . . . , for the present form of this world is passing away" (1 Cor. 7:29–31). By that he did not mean that the whole cosmos, including societal life, was coming to a catastrophic end. He meant rather that the days of the Roman imperial order were numbered, that "the rulers of this age . . . are doomed to perish" (1 Cor. 2:6–8). He thought and taught that "the day of the Lord" would come soon, and at that point "the kingdom of God" would be fully established. The assemblies that he and his coworkers were helping get organized were, in effect, the beachheads of a new age. The nascent assemblies of Christ were thus, in anticipation of the full establishment of the kingdom at the Parousia of the Lord, the local communities of a new international society that was an alternative to the Roman political order.

Economic Features of the Assemblies

Most members of the fledgling assemblies catalyzed by Paul and his coworkers must have eked out a living as poorly paid artisans or unskilled workers. Paul's admonition to the Thessalonians "to work with your hands . . . and be dependent on no one" (1 Thess. 4:11–12) indicates just such modest economic circumstances. Some members were slaves or former slaves. It is quite unsound to argue from Paul's rhetorical flourish mocking the Corinthians who were boasting of their high spiritual status that "not many of you were powerful, . . . of noble birth" (1 Cor. 1:26) that therefore some were at least relatively well-off. Those terms were used of the tiny aristocracy in a city who were extremely wealthy. There is no indication that any member of the assemblies of Christ was from the extremely wealthy urban or provincial elite. As noted above, there was a deep divide between the extremely wealthy magnates who controlled the cities and the vast majority of people (over 90 percent) who lived at or around the level of subsistence. The picture in the book of Acts of a few well-off members is historically unreliable, certainly for the first generation or two.

Beyond the recent discussion of whether some members of the assemblies were well-off, the economics of the earliest assemblies of Christ in Greek cities are almost never discussed. Yet Pauline and other texts do offer at least some information. It is clear that the communities of Christ established common funds. However idealized the portrayal in the early chapters of Acts may be (Acts 2:44–45; 4:32–37), the community established in Jerusalem after the crucifixion and resurrection of Jesus practiced the sharing of resources. The disciples who provided the leadership, for example, and perhaps others as well had left their source of livelihood in Galilee. Others surely were poor residents of Jerusalem. Yet others may have been those pushed off the land because of debts and gravitated to the city looking for work. In any case the community expected those with some property to divest it and contribute the proceeds to a common pool from which all could live, somewhat parallel to the practice of the community of scribes and priests at Qumran, by the Dead Sea.

> There was not a needy person among them, for as many as owned lands or houses sold them and brought the proceeds of what was sold. They laid it at the apostles' feet, and it was distributed to each as any had need. (Acts 4:34–35)

While other assemblies of the Jesus movement(s) may not have "held all things in common," they did have some sort of a common fund. Critics of the assemblies generations later, when the Christian movement had expanded considerably, mocked them for taking care of one another economically. It had become common for assemblies to have a community fund that was used for burial of members or to buy a member out of slavery. We know that common funds were used for the latter in the assemblies in Asia Minor fifty years after their origin from a letter of Ignatius, bishop of Antioch, urging that slaves "not desire to be set free at the assembly's expense" (Ign. *Poly.* 4.3).

The one early use of a common fund in the assemblies that we know about is for support of the apostles who were working among them. In apparent continuation of the practice mentioned in Jesus' mission speeches in Q and Mark that his envoys eat what was put before them in local households, the wider movement recognized the "right" of the apostles to food and drink (1 Cor. 9:3–6, 13–14). This enabled them to concentrate on the mission without having to worry about supporting themselves. Whatever his motives, Paul did not accept such support (1 Cor. 9:12, 15–18), at least from the assembly in which he was working at the time. He indicates that he did accept support at least from the Philippian assembly. "When I was in Thessalonica, you sent me help for my needs more than once" (Phil. 4:16). Paul interprets their economic support as a gesture to which God will respond with economic sufficiency. "I have received from Epaphroditus the gifts you sent, a fragrant offering, a sacrifice acceptable and pleasing to God. And my God will fully satisfy every need of yours according to his riches in glory in Christ Jesus" (Phil. 4:18–19).

The Collection for the Poor in Jerusalem

The most distinctive economic feature of the assemblies of Christ was the collection that Paul and his coworkers were gathering "for the poor among the saints in Jerusalem." This was also, so far as we know, a unique economic innovation in ancient and subsequent history. The collection was an historically unprecedented horizontal movement of economic resources among peoples subject to imperial rule. As noted in chapter 6 and earlier in this chapter, in ancient hierarchical societies and imperial economic systems, economic resources invariably moved upward from the producers to the rulers and to the imperial center from subject peoples and client rulers. But in the collection the assemblies of Christ among some peoples in the eastern Roman Empire were sending resources, however limited in quantity, to help the poor in the Jerusalem assembly of their "international" movement.

The project evidently originated in the "apostolic council" (Gal. 2:1–10; cf. Acts 15:6–41). Peter, John, and James the brother of Jesus agreed to have Paul and coworkers proceed with his mission to non-Israelite peoples, asking "only one thing, that we remember the poor" (Gal. 2:10).

From Paul's longer phrase in Romans, "the poor among the saints in Jerusalem" (15:25–26), it is clear that this meant those in the Jerusalem community who were literally poor, probably because they had no means of self-support. The limited resources they had pooled were hardly sufficient to sustain them long-range. Thus other nascent assemblies of Christ were to send economic assistance to the poor in Jerusalem.

Earlier interpreters suggested that "the poor" was an honorific title indicating "the pious righteous ones" (as in certain psalms) or even God's chosen eschatological people. The scribes and priests of the Qumran community that left the Dead Sea Scrolls understood themselves as the pious, persecuted, humble "poor," as well as "the children of light" (as in the *Thanksgiving Hymns*, 1QH 13:13, 14, 16, 22). But it is hardly justified to reason from the pious self-image of a scribal-priestly group to the concretely poor common people who joined the Jesus movement. Neither Paul's Letters nor accounts in Acts give any indication that these "saints" were only figuratively poor, that is "the 'poor' who are the saints."

The origin of the very idea of initiating the collection was surely connected with the sharing of resources in the Jerusalem community and the traditional Israelite covenantal understanding of mutual aid and reciprocity within the village community. In the sharing or pooling of resources they made the jump from a residential village community in which people shared the produce of their ancestral land to an urban community in which most did not have (or no longer possessed) land on which to produce food. Leaders of the movement now made the unprecedented move from sharing within a local community to sharing across local communities in a wider movement. The agricultural analogy that dominates one of Paul's exhortations to the Corinthians about "the service (*diakonia*) of the saints" (2 Cor. 9:6–11) certainly suggests that he understood the collection as the traditional economic reciprocity of villagers with one another, only now expanded to an international scale among urbanites. It may also have helped that the same concept, "assembly," was used both for the gathering of a local community and for the whole of the people of Israel. It seems clear that, virtually from the origin of the assemblies of Christ, this term was also used both for the local community and for the wider movement, the assembly (*ekklesia*) composed of all the local assemblies (*ekklesiai*).

The collection has also been interpreted theologically in the context of the highly synthetic construct of the "eschatological hopes of Israel." Key in this interpretation are several late prophetic texts that picture Zion transformed by God into the highest of mountains and Jerusalem exalted as the imperial city. Other nations that had previously conquered Israel would come bringing gifts in service of God and/or the Judeans (e.g., Isa. 2:2–3 = Mic. 4:1–2; Isa. 61:5–7; Hag. 2:6–9). Paul's intention of sending representatives of the assemblies in the various cities (1 Cor. 16:3) might fit into this interpretation. But nothing in Paul's several discussions of the collection suggests such an imperial conception. Far from relating the "service" (*diakonia*) to the fulfillment of prophecies about Jerusalem as the future imperial city, Paul compares it to the paradigmatic deliverance in the exodus. He cites a passage from the exodus story of God's supplying food from heaven for the hungry people just delivered from bondage, where each person had enough but not too much (Exod. 16:18 in 2 Cor. 8:15).

Paul went about the collection systematically, fully aware of the marginal economic level of the assemblies.

> Now concerning the collection for the saints: you should follow the directions I gave to the assemblies of Galatia. On the first day of every week, each of you is to put aside and save whatever extra you earn [literally, "whatever s/he has succeeded in"], so that collections need not be taken when I come. (1 Cor. 16:1–2)

These are the instructions that Paul had evidently been giving in all of the assemblies, ever since his mission in Galatia. By the time he was organizing the Corinthians, the collection was underway in the assemblies in Philippi and Thessalonica ("Macedonia," 2 Cor. 8:1). The funds that were to be taken to "the poor" in the Jerusalem community were being collected little by little by wageworkers or artisans who were to eke out a bit more than they needed to support themselves each week, and set it aside. This must have involved considerable personal and community discipline. Paul used the generosity of the assemblies of Macedonia to encourage the Corinthians to respond in kind.

> During a severe ordeal of affliction, their abundant joy and their extreme poverty have overflowed in a wealth of generosity on their part. . . . They voluntarily gave according to their means, and even beyond their means. (2 Cor. 8:2–4)

We should not be misled by Paul's exaggerated language about the assemblies of Macedonia "overflowing in a wealth of generosity." It was impressive that they had given even "beyond their means," since they were mired in "abysmal poverty." The collection for "the poor among the saints in Jerusalem" was coming from the poor among the assemblies of Christ.

It does seem likely that the collection became increasingly important to Paul himself as a way in which he could demonstrate the value and validity of his mission among the non-Israelite peoples to Peter and other apostles headquartered back in Jerusalem, whose mission was to Israelite people. But the motivation was far deeper for Paul himself and clearly shared by the members of the assemblies.

This deeper understanding comes through powerfully in the inter-relationship of key terms that Paul uses repeatedly in discussion of the collection. Most fundamentally it is "the service (*diakonia*) of the saints" (2 Cor. 9:1). It is also a "community/sharing" (*koinonia*) with the poor in Jerusalem. And it is "grace/gift" (*charis*) from God while also "grace/gift" of the Macedonians and Achaians and other assemblies. It is also a "dem-onstration of love" (*endeixis tes agapes*, 8:24), which binds a community together in mutual aid, and a "good work" (*ergon agathon*, 9:8). Several of these terms come together in Paul's explanation that the collection is

> The grace (*charis*) of God that has been granted to the assemblies of Macedonia [who were eager for] the grace (*charis*) of the community/sharing (*koinonia*) of the service (*diakonia*) of the saints. (8:1, 4)

Besides the grace being both the grace of God and the grace of the assemblies, the service and the sharing-partnership are also both the service and sharing of God and the service and sharing with other people. As Paul says to the Corinthians about "the service of the saints,"

> The service of this service (*he diakonia tes leitourgias tautes*) not only supplies the needs of the saints, but also overflows with many thanks-givings to God. Through the testing of this service (*diakonia*) you glorify God by your obedience to the confession of the gospel of Christ and by the generosity of your sharing/community (*koinonia*) with them and with all others. (9:12–13)

Interlaced through the understanding of the collection as grace, ser-vice, and sharing-partnership is a mutuality of cooperation and shar-ing with one another. Paul speaks to the Corinthians of "a fair balance between your present abundance and their need, so that their abundance may be for your need" (8:13–14). To the Romans he explains he is going to Jerusalem in a service of the saints, for Macedonia and Achaia have been pleased to establish this community/sharing (*koinonia*) with the poor among the saints at Jerusalem. They were pleased to do this, and indeed they owe it to them; for if the peoples have come to have community/sharing (*koinonesan*) in their spiritual blessings, they ought also to be of service to them (*leitourgesai*) in material things. (Rom. 15:26–27)

Through all of these discussions of the collection we detect the influence of the covenantal economics of mutual sharing and cooperation that was to be practiced in village communities, only now extended to the communities of a wider international movement. We can even detect echoes of Jesus' renewal of the covenant, such as the mutual indebtedness and therefore the mutual cancellation or forgiveness in the Lord's Prayer. As the people petitioned God to cancel their debts, they also affirmed that they were canceling one another's debts. As God was bringing the kingdom to the poor and hungry, so they responded by renewing the mutual aid and cooperation central to covenantal teachings. Just as in the covenant the people's loyalty to (service of) God entailed mutual obligations among members of the covenanted communities, so the assemblies' "loyalty" to (a better translation of *pistis* than "faith in") Christ entailed mutual obligations for reciprocal service and partnership.

Surrounded as we are today by all sorts of ecclesiastical, national, and international funds for relief of famine, natural disaster, and general economic distress, it may be difficult to sense what a remarkable innovation the collection was. Within a decade or so of its origins, the nascent "Christian" movement had developed an "international" economic dimension diametrically opposed to the tributary political economy of the empire. Even before Paul set out on his independent mission into Asia Minor and Greece, the followers of Jesus had developed their own distinctive practice of economic solidarity and horizontal reciprocity, the relative haves with the have-nots. Belonging to an international assembly, the local assemblies shared economic resources across the subject peoples (*ethnoi*) and across considerable distances. The international aspect of the movement of Christ believers and especially their international economic reciprocity were unique in the Roman Empire or in any ancient empire. In striking contrast with the vertical and centripetal movement of resources in the tributary imperial economy, Paul organized a horizontal movement of resources from one subject people to another.

Study Questions

1. What difference does it make to recognize that Paul understood the assemblies of Christ as much more than a group of people gathered for worship, but as communities of an alternative society?

2. What difference does it make to recognize that by "saints" or "holy ones" Paul means not people who are particularly holy or pious, but people committed to justice in social-economic interaction?

3. How does the collection for "the poor among the saints in Jerusalem" seem like an extension of the reciprocal sharing of resources among families in covenantal village communities to what was in effect an "international" sharing of resources among communities of peoples subject to the Empire?

Chapter Ten

Covenantal Community
in the Gospel of Matthew

Like Paul in his letters, so Matthew in his Gospel addresses new communities of the assembly of Christ, in areas beyond Galilee and Judea.[1] But while Paul addresses mainly new communities of non-Israelites, Matthew addresses new communities of Israelites (Judeans). More explicitly than Mark, whose Gospel narrative he follows, Matthew highlights Jesus' renewal of covenant community and covenantal economics, mainly by inserting long covenantal speeches by Jesus into the Gospel story. What Jesus had originally focused on Galilean villages, however, Matthew adapted for application to small minority communities of Judeans striving to live as alternative communities in Syrian towns under the increasingly oppressive impact of centralized Roman imperial power.

Far more boldly and unambiguously than Mark, Matthew presents Jesus as the Messiah/Christ—from his genealogy at the beginning, to his trial before Pilate and crucifixion at the end, and in Peter's declaration in the middle. But Matthew also presents Jesus more clearly and dramatically as a new Moses. As an infant he descends to and then journeys out of Egypt, recapitulating Israel's exodus from Egypt (Matt. 2:13–23). He is then tested in the wilderness, like Moses (4:1–17). Jesus is still in the role of the new Moses at the climax of Matthew's Gospel when, at the Passover Festival celebrating Israel's exodus, he presides over the Last Supper as a meal of covenant renewal (26:27–28). Thus the symbolism is unmistakable when Jesus goes up on the mountain and gives commandments that intensify some of the original covenantal commandments

---

1. Have a Bible handy so that you can read Matthew 5–7 (the Sermon on the Mount) and other key passages in Matthew discussed in this chapter.

(5:20–48). The "Sermon on the Mount," as the long speech in Matthew 5–7 is known, is clearly Jesus' renewal of the Covenant given to Israel at Mount Sinai. Jesus delivers further covenantal teaching in the speech on community discipline and the immediately following dialogues (Matt. 18–20). Matthew's Gospel, moreover, expands Jesus' condemnation of the rulers of Israel for their economic manipulation and exploitation of the people, all clearly on the basis of covenantal commandments and principles (17:24–27; 21–22; 23).

The Communities That Matthew Addresses

Before examining covenantal economics in Matthew we should clear up possible confusions about a couple of key terms and establish a clearer sense of the communities that Matthew is addressing. First, since Israelites were prohibited from speaking the name of their God, "Yahweh," they substituted "heaven," and Matthew uses "the kingdom of heaven." This has misled many moderns into thinking that Matthew's Jesus is promising "the poor in spirit" that they are going to heaven. But the opening of the Lord's Prayer indicates that the coming of "the kingdom of heaven" is unmistakably to be on earth: "Your kingdom come, your will be done, on earth as it is in heaven." Second, the Greek term *ekklesia* has conventionally been translated "church," which signals a religious community to modern Westerners. As noted in the previous chapter, however, *ekklesia* referred to the popular citizens' assembly of a Greek city-state, just as *synagoge* referred to the assembly of a village (or the assembly of all Israel), that is, a community with its political-economic aspects inseparable from its religious aspect.

While Jesus had worked primarily in Galilean villages, Matthew's Jesus (and Matthew) appears to be addressing the assembly (*ekklesia*) of Christ at a point when the movement has already spread well beyond Galilee and Judea. In contrast to Paul and his coworkers who were working among the other peoples, however, Matthew is addressing Judeans/Israelites. Matthew's Jesus declares that he is building his assembly (*ekklesia*) "upon this rock," referring to Peter (whose name means "Rock"; 16:13–20). As we know from Paul's account of the division of missionary territory, Peter continued to work among "the circumcised" (Israel), while Paul went to the (other) peoples (Gal. 2:7–8). In the overall plot of Matthew, like that of Mark, Jesus is carrying out a renewal of Israel in opposition to the rulers of Israel. But Matthew's Jesus instructs the disciples to go "to the lost sheep of the house of Israel," just as he "was sent only to the lost sheep of the house of Israel" (Matt. 10:6; 15:24). These are clear clues that the Gospel of Matthew addresses people who still thought of themselves as part of Israel, or rather as (communities of) Israel now undergoing renewal over against the rulers of Israel, that is, the Pharisees and high priests, along with the Romans.

The assembly(ies) of Judeans/Israelites that Matthew addresses, however, lives beyond Galilee and Judea among those other peoples. Matthew also gives several indications that the assembly addressed consisted of minority communities contending with persecutors in larger towns or cities. The report in Matthew that Jesus' "fame spread throughout all Syria" (4:24) suggests that the Matthean communities were located in Syria. Because it had a large number of Judean residents, Antioch in Syria has been a leading contender for the location of the Matthean addressees. But considering how widespread the Diaspora of Judeans had become, the Gospel could just as easily have been addressed to an audience of Judeans in any or all of the following: the city of Caesarea on the Mediterranean coast, the other city of Caesarea (Philippi) to the north of Galilee, cities of the Decapolis, or other cities and towns in Syria.

Matthew also indicates that the communities addressed understand themselves as a continuation of the renewal of Israel inaugurated by Jesus over against the rulers of Israel, the high priesthood in the Temple as well as the Romans. Yet the Gospel gives several indications that the Temple and Jerusalem have been destroyed by the Romans (in their devastating reconquest following the great revolt, 66–70) and the client priestly aristocracy is no longer in power. Thus, as recent interpreters have suggested, the sustained attack on "the scribes and Pharisees" (see especially Matt. 23) reflects the Matthean communities' struggle to maintain their independence of those who attempted to assert authority over communities of Judeans following the Roman destruction of Jerusalem and the Temple. Matthew presents Jesus' prophetic condemnation of the Temple and high priests, which he took over from Mark's Gospel, as an historical account of Jesus' mission of renewal of Israel versus its rulers. But Jesus' prophetic pronouncements focused on Roman rule and Rome's client rulers in Jerusalem have wider implications also for Roman rule and Rome's client rulers in the towns and cities of Syria, all the more after the destruction of Jerusalem.

The Gospel of Matthew thus addresses minority communities of Judean/Israelite heritage who, while no longer under the authority of the Temple and high priests, are living under the authority of the local rulers in other towns and cities subject to Roman imperial rule. Matthew's

Gospel thus provides a window onto how covenantal economics in Isra-elite tradition and in the teaching of Jesus was adapted for small minority groups of Judeans striving to live as alternative communities in the domi-nant Roman imperial order.

The Sermon on the Mount

Jesus' first long speech in Matthew 5–7 ("the Sermon on the Mount") is often recognized as a covenant speech, although that recognition fre-quently plays no role in its interpretation. Most obvious is that in the "antitheses" in 5:20–48 Jesus starts by citing some of the ten command-ments or other principles familiar from covenantal law codes and then intensifies them in sharp restatement. Comparison with Jesus' covenant renewal speech known from the version in Luke 6:20–49 shows that the Sermon on the Mount follows the same basic outline and steps: the beginning blessings (Luke 6:20–22; Matt. 5:3–16), the closing double parable (Luke 6:46–49; Matt. 7:24–27), and covenantal teachings in the middle (e.g., "love your enemies"; "do not judge"; Luke 6:27–36; Matt. 5:38–42, 43–48; Luke 6:37–39; Matt. 7:1–5). We can thus easily recog-nize that, like Jesus' covenant renewal speech known from Luke 6:20–39, the Sermon on the Mount also follows the structural components of the Mosaic Covenant, beginning with a new declaration of deliverance (the blessings), continuing with covenantal demands or teachings in the body of the speech, and ending with the double parable as motivational exhor-tation to observe the teachings. Matthew expands the speech, however, with considerable additional instruction. The Sermon on the Mount is thus a far more elaborate covenant renewal speech. It seems to be a sort of charter for the Matthean communities.

All of the features that we recognized in Jesus' covenantal renewal speech known through Luke 6:20–49 are also present in the Sermon on the Mount. But Matthew adds some features, as we can see in a short survey of the speech. Previous interpretations suggesting that Matthew has watered down or "spiritualized" the concrete social-economic focus of Jesus' teaching have been based on mistranslations of key Greek terms and traditional Judean/Israelite concepts. Such interpretations are themselves the source of the spiritualization they find in the text. The first "beati-tude" announces the general agenda of the sermon: Jesus is announcing God's new act of deliverance in establishing the kingdom of God—which Matthew and other faithful Judeans refer to as "the kingdom of heaven"—among the poor. The different wording of "the poor in spirit" and "those who hunger and thirst for justice" instead of "the poor" and "the hungry" does not spiritualize the addressees, who remain concretely poor and hungry. The additional blessings stack up the qualities desirable, even necessary, in the renewed covenantal community, such as "meek," that is, not covetously striving to take control of others' goods, and "merciful," with its implications of economic sharing and mutual aid. The keynote is sounded by the blessing on "those who hunger and thirst for *justice*, for they shall be filled." The traditional translation ("righteousness") has led to a pious individualist interpretation. The point rather is that with the coming of the kingdom of God to the poor, *justice* will be realized or effected for them, with sufficient food, clothing, shelter, and so on, for a basic livelihood. Jesus reaffirms the same basic point later in the speech in the paragraph concluding with "strive for *the kingdom of God* and its *justice*, and all these things will be given to you as well" (Matt. 6:25–33).

The last two "beatitudes" (Matt. 5:10, 11–12) are a notable intensification over the final blessing in the earlier covenantal speech of Jesus. Persecution has clearly become a more serious problem for the communities addressed by Matthew. Significant is the reason stated for the persecution: their commitment to *justice* (in social-economic relations). The blessings on the persecuted, moreover, indicate that Matthew's Jesus is addressing a community (or communities), not just individual persons, in accord with the very character of the making or renewal of the Covenant, which was between God and a whole people, not just God and an individual.

The move from the declaration of deliverance (the blessings) to the covenantal commandments and teachings in the Sermon on the Mount could not be more explicit. Far from an abolition or supersession of the traditional Mosaic covenantal Law and the Prophets, Jesus' renewal of the Covenant is a fulfillment of them, the very foundation of his renewal of Israel. Far from the ensuing antitheses ("you have heard that it was said . . . , but I say to you . . . ," 5:21–48) being new laws or commandments replacing the original ones, they are intensifications focused mainly on inner motivation of observing the commandments, such as anger and lust. In the antitheses Matthew's Jesus is addressing communities that are more than just religious. As one can see in the antitheses focused on social conflict, adultery, swearing falsely, and reciprocity ("give to one who wants to borrow"; 5:27–32, 33–37, 38–42), Jesus is delivering new covenantal teaching addressed to social-economic interaction in small communities in which families are the most basic social unit. In these intensifications of the traditional covenantal commandments Matthew's

Jesus is demanding from those who have received the blessings of the new deliverance rigorously disciplined justice in social-economic relations, a justice that surpasses that of the scribes and Pharisees (5:20).

The intensification of the commandment "not to murder" in the first antithesis (5:21–26) focuses on the social conflict between community members that might lead to fratricidal violence. It is not difficult to discern that many of the conflicts that might lead to intense anger and taking a neighbor to court would likely have involved economic matters such as borrowing and lending. The intensification of the commandment against "bearing false witness/swearing" would also have been addressed to economic interactions. Matthew divides the covenantal admonitions that begin with "love your enemies" in the earlier speech of Jesus (Luke 6:27–36) into the last two antitheses (Matt. 5:38–42, 43–48). In covenantal law traditions, "an eye for an eye . . ." usually indicates the general area of bodily injury. This is what the cue in 5:38 might lead us to expect. But the examples given to illustrate the radicalization of "do not resist an evildoer" do not fit the general category of resistance. They pertain rather to an insult and to borrowing and lending. Perhaps not only "an eye for an eye" but also "going the second mile" had become a proverb with such broad application that it was used with reference to borrowing and lending. The thrust of this antithesis is to exhort community members to provide economic assistance to other community members despite their having done so before and despite being marginal themselves. In the final antithesis, however, Matthew shifts the focus of the "love your enemies" from economic relations with community members to outsiders such as those who persecute the communities he addresses.

Immediately following the demands for higher justice articulated in the antitheses, however, Matthew has additional instructions and exhortations on economics. First come three standard Judean ways of practicing justice (6:2–4, 5–15, 16–18; the NRSV translation "piety" in 6:1 is misleadingly narrow). Matthew's attention to the manner in which it is done may distract from the economic substance of giving alms. Given its prominence in scribal instruction (Sir. 3:30–4:10; 7:10; Tob. 1:16–17; 4:5–11; 12:8–10), giving alms must have become a standard way of aiding the poor, parallel to the mechanisms in the "moral economy" of the village community, such as making fields available for gleaning or taking a portion of the harvest in the seventh (fallow) year. Like these other forms of aid for families having difficulty, giving alms also was understood as a form of "laying up a good treasure for yourself against the day of necessity" (Tob. 4:9). That is, giving alms was a form of insurance against a time when a family might itself need such help from others. Giving alms was also seen as an offering to God (Tob. 4:11), a form of love of neighbor that the scribe may have had in mind in his agreement with Jesus' emphasis on the second of the two greatest commandments (Mark 12:32–33). Surplus goods that one did not need were to be given as alms rather than to be stored up as treasure (Tob. 12:8–10).

What begins as instruction on the place and manner of prayer focuses on the Lord's Prayer (Matt. 6:9–13). Matthew's version is longer than the earlier form followed by Luke. Adding to the economic emphasis of the Prayer, in the central petitions for subsistence bread and release of debts are two other features familiar from the Matthean version. We modern Westerners think of the phrase "hallowed be your name" as an acknowl-edgment of the transcendent sacredness of God. In Israelite tradition, however, even in texts closely identified with the Jerusalem temple, God "hallows" or "sanctifies" God's name by delivering the people from foreign empires, inspiring them to observe the covenantal statutes and ordinances, and ensuring that they have sufficient food (Ezek. 36:22–32). In the prayer, hallowing God's name points directly to the mutual forgiveness articulated in the petition to "release our debts, *as we herewith release those of our debtors.*" The exhortation to "forgive others" attached to the end of the prayer (6:14–15) makes unmistakably clear that the cancellation of debts is the emphasis of the prayer in the covenantal speech in Matthew 5–7.

The third act of justice is fasting (6:16–18). Fasting, which is closely connected with covenantal life, means going without food, of which there is never enough to feed everyone in a poor urban community, same as in a marginal rural community.

The exhortation in the next step in the Matthean covenant speech (6:19–24), ending with the principle that "You cannot serve God and Mammon," reinforces the practice of mutual sharing, of those with sufficiency aiding those without in the Matthean communities. It must have been a constant pull, for those who were marginal economically, to want to "lay up treasures on earth" (surplus goods, wealth). To share those "treasures" with needy community members, however, in keeping with covenant principles, would be "laying up treasures in heaven," that is, with God, whose covenantal will was supposed to be done.

Two aspects of the principle "You cannot serve God and Mammon" are notable. First, Jesus and his movements understood the drive to accumulate wealth as service of a powerful force, like another god. They had been the victims of just such obsessive service of Mammon in the predatory practices of their rulers. They understood full well that this is just what the covenantal principles were designed to guard against. Thus, second, this principle in effect restates the first two commandments in their economic aspect: exclusive loyalty to God means one cannot pursue wealth. God's will is for justice to prevail in society, for the economic rights of all to a livelihood to be respected and realized.

Completing the section of the speech devoted to economics Matthew includes other teaching of Jesus (6:25–33, known also from Luke 12:22–31) that reassures the people of God's care for them and admonishes them to stay single-mindedly focused on striving for the kingdom of God and its justice. Following further teaching on social conflict, the sermon concludes with extensive exhortation on keeping Jesus' covenantal teachings, including the double parable as sanctioning motivation on doing his intensified commandments (Matt. 7:24–27).

In sum, the Sermon on the Mount is a covenantal charter to guide the community life of the assembly(ies) of Christ. The overall outline of the "sermon" is the same three steps of a (renewed) covenant as in the earlier covenant renewal speech of Jesus (in Luke 6:20–49). The contents of the Sermon are covenantal blessings, teachings, and motivations rooted in the covenantal tradition. Most of the additions Matthew has made in this expanded covenant renewal speech bolster its focus on economic matters that was already clear in Jesus' earlier covenantal speech. The additional blessings announce and require qualities (mercy, a hunger for justice) among the renewed covenantal community that bolster economic mutuality and communal cooperation. In the central section on covenantal principles the antitheses do not replace but intensify the original covenantal commandments as guiding principles for social-economic interaction in community life. To these principles Matthew adds admonitions on alms, prayer, and fasting, with the emphasis on sufficient livelihood for all and mutual forgiveness and cancellation of indebtedness. In the midst of this exhortation, Jesus' declaration "You cannot serve God and Mammon" is a powerful restatement of the second commandment with its focus on justice, cooperation, and sharing in economic interaction based on exclusive loyalty to God (as opposed to the false god of acquiring wealth by taking advantage of others' difficulties). The covenantal sermon concludes with strong exhortation to faithful adherence to the intensified covenantal commandments and principles that Matthew's Jesus has just declared.

Reinforcing Community Economic Solidarity

Jesus' fourth major speech in Matthew (Matt. 18) strongly reinforces the covenantal community of Matthew's audience and its internal economic relations already addressed in the first major speech, the Sermon on the

Mount. The instructions for handling conflicts within the community in 18:15–20 bear strong resemblances to the similar instructions in the Qumran *Community Rule* (1QS 5:25–6:1; CD 9:2–8). That the latter were designed for a renewed covenantal community striving to live as an alternative society suggests that the instructions in Matthew 18 were also designed for such a covenantal community. In both sets of instructions, steps are to be taken systematically to work out the difficulties, first between the parties in conflict, then with the help of mediators, and finally before the whole assembly. If the offending party refuses to listen, however, he is expelled from the community (which is thus obviously not an agrarian village where families have ancestral lands). Such tight group discipline is essential for minority communities under persecution by outsiders.

The other way community solidarity was maintained was by forgiveness of offenses, not just seven times but "seventy-seven times" (Matt. 18:21–22). This adamant instruction from Jesus to Peter, the rock on which the assembly was founded, is supported by a parable (18:23–35) that powerfully reinforces the petition for release of debts in the Lord's Prayer, already emphasized in the covenant renewal speech (6:12, 14–15). As in the Lord's Prayer, where Matthew's version pointedly has cancellation of "debts" (not forgiveness of "sins," as in Luke's version), the parable (in Matt. 18:23–35) focuses on concrete material debts. Again translations give modern Western readers a narrower sense than the Greek terms indicate. In 6:14–15 Matthew moves from the highly concrete debts of the prayer's petition to the more general *paraptomata* (NRSV "trespasses"). But in context *paraptomata* refer to violations of covenantal laws or principles in the course of social-economic interaction. The parable about the disastrous result of not releasing relatively limited amounts of economic debt reminds us that Matthew is focused on just such social-economic interaction in the community.

The Matthean charter of covenantal community continues with Matthew's reproduction (Matt. 19–20) of the Markan covenant renewal dialogues (Mark 10:1–45). As in Mark, the first dialogue, grounding marriage (hence family) in the creation and forbidding divorce and remarriage (Matt. 19:3–9), insists on women's economic rights as members of families. The teaching Matthew adds about "eunuchs for the sake of the kingdom" (19:11–12), which authorizes an ascetic unmarried life for some members of the community, offers another indication that Matthew is not addressing village communities composed only of patriarchal families but communities recently formed in towns and cities.

In Jesus' encounter with the wealthy man, Matthew (19:16–22) deletes Mark's "you shall not defraud" from the list of the covenant commandments and adds the summarizing "love your neighbor as yourself." This Matthean reformulation gives another indication that the communities addressed may be a step removed from the immediacy of the agrarian village in which peasant families know only too well how someone becomes wealthy. Yet Matthew's statement of how the covenantal commandments are to guide community economic relations is every bit as strong as Mark's.

Matthew even reinforces the political-economic thrust of the cove-nantal teaching by inserting Jesus' prophecy about the *renewal*, when the disciples would be seated on twelve stools effecting justice for the twelve tribes of Israel (19:28). The political-economic focus of Jesus' declaration here is obscured by misleading paraphrases or translations. The NRSV paraphrase "renewal of all things" ignores that the term *palingenesis* was used for the historical restoration of the people of Israel, a long-standing prophetic tradition, and does not refer to the regeneration of the cosmos in Greek (Stoic) philosophy. Bible translators, moreover, have habitually translated the Greek *krinein* and the corresponding Hebrew *shaphat* with "judge." But the connotations of "judging" in English are misleading. In the Psalms, for example, God does not so much "judge" the orphan and widow as "do justice for" them. Yahweh did not "judge" but "liberated" Israel from Egypt. Thus in Jesus' declarations about economic relations in the renewed covenantal community, when the restoration of Israel comes to fulfillment, the twelve will be liberating or *establishing justice for* the twelve tribes of Israel. In Israelite tradition, the criteria for the justice that is to be established are the principles of the covenant.

Matthew's inclusion of 19:28 in the dialogues focused on the renewal of covenantal community also indicates that the covenant renewal is the basis of Jesus' broader program of the renewal of Israel in anticipation of the direct rule/kingdom of God that is at hand. In Matthew's Gospel as in Paul's mission, the formation of new covenantal communities was the form taken in the expansion of Jesus' movement of renewing Israel. Once the movement spread beyond the village communities of Galilee and Judea, however, the newly formed communities were effectively local communities of a wider alternative society in which covenantal coopera-tion and justice were maintained.

Opposition to the Economic Demands of the Rulers

As with Jesus' original movement of the renewal of Israel in Galilean vil-lages, the newly established communities of an alternative society were not only under Roman imperial rule, but were clearly defined over against Roman rule and local Roman client rulers. Matthew takes over from Mark virtually all of Jesus' condemnation of the Temple and high priests and their economic demands on the people (Matt. 21–22). He also takes over the protest against diverting people's resources to the Temple by inducing them to "devote" their produce to the Temple (15:1–20). He takes over Jesus' declaration, in effect, that it is indeed not lawful to render tribute to Rome, and even adds another episode in which Jesus makes somewhat the same point. Matthew may have presented these as historical statements and actions of Jesus, but they clearly had indirect implications for covenantal communities of Israel in Syrian towns beyond Judea and Galilee after the Roman destruction of Jerusalem.

Jesus' condemnation of the Temple and high priests for exploitation of the people could have involved several interrelated interpretations. One might well have been that Jesus' prophetic demonstration against the Temple had been confirmed by the Roman destruction interpreted as ultimately God's action through the Romans. This interpretation would have flowed easily out of a long tradition of interpretation of the Babylonian destruction of Jerusalem centuries earlier as a vindication of the prophets' protests and oracles. Jesus' prophetic action and declaration against the exploitative rulers and ruling institutions in Jerusalem—now taking their place in that long tradition of prophetic protest against unjust rule from Jerusalem—would also presumably have strongly reinforced the Matthean communities' resistance to any Judean authorities who attempted to assert centralized direction of Judean communities beyond Judea. Many interpreters now think that Jesus' sharpened attacks on "the scribes and Pharisees" in Matthew (especially Matt. 23) are an expression of just such resistance.

Simply the perpetuation of Jesus' prophetic declarations of God's condemnation of oppressive central control and expropriation of resources produced and needed by the people would have been a strong restatement of the whole covenantal and prophetic message of God's insistence that the people have economic rights. People who belonged to the Matthean communities had identified themselves with Jesus' message and martyrdom and with the Jesus movement that had originated in Galilee and Judea. Matthew's Gospel reminds them in dramatic fashion of Jesus' condemnation of exploitative rulers. The accounts of Jesus' prophetic statements may well have also had implications for Matthean communities' resistance to any Roman-supported local rulers in the towns and cities of Syria where the Matthean communities were located, at least for their struggle to constitute an alternative society of cooperation and justice.

Matthew also takes over from Mark Jesus' statement about the tribute to Caesar, that the people do not owe it (Matt. 22:15–22). Jesus' declaration about the tribute would have had direct or indirect bearing on such communities depending on whether they were in towns subject to the tribute. Even if not subject to it, however, they would have known about the tribute, which also served as a symbol of the general Roman drain of local resources to the imperial center, to support the military that maintained the imperial order, to enhance the lifestyle in the imperial center, or to expand the wealth of the imperial elite. Speaking craftily in the face of power Jesus had declared that those local resources belonged not to Caesar but to God—who of course had given them to the people for their livelihood in mutual support and cooperation.

In addition to carrying over from Mark Jesus' condemnation of rulers and ruling institutions for their economic exploitation of the people, Matthew has two further sets of material in which Jesus takes a stand against economic exploitation: the episode of the temple tax and the long sequence of woes against the Pharisees.

How to interpret the episode of the Temple tax (17:24–27) is a puzzle. The tax was an annual payment of a half shekel by all Judean and other Israelite males to the Temple. It had been raised from the earlier rate of a third of a shekel only a few generations before. There was considerable grumbling about the tax. The Qumran community interpreted the obligation as only once in an adult male's lifetime. The analogy that Jesus asks Peter to draw in the dialogue (of 17:25–26) fits very well in the situation prior to 70 CE when the Temple was still standing and the tax was still paid to the rulers in the Temple. In the wider context of the Roman Empire the question, "From whom do kings of the earth take toll or tribute? From their children or from others?" was an obvious reference to Rome's demanding tribute from conquered peoples, not from Roman citizens. When Peter answers "from others," Jesus draws the conclusion, "Then the children are free" from the tribute. By analogy with the Roman tribute that the Romans themselves do not pay, the "sons of Israel" are, in principle, free from the Temple tax. This fits well with Jesus' other declarations, known from Mark and elsewhere, objecting to the Temple establishment's exploitation of the people. So as not to give offense, however, Jesus instructs Peter to pay the tax from a coin that will miraculously appear in a fish's mouth—leaving us to wonder whether his instruction was tongue in cheek.

By the time Matthew's Gospel was composed, however, the Romans had destroyed the Temple and had transformed the temple tax into a payment by all Judeans in the Empire to the imperial treasury for reconstruction of the temple to Jupiter on the Capitoline hill. In this new situation of the tax being paid to Rome, the analogy in the dialogue no longer applies to the Temple, and the conclusion Jesus draws does not fit Judeans' payment of the tax to Rome. That the tax was still understood as paid to the Temple, though it was no longer standing, and then secondarily redirected to Rome seems unlikely. More likely is that this episode, which occurs only in Matthew among the Gospels, was meant and understood in historical terms as yet another of Jesus' declarations of economic independence from the demands of the rulers in Jerusalem. Matthew's placement of the episode in the midst of narratives of Jesus' mission in Galilee reinforces the likelihood that this was intended as an historical incident, not an instruction to the Matthean communities on payment of a tax to Rome. But it may have had indirect implications for the payment of taxes to Rome: the people did not owe them, but should pay them in order not to bring the authorities down on their heads.

Following directly upon Jesus' confrontation with the high priestly client rulers in Jerusalem taken over from Mark, Matthew expands the earlier version of woes against the scribes and Pharisees (Matt. 23). In some of the woes (23:8–12) Jesus declares that his movement is radically egalitarian and is not to imitate the previous hierarchical structure of authority. In others he mocks the Pharisees' obsession with casuistry (23:16–22), which is perhaps necessary in elite culture but is alien to the popular concerns articulated by Jesus.

In the traditional Christian caricature of the Pharisees as representative of Judaism in their obsession with ritual laws, however, interpreters usually miss the economic charges leveled against the Pharisees in these woes. These woes evidently depend on oral tradition of prophetic indictments that fit the historical situation in Galilee and Judea. The religious-political-economic position and role of the scribes and Pharisees was to represent the interests of the Temple and high priesthood. As in the episode focused on the dedication (*korban*) of local resources to the Temple, it was important to keep revenues flowing in tithes, offerings, and other ways. In this connection it is not difficult to hear the economic dimension in several of the woes.

"They tie up heavy burdens, hard to bear, and lay them on the shoulders of others" (23:4). It is clear whose shoulders bore the load in Galilee and Judea. "But they themselves are unwilling to lift a finger to move them." Scribes and Pharisees were legal advisers of the temple-state, the only people in the society who could read and write, and they used their writing skills, along with their expertise in interpretation of the laws, to keep the temple-state running. But they were unwilling to use their scribal finger (interpretation of the laws) to alleviate the burden on the producers.

"You tithe mint, dill, and cumin, and have neglected the weightier matters of the law: justice and mercy and faith" (23:23). They are so fastidious themselves about tithing that they are scrupulous even about herbs. But they fail to consider justice and mercy for the peasant producers when it comes to the tithes demanded from the people, whose lives are disintegrating under the demands of the Temple as well as those of Caesar. Similarly, "You clean the outside of the cup and of the plate, but inside they are full of plunder and self-indulgence" (23:25). The NRSV blunts the sharpness of the charge by changing "plunder" to "greed." Jesus charges that while the Pharisees exhibit scrupulous care about purity codes, their application of the laws in effect plunders the resources that belong rightfully to the people. The Pharisees had their own interest in the application of the tithing and other laws, since they were economically dependent on the revenues of the Temple and high priesthood. The indictment that they block people from entering the kingdom (23:13) is almost a summary of the others. Because the effect of the Pharisees' role is to prevent people from keeping the covenantal commandments (as articulated in the example in 15:1–20), they block entry to the kingdom in which the will of God would be done and thus justice realized.

Jesus' woes against the scribes and Pharisees in Matthew 23 are a more sustained attack than he makes in Mark and the earlier set of woes taken over in Luke 11:39–52. This may well be an expression of the Matthean communities' declaration of independence of any attempt at central control of Judeans in the historical circumstances of the late first century. As noted at the outset, Matthew's addressees must understand themselves as part of the renewal of Israel over against the rulers that Jesus inaugurated. We do not know exactly who attempted to become the authoritative successors to the high priests and their scribal representatives after the Romans destroyed the Temple. According to rabbinic legend, the distinguished teacher Yohanan ben Zakkai called together a council of other teachers to provide leadership for the devastated Judean people. Matthew clearly represents "the scribes and Pharisees" as such authorities, but authorities that his communities resist rather than obey. The historical traditions of Jesus' indictments of the Pharisees in Galilee and Judea that Matthew adapts here (Matt. 23) provide historical precedent in the teaching of Jesus for later resistance to Judean authority figures, including whatever economic claims they might make on communities of Judeans in Syrian cities.

Matthean Covenantal Community as an Alternative Society

Many have suggested that in the generation or two after Jesus his followers relaxed the intensity of his pronouncement of the direct rule of God and watered down the rigor with which he demanded that people respond to God's new act of deliverance. If anything, however, the Gospel of Matthew, composed fifty years after Jesus' mission in Galilee, has made more explicit his renewal of covenant community and his emphasis on economic rights and justice. Matthew has expanded the good news of God's new deliverance of the people from their suffering and disintegration under centralizing foreign imperial rule into what is also a handbook for newly established covenantal communities in the cities beyond Galilee and Judea. Matthew addresses communities in the assembly of Christ that have expanded the renewal of Israel inaugurated in Jesus' mission to include minority communities of Judeans/Israelites in Greek-speaking cities where they are under attack precisely for attempting to embody the justice involved in establishing covenantal communities.

The long "sermon" from the "mountain" by Jesus, as the new Moses, far from being a set of sayings of individual morality, presents a foundational charter for establishing and maintaining covenantal community. If we can move past previous mistranslations that reduce Jesus' Sermon on the Mount to maxims of personal piety, we can clearly discern Jesus' demand for justice in community life in response to God's new deliverance. Far from spiritualizing or superseding the traditional Mosaic covenantal law, Matthew's Jesus presses an intensification of the covenantal commandments that extends to the very motivational dynamics of social-economic relations in community life. The basic concern in Jesus' intensification of covenantal commandments and principles is ensuring sufficiency and justice in each family's livelihood. To this end emphasis falls on cooperative and reciprocal sharing and lending, giving alms, and canceling debts. Jesus even summarizes the mutual sharing and cooperative support that are necessary for justice in this alternative society in the fundamental covenantal principle directly reminiscent of the second commandment: "You cannot serve God and Mammon."

The counterpart of economic justice in the covenantal communities of an alternative society in the coming kingdom of heaven is God's condemnation of oppressive rulers and ruling institutions that consolidate their power and privilege by expropriating the produce and resources of the people. Matthew continues and intensifies Jesus' woes against the scribes and Pharisees for aiding and abetting the expropriation for the Temple of the people's resources needed by local communities and Jesus' prophetic declaration of God's condemnation of the Temple. He even expands on the rejection of the central control of people's resources in the statement that the people do not really owe the Temple tax, which had been appropriated by Rome after the destruction of the Temple. And he continues Jesus' declaration that it is not lawful, according to covenantal commandments, for the people to render tribute to Caesar, who may be the Lord of the Empire, but cannot be their lord, since in the first commandment of the covenant they have exclusive loyalty to God as their sole lord and master.

Study Questions

1. What are the various ways in which Matthew's Jesus presses people to establish social-economic justice in the covenant renewal speech known as the Sermon on the Mount?
2. Jesus' statement, with regard to "storing up wealth on earth," that "You cannot serve God and Mammon" sounds suspiciously like a restatement of the second commandment, against serving other gods. How would building up wealth be analogous to serving another god, a god other than the God of the Covenant?
3. A few generations after the time of Matthew, well-off intellectuals criticized the communities devoted to Christ for taking care of one another. How does Matthew's Jesus in the Sermon on the Mount and in the additional covenantal teaching in Matthew 19–20 urge people to take care of others in the community?
4. How would Matthew's inclusion of Jesus' many pronouncements against rulers' economic claims on the people's produce have reinforced the resolve of the covenantal communities of Christ to maintain mutual cooperation as an alternative society?

Conclusion

". . . With Certain Unalienable Rights"

We come back around, finally, to the question posed toward the end of the Introduction: How might the principles of the Covenant concerned with economic rights apply to United States society, which was founded on covenantal ideals, but has recently come so much under the power of huge corporations that operate with little regulation? How might principles of Israel's Covenant, designed for a simple agricultural society, be applied to an extremely complex economy dominated by interrelated transnational corporations? Is it possible that churches, synagogues, mosques, and other communities deeply rooted in the Bible could find in the biblical Covenant the basis for insisting that people's economic rights be protected? Might American civil society which was founded on covenantal ideals rediscover in the Covenant the basis for insisting that its government, which is supposedly governed by a Constitution grounded in the covenantal tradition, take steps to protect people's economic rights?

(Note to readers: In exploring the implications of the biblical Covenant for economics today I am moving well beyond my area of professional expertise. Many readers will have a fuller grasp and deeper insight on the complexities of economics, and particular experiences of and critical reflections on how the economic system we live in is undermining people's livelihood and eroding the economic rights that the Declaration of Independence as well as the Covenant affirm are unalienable. My hope is that the thoughts sketched out here will become part of a much broader conversation on what we can be doing to become more faithfully responsive to the principles of the Covenant.)

Economic Rights

The first step in exploring these possibilities may be to think critically about economic rights today that correspond to the economic rights assumed and protected by the principles of the biblical Covenant. As discussed in chapter 2, the covenantal commandments cover explicitly the right to the integrity of people's life, the right to the integrity of marriage and the family, the rights of the elderly, and the right to the basis of a livelihood for individuals and families or households (protected by the last three commandments: you shall not covet, steal, bear false witness). The various covenantal mechanisms—such as no interest on loans, cancellation of debts, and release of debt-slaves—all attempted to guarantee these rights, which are centered in the basis of a livelihood, which in ancient agrarian societies meant ancestral land.

It is not by accident that these rights protected by the covenant commandments remind us of the statement in the Declaration of Independence that we all know virtually by heart: "We hold these truths to be self-evident: that all men [people!] are . . . endowed by their Creator with certain unalienable Rights, that among these are *Life, Liberty, and the pursuit of Happiness*." As in ancient Israel, so in the agrarian society that Thomas Jefferson (who penned those words) presupposed, "the pursuit of Happiness," for most people, depended primarily on having land as a basis of individual and family livelihood. In an urbanized industrial society, however, individual and family livelihood depends on having a job. The implication is obviously that people have a right to a job or some sort of income. But having a job, like the practice of citizenship in our democracy, depends on having an education. In fact, in the complexities of modern life any number of things are necessary to an adequate livelihood, including decent health care, transportation, day care for children, adequate care for the elderly, clear air and water, safety of life and limb, and so on. Our civil society, through the government, has taken cognizance of these and in many cases taken some steps to guarantee these rights. But in many other cases and, in recent years more often than not, there are fewer and fewer effective safeguards of people's economic rights. Why?

Centralization of Economic Power and Erosion of Economic Rights

What in our world today corresponds to the centralization of economic power, in effect by undermining the people's livelihood and economic rights, by the monarchy in ancient Israel and the Roman imperial order at the time of Jesus? It is clearly not the United States government, which wields little economic power other than attempts at regulating interest and the minting of money, despite complaints about taxes. Economic power today has become centralized in huge corporations, some of them transnational. Although economic power is decentralized in the sense of being wielded by many corporations, the relatively new buzzword "globalization" points to the centralization of economic power in a way that is far beyond the ability even of professional economists to comprehend. The stock-market reports in the media sound like a cycle of myths of superhuman powers whose behavior is mysterious and incomprehensible, like those of the Powers that determined the lives of ancient Mesopotamians. But globalized economy dominated by the many interrelated megacorporations is a far more complex system than an ancient imperial economy, and incomparable in many ways.

Without pretending to understand how the whole system works, we can discern the ways in which the powerful megacorporations have come to resemble ancient empires. It is possible to discern how the huge unregulated corporations have come to have destructive effects on individuals, families, and communities that resemble the effects of ancient empires— effects that contradict the principles of economic justice laid out in the biblical Covenant. This comparison is nothing new. More than a century ago it was standard to talk of how industrial tycoons had built empires in the railroad or steel or oil industries. The only difference is that now the empires are much larger and more diversified and complex.

Just as the ancient empires conquered new territories and peoples to expand their revenues, so contemporary megacorporations have grown by hostile takeovers and leveraged buyouts. Just as ancient "transnational" empires took over many city-states and smaller kingdoms, so modern transnational corporations merged many corporations involved in different industries and countries. Just as one ruler, Solomon, ceded a whole district with its village communities to another ruler, Hiram of Tyre, without regard to the people's lives, so a contemporary corporation closes its factories in one country and relocates in another with much cheaper labor, without regard to the people's lives in either country. In both cases the imperial regime or the imperial corporation acts to expand its wealth, which it then uses for further expansion of its power. Transnational corporations have become so wealthy and powerful that they not only dwarf the economies of many countries, they also have decisive influence on the governments of even the largest countries. In the United States, for example, the huge oil companies determine energy policy and influence foreign policy, and agribusiness determines agricultural and food policy.

The "Great Ones" of the ancient empires manipulated the flow of resources into the control of the imperial regime. Similarly today the CEOs and other managers of huge corporations use their institutionalized power to manipulate the flow of wealth into the hands of management and big investors. As the "COO" of Pharaoh's Egyptian empire, Joseph exploited the people's desperation for food to wrest control of additional resources, demanded increased work, and forced them to accept a lower percentage of their produce to support themselves. Contemporary CEOs of corporations exploit people's desperation to keep their jobs to force them to accept reductions in wages and benefits while they themselves receive huge salary increases and stock options and their investors receive handsome profits.

Contemporary corporations, however, have gone far beyond the ancient empires in devising ways to control people and extract resources from them. Joseph used his control over goods that the people had produced to force them to turn over control of their other goods (the livestock used in production of more food) and eventually their land and future labor to the empire. Big corporations have long since accomplished the same. All that people have left in our centralized industrial economy is their labor, which they give to their company in return for wages or a salary. But in contrast with the ancient monarchies, temple-states, and empires where surpluses were simply stored in the form of gold, silver, and elaborate decor, corporations work by reinvesting profits. To continue generating more and more profits for investors, however, companies must devise ways to sell more and more products and services.

Corporations have done this in two principal ways. First, they induced people to buy unneeded products or to buy necessities in a "value-added," more expensive form. Ancient imperial rulers motivated people to render up tithes and offerings and extra labor by playing on their fear that an angry Storm or River would destroy their villages or overflow the dikes (what we would call a "natural disaster"). Contemporary corporations have, with the help of psychologists and artists, learned how to motivate people by fear and anxiety and by the promise of abundance and security through advertising. Fear of foreign enemies (the "evil empire") makes the populace ready to pay taxes to maintain the excessive destructive capacity of "the military-industrial complex." Anxiety about everything from physical appearance to safety on the road induces people to buy products ranging from cosmetics to SUVs. A 55-horsepower compact car provided adequate transportation for a family of four in the 1960s and 1970s. Marketing in the 1990s induced large numbers of people to buy SUVs—and the gas to fuel them. So essential is advertising to the sale of unneeded products that it has itself become an industry.

Second, corporations issued credit cards to seduce people into the immediate gratification of desire at tremendous cost to themselves, but profits for the banks. Buy now, pay later. Credit cards also induce people to buy far more than they would otherwise because the cost is deferred. This device works best on the poorest people, who cannot afford to pay for their charges quickly. At interest rates of 18 to 25 percent and additional fees and penalties, many people end up paying double or triple the original cost of the purchases to the credit-card companies.

Having grown so large and powerful, transnational corporations used their power to further enhance their power over the United States and other countries in two major ways that are historically unprecedented.

Corporations have come to heavily influence if not effectively control the governments of many countries, even that of the United States. The evidence for this mounts steadily, although it is often ignored. Of the overwhelming number of illustrations we can mention only a handful. In the 1980s corporations lobbied successfully for the deregulation of many industries. Eager to open up additional markets and find cheaper labor, corporations then pressured both the Congress and the presidency to negotiate and approve the North American Free Trade Agreement. Corporations then "exported" jobs from the United States and relocated production in Mexico, where they could pay substandard wages. NAFTA also ruined small corn-farming in Mexico, which in turn led to increased illegal immigration into the United States by people simply looking to make a living. Lobbying, overwhelmingly corporate, became a huge growth industry itself in the last several decades. With donations to election campaigns, corporations exercise decisive influence on United States government policies. Corporate influence and manipulation extend to the local and state levels as well. Since the economy depends on corporations to provide jobs, state governments extend tax breaks and subsidies in the form of supporting infrastructure to companies if only they will keep jobs in, or bring jobs into, their states.

Meanwhile, there is very little public discussion, much less criticism, of ever-expanding corporate power and its influence over the federal and state government. The reason is not far to seek. Corporations control and in many cases own the mass media that determine public attitudes, public discourse, and people's values as well as attitudes. Most obviously the major television and radio networks are owned by multinational corporations. More to the point, however, in addition to corporate ownership, the corporations pay for the programming by buying advertising. One purpose of advertising in the print and electronic media is to generate customers and clientele. Just as General Motors uses materials such as plastic to produce SUVs to sell to drivers, Fox or ABC uses programs to produce consumers to sell to the corporations that pay for the programs. But another purpose of expending huge sums on ads and "sponsorship" is to produce a positive public image for given corporations in particular and the corporate system in general. Constantly consuming such positive images and ideology, the general public is predisposed to participate in the system as good consumers, and not raise questions. Not surprisingly, far from resenting the wealthy or the system that enables them to pile up greater wealth, the overwhelming majority of the U.S. public hope to attain a bit of wealth of their own.

We usually refer to ancient power-holders' use of the media to create a positive aura around the system as "religion." Whatever we call it, the holders of centralized power, both ancient and modern, have used their control of the media of public communication to produce images and ideologies that make the dominant economic system and their own power appear grounded in the nature of the universe ("the way things are") and both (or alternately) benign and threatening.

Finally, it is important to emphasize a fundamental difference in the way the ancient and modern "empires" work. The ancient relation between political and economic power has been reversed in the modern corporate system. In ancient empires from Mesopotamia and Egypt to Rome, the holders of political power could manipulate the economy to enhance their own economic and political power. In the contemporary United States as well as other countries of the world, the holders of economic power can now manipulate the political arm of society in order to enhance their economic and political power.

In both systems, however, the wealth and power of the wealthy and powerful is expanded by exploiting the people, by taking control of more and more of the resources that at one point were understood to be theirs, individually and collectively, the basis of their livelihood. The result now as then is to take away or deny people's rights to retain economic resources that can sustain their life, to remove any basis of economic security. Just as ancient peasants became tenants on land taken over by the rulers and dependent on their decisions, so people today have become dependent on the decisions of CEOs. Like the ancient imperial economy, the contemporary global economy denies people's rights and rides roughshod over mechanisms and devices designed to protect them. As in the ancient empires, the people are at the mercy of economic power exercised at a considerable distance from them, and impervious to their needs and concerns.

Covenantal Principles versus Corporate Power

Ancient Israel's exodus from Egypt and Covenant on Sinai constituted a historical political breakthrough from a tyrannical system to a more egalitarian society of freedom. This breakthrough became paradigmatic for subsequent movements to achieve liberty and equality, as historians have often observed. Closer examination of the Covenant and its persistence in biblical history indicates that the breakthrough was economic as well as political. The ancient Near Eastern economy as well as its political order were indeed powerful and oppressive. But the imperial system was not inevitable and permanent. Through committed cooperative action people withdrew (or escaped) from it and set up an alternative society. And they found ways of resisting when it was powerfully reimposed. From the historical perspective resulting from Israel's breakthrough it was clear that imperial economies had developed and could collapse or be resisted, and that alternative social-economic relations are possible.

As the heirs of this view that reality is historical, that it changes and is changeable, we can remind ourselves that an unregulated global system of megacorporations is not inevitable and permanent. It can be resisted, its abuses opposed. We have the biblical examples of prophetic protests and condemnations of oppressive violations of covenantal principles and economic rights. From the Gospels we know of Jesus' concern to renew mutually supporting covenantal communities in resistance to the oppressive demands of the Roman rulers and their regional representatives. The

Letters of Paul and the Gospel of Matthew offer windows onto the formation of new covenantal communities of a fledgling alternative society and the economic sharing they generated within that alternative society.

If the economic system of megacorporations is measured by the criteria of covenantal commandments and laws, it is every bit as problematic as the tribute to Caesar was for Jesus and other Israelites living under Roman rule. Measured by the covenantal prohibition of interest and cancellation of debts after seven years, 18 to 25 percent interest on credit-card debt is obviously not "lawful," just as the tribute to Caesar was not lawful.

It would be highly impractical, however, for large numbers of people to move into a simple community life that would conform more closely to the biblical covenant, such as the Amish communities in Pennsylvania or the Qumran community in the ancient Judean wilderness. Nor is there much chance that many of the megacorporations will collapse anytime soon, even though there are signs that they may be vulnerable as they undermine their economic base by impoverishing consumers. Perhaps our situation is more like that of the Matthean communities in Syria or the assemblies of Christ in Greek cities. Drawing on covenantal tradition and principles, we can attempt to get out from under the dehumanizing dominance of unregulated centralized economic power as much as possible, and to mitigate its effects while insisting on people's economic rights.

"You shall have and serve no gods besides me"

The first two commandments concern far more than belief in God, the way we think of faith under the modern separation of religion from politics and economics. The commandments "you shall have no other gods" and "you shall not bow down to or serve the heavenly and earthly forces" prohibited serving the Forces/Powers that determined people's lives in the ancient Near East. To ensure that the Forces (gods) were favorably disposed, the people served them with a percentage of their crops and joined labor gangs to construct the palaces of the Forces. The "Great Ones," eager to keep the flow of tithes and offerings coming to the Forces, sponsored elaborate ceremonies focused on impressive statues of the Forces in threatening or nurturing poses, to induce fear of the Forces and a sense that the Forces would provide sufficiency and security.

Serving the Forces of Egyptian civilization is what the Hebrews had been required to do in Egypt, and they found it to be intolerable and unjust, as hard bondage. The first two commandments warned those who had been liberated from such service not to revert, but to maintain exclusive loyalty to the transcendent Force that liberated them. We can see the same principles operating in Jesus' exhortations and dialogues. "You cannot serve God *and* Mammon" is a restatement of the two first commandments focused on the economic implications. The drive to acquire possessions, trust in wealth, is tantamount to service of another god. Jesus' response to the intended entrapment by the Pharisees regarding tribute to Caesar—"Give to Caesar the things that are Caesar's and to God the things that are God's"—is also a restatement of the first two commandments focused on the political-economic implications. Exclusive loyalty to God who delivers from bondage means that the people do not owe tribute to another lord.

The forces that dominate people's lives today, the forces that today's economy is set up to *serve*, are wealth, ever-greater possessions, and the security they supposedly provide, perhaps especially the ever-expanding return on investment that drives the whole complex system. These forces are far more complex in their operations than those in ancient empires, but the pattern of people's service of them is similar to the ancients' service of the gods. The ancients yielded up an ever-larger portion of the produce of their labor to "feed" the Forces (gods) and then also yielded up an additional portion of their labor to build the "houses" of the Forces (gods). Today people yield up an ever-larger portion of the value of their labor for an income a portion of which they then also yield up in buying unneeded goods and in interest payments on credit cards and loans.

Today, of course, the economic forces we are, in effect serving, are not thought of as gods. Rather they are carefully defined in public discourse as secular, as economic, not religious. But this is a disguise, and not a very good one at that. We are surrounded by advertising that induces anxiety and fear yet offers security and the good life, similar to what ancient imperial religion evoked in the "servants of the gods." Indeed, many of the unneeded products, possessions to have as parts of the good life, are glamorized, they are "idolized." But in acquiring them as an addition to their other household "idols," people are "bowing down and serving" the forces that they represent.

Recognizing that we are serving "other gods" in the centralized global economy, however, does not mean that we can be free from its domination. Jesus declared that people did not owe tribute to Caesar, but the communities of the Jesus movements continued to live under the domination of Caesar, who still had power to coerce their continuing service at least in the form of taxes and rents and tribute. Yet they knew that imperial rule and exploitation stood under God's judgment as unjust and oppressive. In anticipation of the imminent establishment of a new society of justice under the direct rule of God, they renewed local covenantal cooperation and created communities of an alternative society, to resist the disintegrating effects of centralized power.

Similarly today those who recognize that economic life dominated by huge corporations is neither ingrained in the structure of the universe or inevitable must continue living under its sway. In the United States today, with many of our political rights still mostly intact, those who choose loyalty to the God who liberates from economic domination have more options than did the ancient Jesus movement and assemblies of Christ. Like the latter, they can in various ways and to various degrees be communities that embody alternative values and alternate social-economic relations, including economic cooperation and mutual aid. But churches and synagogues can also act politically and economically in the larger society, in addition to or in concert with their religious services.

Since megacorporations do not yet have anywhere near the coercive control exercised by ancient empires, their client rulers, and their officers, moreover, there are other possibilities as well. Civil society has begun to disintegrate under the impact of advertising and the fragmenting of the body politic. But political action is still possible. Applying the first and second commandments, recognition that obsession with profits and expanding wealth is a force (but false god) that many people serve in our society can lead to political action to place restraints and regulations on the oppressive powers, actions, and effects of the huge corporations. Since they are false gods, they should not be treated as sacrosanct.

"You shall not covet . . . steal"

Similar to the first commandment, "you shall not steal" and "you shall not covet" have much broader implications in covenantal economics than in a capitalist economy in which most resources have become defined as private property. In the covenantal society of Israelite villages and in Jesus' covenant renewal, resources such as land and the produce of land (the fundamental basis of livelihood) were understood in a much more social sense. Families had unalienable rights to their ancestral inheritances, but they were also expected to share the products of their land-and-labor with others as needed. To understand the scope and implications of "you shall not steal/covet" we must appreciate their close relationship with covenantal mechanisms intended to preserve families' economic viability, such as the prohibition of interest and the sabbatical release of debts. People were not to take advantage of their neighbors' economic difficulties to "steal" from them by taking interest on loans. And if neighbors could not recover economically within seven years, they were to cancel the debts.

Jesus' conversation with the wealthy young man illustrates the point. A rich person had become wealthy by defrauding others, taking their goods via interest on loans and appropriating them as his own possessions. The goods still belonged rightfully to the poor who had thus been defrauded, hence Jesus' command to give them (back) to the poor.

If we apply the covenantal principle of not stealing and the covenantal prohibition of charging interest, as illustrated by Jesus' instruction to the rich man, then an economic system based on the charging of interest can only be deemed systematic stealing. This may be a useful point to remember over against the currently dominant ideology of free-market capitalism. Since interest on investment will not be disappearing anytime soon, however, it is important to understand the more subtle ways that the economy we live in is challenged by covenantal principles.

In American society where most resources have been defined as private property, laws against theft have almost the opposite effect of "you shall not steal" in a covenantal economy. This happens in several ways. For example, corporations, which control vast resources as their private property, pay the lowest wages and offer the fewest benefits that they can get away with. Workers acquiesce because good jobs are hard to find, there is now little job security, corporations have the unrestrained power to move production hence jobs to other locations, and corporations in collusion with the federal and state government have effectively weakened the union movement. Corporations also literally defraud people, largely by bending but not breaking the laws. Credit-card companies in particular, by charging 18 to 25 percent interest plus fees, take possession of huge sums of money which become their (or their investors') private property.

Private property is what is sacred in the American economy. If we applied the covenantal commandment, then low wages, manipulative advertising, and exorbitant interest rates would, like the rich young man's acquisition of possessions and the scribes' urging widows to give to the Temple, be defined as stealing. Such standard practices are fundamental violations of people's economic rights to a livelihood.

"You shall not covet," as we noted in chapter 2, meant more broadly "covet-and-seize," as with those whom Micah described as lying on their beds devising schemes to "covet fields and seize them" (Mic. 2:1–2). That, of course, is precisely what modern corporations do in marketing. They devise schemes to make people give them a portion of their livelihood for often unneeded products. They do this, however, by inducing the consumers themselves to covet, to desire to have all those products. Driving the supersized SUV will give one a sense of power. Driving the high-performance luxury car will give one a sense of unrestrained freedom as well as power. Advertising even induces people to desire certain identities, which can be acquired by acquiring certain products. An important difference between the advertiser and the targeted consumer is that the former covets others' resources while the latter merely covets more possessions.

In the broader global (also imperial) economy, however, the desire for unneeded products induced by advertising leads to coveting-and-seizing other countries' resources. People in the United States and northwestern European countries consume thirty-two times as much as people in third-world African or Latin American countries. Since such consumption is utterly unsustainable, the massive desire induced by advertising means systemic "coveting and seizing" of the livelihood of future generations and the very creation that sustains life.

Covenant Mechanisms to Protect Economic Rights

Covenantal economics in the Bible included many mechanisms designed to protect people's rights to a livelihood. Some of these, such as gleaning, liberal lending with no interest, and not harvesting in the sabbatical year, provided supplementary resources to tide people over temporary difficulties and insufficiency. Others, such as release of debts and debt-slaves and redemption of land, supplied ways of recovering from longer-term poverty and indebtedness. These became all the more important when rulers and their officers with political-economic power escalated their exploitation of the people. Often they were insufficient to counter-act the institutionalized power of imperial rulers, their client rulers, and their officials.

It is not difficult to recognize what some of the corresponding measures would be to mitigate exploitative practices and their effects in the contemporary global economy—practices that systematically and institutionally violate covenantal principles such as "you shall not covet" and "you shall not steal." A centralized economy dominated by huge corporations that is so much more complex than a simple agrarian economy requires a far more complex array of mechanisms to protect people's economic rights.

Today's equivalent to the biblical unalienable right to land as a basis of livelihood would be an income that would cover the basic necessities of livelihood, "the pursuit of happiness," to which people have inalienable rights, at least according to the Declaration of Independence. Those would presumably include but not be limited to housing, clothing, food, education, job training, health care, transportation. Workers' incomes from jobs would thus require greater equity within corporations of payment to workers and to management. Bringing the huge remuneration of CEOs and other top management down and the poorly paid workers up would clearly require considerable political and economic leverage. To compensate for the difficulties that have escalated with the increasing denial of people's economic rights, the fundamental right to a livelihood would also require affordable and quality health care, well-funded job training and retraining, humane working conditions (so that jobs are not tantamount to debt-slavery), and elaborate regulations to prevent the blatant forms of corporations' exploitation of people.

Equivalents to supplementary aid to people in temporary economic difficulty such as gleaning rights and liberal lending without interest would run the gamut from food stamps to unemployment compensation. This would require *expansion* of programs already in place but inadequate.

Programs to aid in recovery from long-term poverty and its results are needed particularly in response to disintegration of family and community life. It has proven naive and inadequate to expect one institution in our society, the public schools, to address a whole complex of interrelated deficits that have resulted from long-range poverty. The increasing power of corporations to wreak havoc by shifting the location of their production demands new and innovative responses. Well-funded retraining programs are required for workers whose jobs are eliminated or "exported." Governments could mitigate some of the worst economic impact on families and communities in both the United States and other countries by restoring regulation on corporations and requiring international economic planning.

Covenant Renewal and Prophetic Protest

The Hebrew prophets protested rulers' violations of the people's economic rights and Jesus catalyzed a movement of covenant renewal among village communities under Roman imperial domination. Again modern-day equivalents would have to be far more complex to address the continuing changes in the global economic system. Since the United States as a whole, like the churches, has deep roots in the biblical Covenant,

covenant renewal is at least conceivable in the wider civil society as well as in churches.

The voluntary associations in contemporary society that see themselves as the continuation and equivalents to the covenant renewal communities addressed by Jesus' speeches and the Gospels of Mark and Matthew are the churches. Synagogues and mosques in the other two Abrahamic traditions see themselves, in a parallel way, in continuity with the Mosaic Covenant and covenantal principles. The covenant renewal of village communities evident in Q and Mark included, indeed focused on, mutual economic support and cooperation. Economic sharing and cooperation continued in the urban communities addressed by Paul and Matthew. Periodically in Christian history, church communities again became alternative societies with strong mutual economic support and cooperation. This long tradition includes, for example, the Hussites and Moravians, the covenantal communities in seventeenth- and eighteenth-century New England, and more recently the "basic Christian communities" in Latin America.

Many modern Western societies, especially the United States, established an institutionalized "wall of separation" between "church and state" and a broader separation between separate spheres of religion and economics as well as religion and politics. But that has not precluded churches as primarily religious communities from being economic communities as well, or taking economic action. The converts of John Wesley and the first generations of Methodists organized miners in Wales and fostered literacy among their members. Preachers in the northeast United States took the lead in organizing mill workers. Evangelical preachers and politicians agitated against slavery in the mid-nineteenth century and pressed for legislation protecting the economic rights of workers in the Progressive Era. Catholic churches were also sources of economic aid and sharing and, in effect, credit unions in immigrant communities. More recently the U.S. Catholic bishops issued a statement on the economy. And in the last few decades, organizations of women inside and alongside the churches have taken innovative initiatives to ensure the economic rights and security of women, which are still grievously unprotected by laws and their enforcement. At least some evangelical churches are beginning to address the seriously detrimental effects of deregulated capitalist corporations.

A major factor in the demise of civil society in the United States has been the decline in activity by voluntary associations in general, including churches and church bodies. Mainline churches in particular have allowed themselves to become more and more marginalized in public life, while what is known as the Christian Right has become aggressive on social and political issues. There is plenty of room for churches to become more active in economic and political matters in progressive (rather than regressive) ways, in the tradition of the covenant renewal communities addressed in Q, Mark, and Matthew.

In a complex society in which residence is often segregated by income and race, however, covenant renewal that goes no wider than the local congregation would only reinforce such segregation. Like the network of covenantal communities in the Jesus movements and the "assemblies of Christ," local churches belong to wider networks of congregations in which covenant renewal can be embodied, including its economic dimension. Ecumenical relations open yet wider possibilities of cooperative economic action.

What churches, synagogues, mosques (along with related voluntary associations) might do to expand the economic dimension of their covenantal communities falls into three interrelated kinds of activity. First, they can expand the ways that they embody economic aspects of covenantal community. Already churches provide funds and services, for homeless shelters, food pantries, or temporary relief of extreme poverty. They could do far more in pooling resources to provide such services—while also pressing government to (again) fulfill its proper function of providing them and establishing programs that underwrite economic rights such as job retraining and affordable housing.

Second, they can serve a prophetic role in protesting the abuses of corporations, or more modestly an educational role in informing the public. To gain public attention in a society where corporations control the communications media, it may be necessary to mount demonstrations even to bring information to people's attention. Jesus carried out a forcible demonstration against the Temple's economic exploitation of the people. Churches have a long history in the United States of supporting demonstrations on political rights. Churches' support of the United Farm Workers strike in the 1970s is one of the few well-known national campaigns on an economic issue.

Third, churches can take economic action as covenantal communities in the wider society. This could take the form of setting up separate economic programs or pressing government at various levels to provide needed services and to cease subsidizing corporations against the interest of the public. Churches can engage in additional campaigns such as those already pursued in organizing communities against large corporations such as Walmart manipulating or forcing their way in and destroying small local businesses and generally lowering wages.

Given the heritage of Covenant in U.S. history, particularly in the foundational events and documents, there may also be possibilities of reviving discussion of and action on covenantal principles and values in state and national covenantal political communities. In the Declaration of Independence, Jefferson had invoked the Covenant: "For the support of this Declaration, with a firm reliance on the protection of Divine Providence, we mutually pledge to each other our lives, our fortunes and our sacred honor." Until very recently presidents appealed to the Covenant in their inaugural addresses. And, as noted in the introduction, at one point the covenant commandments were at the center of public political discussion, including in presidential elections and legislative deliberations.

One important starting point would be for members of the churches, the smaller covenantal communities, to become aware that they are also members of the larger covenantal society with the rights and responsibilities of citizens. They might well think of renewing the relationship between the membership in the one and the other that has deep roots in U.S. history. In the early nineteenth century, while a "wall" separated church and state, the churches were understood as "schools of citizenship." As suggested by thoughtful leaders from John Winthrop to Sojourner Truth to Abraham Lincoln, liberty did not mean the freedom to do as one pleased, but covenantal obligations to consider the good of the whole in all one's actions. The democratic form of government was understood in covenantal terms. Government rested on law, which derived ultimately from a higher source, God of Nature, but in its positive form was created by active participation of those subject to it. Active participation of the citizenry will be necessary for the people to take the "government of, by, and for the people" back from the corporations. And the people will have to insist that their government protect their economic rights from the corporations as well as their political rights from both the corporations and the government itself.

For Further Reading

Chapter 1

On the ancient Near East in general:

Bedford, Peter R. "The Economy of the Near East in the First Millennium BC." In *The Ancient Economy: Evidence and Models*, ed. J. G. Manning and Ian Morris, 58–83. Stanford: Stanford University Press, 2005.

Liverani, Mario. "The Near East: The Bronze Age." In *The Ancient Economy: Evidence and Models*, ed. J. G. Manning and Ian Morris, 47–57. Stanford: Stanford University Press, 2005.

On the ancient world in general, including the Roman Empire:

Morris, Ian, and J. G. Manning, "Introduction." In *The Ancient Economy: Evidence and Models*, ed. J. G. Manning and Ian Morris, 1–46. Stanford: Stanford University Press, 2005.

Saller, Richard. "Framing the Debate over Growth in the Ancient Economy." In *The Ancient Economy: Evidence and Models*, ed. J. G. Manning and Ian Morris, 223–38. Stanford: Stanford University Press, 2005.

Chapter 2

Chaney, Marvin L. "'Coveting Your Neighbor's House' in Social Context." In *The Ten Commandments: The Reciprocity of Faithfulness*, ed. William P. Brown, 302–17. Louisville: Westminster John Knox Press, 2004.

Chapter 3

Early Israel in the hill country:

Coote, Robert B., and Keith W. Whitelam. *The Emergence of Early Israel in Historical Perspective*. Sheffield: Almond Press, 1987.

Finkelstein, Israel, and Neil Asher Silberman. *The Bible Unearthed: Archaeology's New Vision of Ancient Israel and the Origin of Its Sacred Texts*. New York: Free Press, 2001.

Gottwald, Norman. *The Tribes of Yahweh*. Maryknoll, NY: Orbis, 1979.

Hopkins, David C. "Life on the Land: The Subsistence Struggles of Early Israel." *Biblical Archaeologist* 50/3 (1987): 178–91.

The moral economy of peasant societies:
Horsley, Richard A. "Moral Economy and Renewal Movement in Q." In *Jesus in Context: Power, People, and Performance*, 205–23. Minneapolis: Fortress, 2008, 205–23.
Scott, James C. *The Moral Economy of the Peasant: Rebellion and Subsistence in Southeast Asia.* New Haven: Yale University Press, 1976.

Principles of subsistence and mutual support:
Levinson, Bernard M. *Theory and Method in Biblical and Cuneiform Law.* Journal for the Study of the Old Testament Supplement 181. Sheffield: JSOT Press, 1994 (especially on covenant code and ancient Near Eastern parallels).
Marshall, Jay W. *Israel and the Book of the Covenant: An Anthropological Approach to Biblical Law.* Society of Biblical Literature Dissertation Series 140. Atlanta: Scholars Press, 1993.
Wright, Christopher J. H. *God's People in God's Land: Family, Land, and Property in the Old Testament.* Grand Rapids: Eerdmans, 1990.

Measures addressed to mounting debts and disintegration of families/Rights of the poor:
Bergsma, John Sietze. *The Jubilee from Leviticus to Qumran.* Supplement to Vetus Testamentum 115. Leiden: Brill, 2007.
Chaney, Marvin L. "Debt Easement in Israelite History and Tradition." In *The Bible and the Politics of Exegesis: Essays in Honor of Norman K. Gottwald on His Sixty-fifth Birthday*, ed. David Jobling et al., 127–39. Cleveland: Pilgrim Press, 1991.
Lemche, N. P. "The Manumission of Slaves—The Fallow Year —The Sabbatical Year—The Jobel Year." *Vetus Testamentum* 26 (1976): 38–59.
North, Robert, S.J. *Sociology of the Biblical Jubilee.* Analecta biblica 4. Rome: Pontifical Biblical Institute, 1954.
Wesbrook, Raymond. *Property and the Family in Biblical Law.* Journal for the Study of the Old Testament Supplement 113. Sheffield: JSOT Press, 1991.

Chapter 4

Chaney, Marvin L. "Bitter Bounty: The Dynamics of Political Economy Critiqued by the Eighth-Century Prophets." In *The Bible and Liberation: Political and Social Hermeneutics*, ed. Norman K. Gottwald and Richard A. Horsley, 250–63. Rev. ed. Maryknoll, NY: Orbis, 1993.
———. "Whose Sour Grapes? The Addressees of Isaiah 5:1–7 in the Light of Political Economy." *Semeia* 87 (1999): 105–22.
Steinberg, Naomi. "The Deteronomic Law Code and the Politics of State Centralization." In *The Bible and Liberation: Political and Social Hermeneutics*, ed. Norman K. Gottwald and Richard A. Horsley, 365–75. Maryknoll, NY: Orbis, 1993.
Yee, Gale A. *Poor Banished Children of Eve.* Minneapolis: Fortress, 2003.

Chapter 5

Prophetic oracles:
Chaney, Marvin L. "Micah—Models Matter: Political Economy and Micah 6:9–15." In *Ancient Israel: The Old Testament in Its Social Context*, ed. Philip F. Ester, 146–60. Minneapolis: Fortress, 2005.

Coote, Robert B. *Amos among the Prophets: Composition and Theology.* Minneapolis: Fortress, 1981.

Dearman, John Andrew. *Property Rights in the Eighth-Century Prophets.* Society of Biblical Literature Dissertation Series 106. Atlanta: Scholars Press, 1988.

Chapter 6

The Roman imperial economy generally:

Finley, Moses I. *The Ancient Economy.* Rev. ed. Berkeley: University of California Press, 1985.

Garnsey, Peter. *Famine and Food Supply in the Graeco-Roman World: Responses to Risk and Crisis.* Cambridge: Cambridge University Press, 1988.

Garnsey, Peter, and Richard Saller. *The Roman Empire: Economy, Society, and Culture.* Berkeley: University of California Press, 1987.

Scheidel, Walter, Ian Morris, and Richard Saller, eds. *The Cambridge Economic History of the Greco-Roman World.* Cambridge: Cambridge University Press, 2007.

Judea and Galilee under Roman rule:

Broshi, Magen. "The Role of the Temple in the Herodian Economy." *Journal of Jewish Studies* 38 (1987): 31–37.

Fiensy, David. *The Social History of Palestine in the Herodian Period: The Land Is Mine.* Lewiston, NY: Mellen, 1991.

Goodman, Martin. "The First Jewish Revolt: Social Conflict and the Problem of Debt." *Journal of Jewish Studies* 33 (1982): 418–26.

Horsley, Richard A. *Sociology and the Jesus Movement.* New York: Crossroad, 1988, chaps. 4–5.

———. *Galilee: History, Politics, People.* Valley Forge, PA: Trinity Press International, 1995.

Chapter 7

Horsley, Richard A. "The Covenant Renewal Discourse: Q (Lk) 6:20–49." In Richard A. Horsley with Jonathan A. Draper, *Whoever Hears You Hears Me: Prophets, Performance, and Tradition in Q,* 195–227. Harrisburg: Trinity Press International, 1999.

Chapter 8

Horsley, Richard A. *Hearing the Whole Story: The Politics of Plot in Mark's Gospel.* Louisville: Westminster John Knox, 2001, especially chap. 8.

Chapter 9

Greek cities under Roman rule:

De Ste. Croix, G. E. M. *The Class Struggle in the Ancient Greek World: From the Archaic Age to the Arab Conquests.* Ithaca: Cornell University Press, 1981.

Paul and the collection:

Friesen, Steven J. "Poverty in Pauline Studies: Beyond the So-called New Consensus." *Journal for the Study of the New Testament* 26/3 (2004): 323–61.

Georgi, Dieter. *Remembering the Poor: The History of Paul's Collection for Jerusalem.* Nashville: Abingdon, 1992.

Horsley, Richard A. "1 Corinthians: A Case Study of Paul's Assembly as an Alternative Society." In *Paul and Empire: Religion and Power in Roman Imperial Society*, ed. Horsley, 242–52. Harrisburg: Trinity Press International, 1997.

Chapter 10

Carter, Warren. *Matthew and the Margins: A Sociopolitical and Religious Reading*. Maryknoll, NY: Orbis, 2000.
Crosby, Michael H. *House of Disciples: Church, Economics, and Justice in Matthew*. Maryknoll, NY: Orbis, 1988, chaps. 6–7.

Index of Ancient Sources

*Page numbers in **bold** indicate where a passage is discussed specifically.*

185

Index of Subjects

*Page numbers in **bold** indicate where a topic is discussed specifically.*